Amiya's ENCYCLOPEDIA of HEALING

Reclaim Your Sexuality

HOW TO HEAL FROM THE WORDS, ACTIONS, AND BELIEFS THAT DENY WHO YOU ARE

Amma & Friends through

CATHY CHAPMAN, PHD

Other Books by Cathy Chapman

Change Your Encodements, Your DNA, Your Life!
The Creation of Form

Amiya's Encyclopedia of Healing series

From Conception to Birth
The Human Energy Field — Auras
The Human Energy Field — Chakras
The Human Energy Field — Hidden Structures
Trauma and PTSD — Resolve the Pain to Recover Your Life

Amiya's ENCYCLOPEDIA of HEALING

Reclaim Your Sexuality

HOW TO HEAL FROM THE WORDS, ACTIONS, AND BELIEFS THAT DENY WHO YOU ARE

Amma & Friends through

CATHY CHAPMAN, PHD

Light Technology PUBLISHING

For information about special discounts for bulk purchases, please contact Light Technology Publishing Special Sales at 1-800-450-0985 or publishing@LightTechnology.com.

ISBN-13: 978-1-62233-082-9
ebook ISBN: 978-1-62233-822-1

Light Technology Publishing, LLC
Phone: 1-800-450-0985
1-928-526-1345
Fax: 928-714-1132
PO Box 3540
Flagstaff, AZ 86003
LightTechnology.com

TABLE OF CONTENTS

INTRODUCTION

Your Essence as a Human Being

Amiya

Many of you hide the sexual aspects of your lives because of shame. When you fully and rightfully access your sexuality and combine it with your natural inner power, your sexuality integrates with your spirituality and produces even more inner power. When you are fully in tune with your sexuality, you can be fully in tune with your spirituality. The life forces of spirit and physicality come together and make you who you truly are. You might not realize how important your sexuality is to your spirituality or how important your spirituality is to your sexuality.

Why do religions shame sexuality? Religions tend to repress sexuality and make it seem "bad" because they want to be in control. Many religions shame you for your sexuality and for accepting your humanity. Authorities also like to control bloodlines to keep them "pure." The belief that you must have a particular person in charge of you who tells you who you are and what is right or not right limits your intuition. Your religious scriptures, even those you do not know, contain truths and untruths. Your truth is within your heart.

Sexuality, as we, Amiya, use it, is the sense of who you are and your essence as a human being. Sexuality is neither male nor female. It is your relationship with your physical body and your relationship with others in their physical bodies. When religions became involved, they decided people should only use their sexual drives in certain ways, only one gender could love another, and only one gender could have sex with another. They completely threw out what was known and accepted about sexuality in ancient days.

In the spiritual realm, those of us on this side (and we're even speaking of the Creator) accept the fluidity of what you call gender and how you choose to express your sexuality. From your heart source, you know that relationship is based on agreement and sharing love. As long as you have mutual agreement and the wisdom to make that agreement, all is aligned from the heart. Think about what that means. If you lack power and have not gained the wisdom yet to make an agreement, the right to use the physical expression of sexuality does not exist.

Here, we focus on the rightness of sexuality and sexual expression. To prevent emotional pain, like-minded people need a like-minded agreement to have a fulfilling sexual relationship leading to joy and not pain. This includes the age appropriateness of sexual expression. Children have not gained the wisdom and understanding needed for sexual expression. Forcing sexual relations is never from the heart. Heart-based, mutual sexual expression supports each person involved. Heart-based sexual expression includes accepting one another as you are. Heart-based expression is about equality. It is union and oneness. You cannot have heart-based oneness when you are in a position of power over someone.

You might think, "Ah, but you talk about the spiritual hierarchy. Isn't that power over those below?" Members of the spiritual hierarchy look at things differently than members of earthly hierarchies. Members of earthly hierarchies see their positions as having greater status and prestige than others. Those of the spiritual hierarchy view their roles as having greater responsibility and service to others. On your planet, one higher in a hierarchy has greater control over another. We might go into these ideas later.

You as a Sexual Person

This book contains three parts. First, Amiya and her Healing

Friends give us information about sexuality in general. Next, they talk about healing aspects of our sexuality that might confuse us or give us discomfort, such as who we're attracted to and issues related to our sexuality and religious beliefs. Then Amiya and her Healing Friends work with us on abuse issues.

First, we will talk about events that affect you as a sexual person. Why might you have a strong sexual drive and someone else does not? Why might you be attracted to people of the same gender or to both genders? Why might you feel uncomfortable with your prescribed gender? The key is to accept how you are and how others are. Lack of acceptance brings great shame, especially when you're first discovering yourself as a sexual being.

Do you remember when your hormones first turned on? It was a natural and powerful occurrence, but you were likely told the effects of your hormones were not good. What do you do with this influx of power when no one is there to guide you? Ancient indigenous cultures had rituals for this coming-of-age time. They also knew this influx of power had a spiritual transcendence.

From our side, we see the rightness of how you express yourself with another physically, and we do not judge. We work with you to bring healing when the energy between you and another is in conflict and brings emotional pain. We will work with specific areas of sexual trauma such as rape, incest, and molestation.

Some on your planet declare others as evil or unacceptable because they love differently than is conventionally accepted. We will differentiate between those who make free decisions to share themselves with others from those who are forced to give their bodies to others. We will talk about what happens in your energy field and brain when you are in a relationship with someone you are attracted to, and we will discuss agreements between two people who care for each other even if they do not understand what love truly is. We're talking here about adolescence. Adolescents don't completely understand what love is. Those of you who are still in partnership with your adolescent love, think about your understanding of love then and your understanding of love now.

This book is important because we will show you how to dismantle energies of non-acceptance for who you are because of who you choose to love or your confusion about the gender you feel internally versus what you display externally. You might have been born before parents could learn their child's gender before birth. Spending nine months in the womb with parents who wanted one gender while knowing that was not you affects your relationships with your parents, others around you, and most importantly with yourself.

We will also discuss how your sexuality influences every part of your life. It affects how you sit, how you stand, and what you see when you look out your window. You have what is basically called a feminine nature and a masculine nature. Those energies get mixed in the different ways you look at each other, and you discover more about who you are.

Many of you work with fairies, and there is a different sexual energy when you work with fairies than when you work with dragons or elves. Even though you call these sexual aspects of yourself masculine and feminine, they are the spiritual aspects of being proactive or receptive, mentally oriented or intuitively oriented. Your society relates them to specific genders. The energies of being control oriented or passively oriented is not truly gender specific, a difference created by your patriarchal system. When you had a matriarchal system, similar energies were defined differently, and your relationships to them were different.

Choose the Path toward Healing

Your sense of who you are as a sexual being began in the womb with your biological parents' concepts of themselves as sexual beings and their relationship with each other as sexual beings, not with the action of sexual intercourse. There is a difference between having sex and what you call "making love." We will go into these differentiations and show you how to balance those areas in which somebody placed shame on you for your thoughts or actions.

Little boys learn it sooner than little girls, for the most part, but certain religions place great shame on discovering the pleasures of the body when you stimulate yourself. Why is that? We will show you how to release those low-vibration energies that have told you that some parts of your body are shameful. No parts of your body are shameful. That shame has been projected on to you by others.

We will talk about what it is like to have a good relationship with your parents and how that affects your sense of self as a sexual being. They teach you about your sexual identity through example by being who they are and loving each other. They also teach you about who they are when not loving each other. We are not speaking about their sexual relationship through intercourse although that energetically contributes.

Yes, this is a complex topic, and we are sharing some of the complexities we will address. The areas of healing related to trauma are contained in our previous book, *Trauma and PTSD*. In this book, we will work specifically with areas related to gender identification, sexual attraction, sexual trauma, and confusion related to sexuality foisted on you by others. We will work with healing the chakras and energy fields affected by wounds surrounding sexuality and sexual expression. Sexuality is integral to who you are, and when someone damages that, it damages your energy field, depending on who was doing the damaging and how the damage was done — physically, verbally, or "just" energetically.

We will begin slowly. We won't begin with the most difficult cases of trauma. We will begin with what it is like to be someone not yet born, an infant, and a child, and we will heal those wounds. As a child, what messages did you receive about your body and the need to keep it hidden? There is a balance, and we will talk about that. We will talk about accepting balance within yourself and others. We will work at strengthening and healing your energy field and becoming comfortable with the complementary agreement with your partner about how you choose to express your sexuality.

It is interesting that some of you choose to express your sexuality with your bodies and some of you choose to sublimate those energies and make the choice to be celibate. You express your life-giving nature in ways that do not produce human beings, but you can soothe human beings.

Sexual Wounds from Past Lives

Cleo: Will we also be healing sexual wounds from past lives?

You can be assured that sexual wounds from past lives contribute to what happens to you in this lifetime. So the answer is very much yes.

Cleo: I was thinking in particular of the times during the Inquisition and the Dark Ages in general.

What happened to you in other lifetimes definitely affects you. The Judeo-Christian story of Adam and Eve is also a sexual story. You might not realize that.

Think about what it is like when you stand naked before another. This might be difficult for you to imagine if you do not have this concept or experience. Those of you who go to nudist colonies might. Consider living your life without any protection over your body, and then suddenly you feel ashamed of your body and must cover it — not for protection but from shame. A woman covering her breasts because she does not want to burn her nipples in the sun is different from covering her breasts because it is shameful for them to be seen.

You mentioned the Inquisition. These supposedly celibate men developed what you would call horrendous and exquisitely painful tests done on women, but it was not because of their fear of witches. It had to do with their fear of the feminine power; they did not understand it as being of God. They only saw women as evil temptresses. You still have that in today's society in blaming the victims of rape; it happened because of where she was going or what she was wearing. Of course, both genders are raped. Women have the shame that comes from thousands and thousands of years of being inherently evil because they are female and because heterosexual men do not understand their attraction to women. They use women as objects for their sexual pleasure. Does that answer your question?

Cleo: Oh, absolutely. There will be more where that came from.

I'm sure. Anyone else? Have any thoughts or feelings surfaced based on what we have said?

Carolyn: They teach children not to let anybody touch them where their clothing is. If they're wearing a T-shirt and shorts, nobody puts their fingers underneath that part of the clothing.

What does that bring up in you?

Carolyn: I wish I had known about that when I was nine, when I was sexually abused; I was really manhandled.

So what have you and society now learned? They took off the blinders and elevated children from the roles of possessions, of things. This is the same for women — the elevation of women from things for male pleasure and children for male pleasure, sometimes for female pleasure. People are more in control and now able to say no. As a child, as a woman, and as a man, you have the right to say yes or no to sexual activity. Some attempt to say that a child can give consent at a very young age. That is not true. They do not have the wisdom to know what sexual activity means. That's why we mentioned wisdom.

What Source Wants to Experience

Margaret: What's the lesson on Source's side for having such incredible, horrendous things happen to people? I mean, souls obviously must learn an incredible amount from choosing this pain over and over through the centuries. We design our lives. We do this to ourselves on purpose, which is very masochistic, sado-masochistic. So why does Source want to experience that? That's my ongoing question about a lot of things but specifically around sex.

Mimi: Yes, it is a very strange planet. And where does this theory of choosing these things intersect with the concept of feeling we should all be attempting to be our best selves and raise the vibration of the planet? People supposedly ask for something that is totally opposite to that. Do you understand what I'm trying to say?

Are you trying to say that we are talking about consent and acceptance, yet people are asking for a learning experience that does not involve consent and acceptance?

Mimi: Yes. I just can't believe that anybody would want to learn about being violated and that the other person would say, "Yeah, I'll volunteer to be a serial rapist for you to have that experience."

So we will need to go into detail about the difference between the potentials and the actualities of choice. Does that make sense?

Mimi: No.

One potential is that you might choose to be in a relationship with someone who has the potential to be a perpetrator. You have the potential to be a victim or a perpetrator. It is complex. We will put that on the list to discuss.

Cleo: Does karma play a part in this?

Saying you would choose something over and over again is karma. And this is a major question as to why and how this works on a spiritual level. This will just throw more confusion into everything, but the Creator does not wish harm for anyone. The Creator does not even need to learn about rape. It all goes back to human beings learning about control, service, and imbalance in life. We might have you talk to Amma about some of the things that she doesn't talk about very much, which are the other forces that have come to this planet and brought about such things. But we might not do that for the book itself. We'll see.

Cleo: And will we be touching on child trafficking?

Yes. We will touch on the wounds that cause such things and what happens to children who are victims. It is not the Creator's desire that children be trafficked or that they be violated. We will talk about what that does to people and how we can go about working with people who want to be healed from those assaults.

Healing Means Letting Go of Pain

Cleo: Is the same true of altar boys who were abused by priests or Boy Scouts by their leaders?

That's what this book is about: to heal those wounds as well as other wounds. There is no separation between what is important and what is not important. Any wound is important. It all begins in the womb with the parents' view of sex and sexuality. Additional wounds layer on the child and then the adult. Each layer causes greater pain, greater woundedness. You will not find a pedophile who was not sexually violated as a young child.

Carolyn: Okay, so we have some learning to do from soul to soul or as a soul from lifetime to lifetime.

As always, yes.

Carolyn: Are you going to talk about areas of the planet where sexual abuse has happened, is happening, and how we can relate to or even learn from that?

We are going to touch on the healing of sexual abuse.

Carolyn: Can we heal from these areas where there is sexual abuse?

Have you been able to heal from anything in your life so far with the work we have given you?

Carolyn: Yes.

So the answer is yes. You have your choice, do you not? You can become upset and frustrated and say, "No, it doesn't work because it only healed 25 percent." Or you can be thankful for the 25 percent and continue working with the healing. As we and Amma have often said, healing happens in layers. Your desire (and anyone's desire) is to be healed immediately of all layers. The only way to heal immediately from all layers is to let go of all your pain.

Carolyn: So if you do that, does that mean you won't get any kind of remembrances, flashbacks, or feelings from different areas on the planet?

When you are healed, you are healed. There will be no signs of what happened.

Carolyn: Okay. Thank you.

Anybody else?

Cleo: Does that involve healing the pain body?

Yes, and more.

Margaret: Will you present ceremonies and ways to celebrate the child to fully accept herself or himself?

We will be glad to share some things with you.

Cleo: If a person doesn't feel any real interest in sex, then is that due to past experiences in this life, past lives, or parental influences?

It is due to what people choose to experience in this lifetime.

Cleo: Oh, I didn't know that.

If it is truly a decision to not have sexual energy, then that's a good thing to discuss. Your many questions show how precious and important this topic is to you. Blessings to you.

CHAPTER ONE

Embrace Your Sexuality

Amiya and Dr. Cathy

Amiya: Let's talk about what sexuality is. Very succinctly, sexuality is you. How about that? I guess we can end the book, can't we? It is you and your expression of love to the world. Whether your gender is masculine or feminine, it is how you approach the world. It is connected to your spirituality. If you want to have a healthy sense of sexuality, have a healthy connection to whatever you identify as the Creator/Source/All That Is/Love Itself.

When you express your sexuality through the physical act of what many of you call making love (we won't use some other terms because we like to refer to it as the exchange of love from one to another), you have the ultimate expression of oneness — that experience of not knowing where one ends and the other begins. That is oneness. We know it does not always occur from love, but when your union produces the fruit of the womb, a child, then you have a true example of the energy of creation. Source, in loving oneness, created this Earth and each of you.

Most of you in the world do not question yourselves as male or female. But some of you struggle, with many overlays of emotion, whether you are male or female or attracted to men or to women. This is where the healing comes in. Remember who created you: Love created you. No matter what societies, religions, governments, or people walking on the street think, you were created from love and are love. Any attraction you have based on love is *perfect*. Any relationship you have based on mutual love (true love, not lust) is perfect. This love comes from your heart, one to another, in complementarity. Of course, many other things that we will discuss can cause a few complexities or problems and pain in life.

Sexuality Is Connected to Spirituality

We will first talk about the usual person, the greater preponderance of people on this planet, and we will begin with what you call the heterosexual relationship. Then we will move into other expressions of love. (We will start from the majority and move to the minorities.) As we do this, please know that even if it is a minority of one, there is love. When you can express yourself through giving love and receiving that same love from another, you express sexuality and spirituality at the same time.

In her practice, this one we speak through has found that couples have the most difficulty talking about their two most sacred parts: sexuality and spirituality. You have sexuality even when you do not have a partner. You have sexuality when you have more than one partner. As long as you all agree from your hearts, there is love. We are talking about the essence of love: giving yourself and receiving another. And yes, even if you are your own partner, you are giving love to yourself and receiving that same love.

Sexuality was created to have relations with anything on this planet. If sexuality was not spiritual, you would not find many of the great saints and mystics expressing their love relationship with the Creator in sexual terms. Those of you of the Judeo-Christian tradition, a book in your Hebrew scriptures called the *Song of Songs* is the relationship of one to another, but it is about the relationship with God, Love Itself, in sexual terms.

Check your feelings right now. Do you feel absolute joy and delight, or is there an underpinning of shame? Is there a "how could this be?" It would not be unusual to have underpinnings of shame due to your instruction when you were younger. The joy of sexuality and sexual expression is rarely taught. That book, the *Song of Songs*, is not taught. In fact, it's not included in every Bible because people have separated sexuality from the Creator.

Even though heterosexuality is the ultimate source of the creation of life through the joining of a male and female body, that expression was never intended to be the primary purpose of your sexuality and your sexual relations. Does that confuse you? The primary purpose — are you ready? — is to create more love. That is all: to create more love. Sometimes that love creation produces a child. Sometimes it produces a project such as art. Sometimes it produces a wonderful relationship of one to another in which you both grow tremendously. Sometimes it produces a garden, purifies water, or cleans trash out of an area.

You might ask, "But what does that have to do with sexuality?" Sexuality is about love. Spirituality is about love. Sexuality is love with spirituality as the head. It is love with the Creator, with Source. Sexuality is an expression of love with what has been created.

Remove Victim Consciousness

This was a short message today, and the healing will be different than usual. We will take more time with the healing steps as we speak to you. Through our words, thoughts, and your healing team's actions, discordance might have surfaced that perhaps you no longer believe but hold deep within because you grew up with it. Connect with your healing team, and ask them to locate that wound buried within (or that has already surfaced) of conflicted feelings. What wound is most in conflict with our words? Its energy might come up, as it has for this one. She doesn't know what it is, but the energy is there.

Be very present to that wound. Be present in love with that younger you or the soul energy from other lifetimes. Set your intention to be truly free of the world's view of sexuality and the separation between sexuality and spirituality.

We now command: Healing team, first please use the Basic plug-in to heal the wound that has surfaced. The Basic plug-in includes steps to bring back parts of yourself. Your soul-healing angels are out everywhere looking for all the pieces you lost.

Now we ask your healing team to please use the Healing over Lifetimes plug-in to find those wounds that separated you as a sexual being from yourself as a spiritual being. We ask them to go back to heal those times when the sexual act was not used with love and therefore separated you from the deep spiritual connection that can occur during the sexual act of love.

We remind you that this energy occurs in layers. Now we ask for the Remove Victim Consciousness plug-in, and we'll do it in several layers: First, remove the victim consciousness that comes from the experience of being treated as a sexual object. Yes, you wonderful females, males are treated the same way at different times. Now remove the victim consciousness of authority figures (speaking of churches right now) who have made you a victim to your biology, to your gender.

Now we ask for your healing team to find the biggest implant within you. We're going to start with the biggest implant that has to do with sex, sexuality — anything in that realm. Please find that implant. For most of you, it's in the second chakra. For some of you, it's in the third, and for others, it's in the heart. Still others experience it in the first chakra. It does not matter where. We ask that the implant be removed. Remember, the Basic plug-in is contained in each plug-in, so a specific wound will be healed. There you go. We ask your healing team to heal another layer of victim consciousness — the false information you were given that caused you to become afraid of loving relationships.

Heal Your DNA

Now, let us work with the DNA in several layers. The first layer we'll work with is removing miasmas, the energy along the double helix that passes from generation to generation. It does not necessarily affect the DNA, but it left its information there. This is the fear of being truly honest and transparent with your partner or yourself, causing you to fear relationships in general. We ask your healing team to remove this miasma and to repeat the cleansing for sexual relationships particularly. Now your healing team is going through the genetic level, through your DNA, searching for any places back through your genetic line, both male and female. Your healing team spreads out to find those wounds where your genetic material was changed through pain, suffering, or abuse.

Now we go to the mitochondrial DNA, the DNA within your mitochondria that comes from the feminine line: your birth mother, birth grandmother, and back throughout that line. We asked your healing team to remove any implants; any wounds that have influenced your expression of sexuality with yourself, with others, and in the physical act of making love; and any barriers of your transparency as an individual with another. We ask for that healing to occur now.

We now ask for your healing team to send energy of the exact vibration needed to clear your aura of anything that has surfaced and is a low vibration. Just let the energy come down.

We now ask your healing team to do what is needed to connect your first chakra to your heart chakra, your second chakra to your heart chakra, and your third chakra to your heart chakra. These are known as your physical chakras. They are connecting them with your heart chakra.

Now just breathe. When you inhale, bring in energy from the earth to your heart chakra. Command, "Heart chakra, spin." Bring energy down from above to the heart chakra. Command again, "Heart chakra, spin." You have the energy from above and below. That is the creative energy from your planet. You might wish to call her Gaia, Mother Nature, or the creative energy that you see when you look out your window: plants, trees, grass, and from above, the creative energy of Source. Say, "Now all chakras spin."

Your healing team is now harmonizing your entire encodement system, as they've done after each plug-in. Here's a secret that we're now proclaiming to the world: The more comfortable you are with your sense of self as a sexual being, even if you are a celibate sexual being, the more you will love yourself and be able to extend that love to others, human and non-human — those who move with feet, slither, swim, fly, or are rooted. In other words, you come into oneness again with all. As you know, love is required for oneness, along with a recognition of the sacredness of every human being and molecule on this planet.

So we leave you with that for today. Notice your body. Notice any feelings of freedom, a lessening of tension, or a deepening within yourself of who you are, the marvelous exquisite being that you are. Our love to you, learned scholars.

Why Healing Can Be Painful

Margaret: Healing is often painful. What causes that pain? You think it would be the opposite.

Dr. Cathy: Speaking personally, there are times I experience pain and there are times I experience freedom. Well, here is Amiya. Let's let her say what it is.

Amiya: There are several reasons why healing can be painful. One, you know that you are releasing something from the past, and you hold on to the past. It could be grief surrounding what happened, or you identify yourself with the memory. Even though you are letting it go, you hold on to it for that bit of time. That can be painful. It can also be painful when another wound grabs hold of the wound you're releasing and wants to hold on to it. That is when you call your healing team in and say, "Please use the Basic plug-in to heal the wound that wants to hold on to this wound I'm attempting to release." That's part of the healing in layers.

Victoria: I wish to share an experience. About a year ago, I found out my husband was cheating, and I realized he was hurting. This helped me see a different perspective of the situation, and I decided to forgive him. We went to bed that night and made love. It was the most profound love we had experienced with each other. The profoundness was so deep that the orgasm stayed with me for two weeks. I had a kind of kundalini experience afterward. My only focus was on love, just a feeling of love. That two weeks healed the whole situation. It stemmed from love and my point of forgiveness of choosing to look at what happened from a different perspective.

Dr. Cathy: What an amazing experience. The fact that you were able to freely accept his pain created something new in you and in the relationship.

Victoria: Yeah, it's been completely transformational.

Thank you for sharing that. Anybody else?

Brenda: I had a very positive experience with the healing. I'm still trying to figure it out. Light came in, and I released the shame and separation I felt of not fitting in and believing something is wrong with me. My whole digestive system, my whole abdominal cavity, feels more at peace, as if the tension has lessened. I feel more self-acceptance and self-love and being okay with what is. So thank you for that. That was very profound for me.

You're welcome. And thank you for sharing that, Brenda. I think these are examples of some of the things we're going to experience as we work through this particular book and the healings we'll be given. Some of the healings will relate to us as individuals, and others will be for the larger group. They are examples of how the love given and the love received open us in a way of transparency. It's a very vulnerable place to be, and I am so thankful and appreciate all of you who are sharing that vulnerability. Thank you.

CHAPTER TWO

Heal Your Perception of Sexuality

Amiya and Dr. Cathy

Amiya: To determine where to begin healing sexuality issues when working with a client, you can refer to the information on healing trauma in the book *Trauma and PTSD*. But since we are instructing people as if this is a textbook, we will begin in a more linear way — in the DNA.

We're going to use methods we learned in the book *Healing from Conception to Birth*. As we do the work, there is little for us to offer in instruction other than to take you through the healing processes. This will be a section on healing.

Go into your heart source, into your sacred space. Notice your consciousness, your energy, and your body. In your sacred space, create a screen, such as in a movie theater, or something on which you can see an image. Develop whatever mode of viewing you wish. It could even be a hologram that appears before you. We will show you how to use your healing team to heal your past.

It's important to know that aspects of you have their own consciousnesses. Those aspects include you as a husband, wife, partner, or friend, and that friendship aspect can change depending on which friend you are with. If you are a parent, you have a parent aspect. Your body-soul aspect works with the physical body, and it affects all other aspects of you, including all levels of consciousness within you.

Connect with Your Sexuality

Today you are going to meet the consciousness of your sexuality, which includes your sexual self. Connect with your healing team and ask to meet that consciousness. Notice your emotional and physical responses when this consciousness comes up. If you are working with gender identification issues, notice the gender of this consciousness. Is it male, female, or fluid? Do you sense a combination of the two — male and female? Have you considered that it is not either/or; it is both/and?

Now imagine the two of you side by side: you, the one going through this exercise, and your sexual aspect. First greet that part of yourself. Can you embrace that part of you, or are you wary of it? Perhaps our first step is to do encodement work.

Connect with your healing team. Ask them, "Please remove any artificial encodements between me and my consciousness of sexuality and me as a sexual being." Notice what happens in your body. Ask your healing team, "Please repair any damaged or altered natural encodements interfering with the relationship between the consciousness of my sexual self and my sexuality." Again, notice changes in your body. You might feel energy depending on where your particular wounds are, such as in the second chakra (or what can move the energy of the second chakra).

This can produce physical changes, physical energy within your genitalia. Some of you might actually experience some sexual arousal. Some of you might feel it in your third chakra, and the energy moves downward. Others might find these changes in the heart chakra that move outward to the consciousness of sexuality. Where you feel these changes, these energy movements, gives you an idea where you need to heal. When you're doing this with a client, where they experience the energy gives you a clue where to work for healing.

Remove Trauma from Conception

You can work together — your awareness of you as a whole and your consciousness of sexuality. Experience the two of you together as partners. Ask your healing team to see the beginning of your life, when that egg and sperm came together, which, as you know, does not happen at the moment of intercourse. It can happen up to forty-eight hours later while you're washing dishes or driving the car. The first focus on healing sexuality and sexual expression begins here.

Ask your healing team, "Please remove any trauma that might have occurred in the sexual act that produced me." People who were the product of rape have definite trauma. Those who were the product of love can also experience trauma. This happens especially in the oldest child of a woman who became pregnant the first time she had intercourse. Trauma surrounds the uncertainty of the sexual act and the pain produced by the rupturing of the hymen. That trauma energy can go into the sperm, which are swimming their way up, and the egg, which waits impatiently for fertilization. This happens through the sexual act even when there is love.

You're a multidimensional human being. You might have experienced — like this one we speak through, who was the product of the honeymoon with a mother who was a virgin — trauma from your parents' pain and from such fears as, "Am I good enough? Am I good enough to pleasure my new wife, my new partner?" That energy can come into the egg or the sperm. It does not matter, by the way, if the woman has the concerns; the energy of uncertainty can still enter the sperm, which move upward and carry it to the egg. So the energy can enter both places.

Ask your healing team, "Please remove, from that very beginning of life, any sense of 'I'm not good enough' related to the expression of love through sex." Become aware of any energetic changes you feel. Don't worry if you don't experience any changes.

The egg and sperm come together and form the very beginnings of you. Let's do a type of freeze frame of that combination of the sperm fertilizing the egg, those first two cells, or even the first four cells of the you that began. Let's use the Healing over Lifetimes plug-in to heal any energies on a soul level from any lifetime regarding your comfort level, confidence as a sexual being, and confidence as a man or a woman. Bring together the history of those who came together to form you and your soul history. These are the energies needed for you for this lifetime of your soul. Allow your healing team to look for areas in those lifetimes that need healing.

Heal Family and Galactic Influences

Now we ask your healing team to work with your genetics. First, you did your soul history (which, by the way, might include some genetics further back in your soul history). You could be your own great-great grandparent. We're going to work with the genetics themselves.

Let us begin with the genetics from your birth mother's DNA. As you know, your genetics come from your birth parents; however, your genetics can be altered by your relationships with the family you grow up in. We are working during the time you were no more than four cells large. Ask your healing team, "Please follow the thread of energy that entered me at the time of fertilization. Heal any discomfort with me as a male or female and as a sexual being," which might have begun then.

We asked your healing team to follow that through the female line first. As you follow that through the female line, you go to your mother, grandmother, the two great-grandmothers, and the four great-great grandmothers. Do you see how it expands outward? Allow that energy to move through you, and ask your healing team, "Please use the Basic plug-in to heal each wound encountered while following that line." Breathe.

Now, we'll clear your father's line. We follow the same procedure, beginning with your father, then your grandfather on the father's line, two great-grandfathers, four great-grandfathers, and eight great-grandfathers. Your healing team follows that line of discomfort with sex and sexuality. Now your healing team has told me it is permissible to continue even as they are doing that work.

Let's work with something that adds to your sexuality — your comfort level as a female or as a male. We are speaking of your family line in addition to you in this lifetime. We will deal with the female line first because this has to do with sexuality, how you feel as a female and how your family has felt about females. This will bring greater understanding and awareness, as you live in a patriarchal society. The female line is not honored except for the purpose of giving birth to males. That has begun to change in the past hundred years, but it is still present in some cultures.

Ask your healing team, "Please go through the female line." It does not matter whether you are male or female. They start with your birth mother and then move on to your birth grandmother and their great-grandmothers, all genetically, that have the energy of females being "less than." This also occurs if you are male, but we're going to do it differently there. We ask for the healing of the energy you received from your biological mothers that women are less than.

Now ask you healing team, "Please heal the energy of the birth father's line back through the generations that said women are less than." As your healing team performs this healing, they do many things on the encodements level that would be pages and pages long if we wrote it out step by step. Know that healing is happening.

Still with that four-cell stage on the birth mother's side, all the way back through birth mothers and birth grandmothers (even if you didn't know that one was adopted), we go through the birth line for females to remove the energy that it is wrong, sinful, and inappropriate for a woman to enjoy sexual expression. And now your healing team removes that same energy from the male line — that it is wrong for a woman to have sexual pleasure. We will add, on this line, the healing of women seeking sexual pleasure outside the partnership or marital bed. This is why some cultures have female genital mutilation or genital circumcision. Remember, men do not have, but women do have, one organ devoted totally to sexual pleasure. Allow that healing to happen.

Moving back to the female line, we ask your healing team to remove all energies of the belief that the woman should be subservient to the male. Then we ask for the same energy to be removed from the male line. Included in this view of subservience is that the woman is the servant, the slave, of the male in the areas of keeping the house as well as providing him sexual release. All that is being healed.

Next, imagine your genetic family line, both male and female. See those thousands of beings before you. Ask for the creation and activation (or simply the activation if the encodements are present) of the encodements that males and females are partners. Continuing the healing with you as a four-celled being, we will go back into that genetic history and do both male and female at this time. We will explain the energy, and your healing team will do all the particulars.

Although children are produced from a male and a female, a love relationship can be with any gender. Ask your healing team, "Please install the belief that a love relationship can be with anyone of any gender as long as there is mutual consent."

Now ask your healing team, "Please repeat this for my genetic line; apply it throughout my soul's history." They will apply the Healing over Lifetimes plug-in for each individual incarnation within your soul line. Again, notice any changes in your physical or energy body.

Heal from Week One through Birth

Now you get to expand from four cells to eight, sixteen, thirty-two, and all the way to the number of cells you were when you were born. This might take a few minutes.

Ask your healing team, "Please go week by week of my gestation to bring healing to any imbalances I acquired regarding sex and sexuality from my mother or father, their relationship, and them as male or female." It doesn't matter where the energy of imbalance came from, only that it be removed. Just to be clear, it does not matter whether something happened between your birth mother and your birth father, your birth mother and another male, or your birth mother and a female. Your healing team will clear anything that brings an imbalance to your sense of self as a perfect, whole, happy, healthy, sexual being. The imbalance could be guilt, shame, or anger. It could even be boredom or resistance.

We ask your healing team for that energy to be released in the first week of gestation (remember that in the first week you have no definite knowledge that you are there), the second week of gestation (yes, we will be counting to forty), and the third week of gestation. Note where you have a feeling of great change. Perhaps it was in the third week. Something might have happened to your birth mother that needs to be healed on a deeper level.

Now we ask your healing team to release that energy from the fourth week of gestation and then the fifth week. At the fourth or fifth week, there might be anxiety or anticipation, as the woman has missed her period and is two to three weeks late. We ask your healing team to clear the sixth week, then the seventh, eighth, ninth, tenth (keep breathing), eleventh, twelfth, thirteenth, fourteenth, fifteenth, sixteenth, seventeenth, eighteenth, nineteenth, twentieth, twenty-first, twenty-second, twenty-third, twenty-fourth, twenty-fifth, twenty-sixth, twenty-seventh, twenty-eighth, twenty-ninth, thirtieth, thirty-first, thirty-second, thirty-third, thirty-fourth, thirty-fifth, thirty-sixth, thirty-seventh, thirty-eighth, thirty-ninth, and the fortieth weeks. This continues if you were in the womb longer than forty weeks.

Your healing team removed much of your mother's energy from you, including the following:

- any discomfort she felt as she underwent examinations to be sure you were okay
- the desire, or lack of desire, of having sex with anybody during that time
- any discomfort or feeling that she was as big as a whale and not attractive
- any resentment she felt about the pregnancy (not necessarily about you but about the pregnancy as she got larger and larger and perhaps experienced pain or extreme morning sickness)

After you go through this process, if you still have the sense that more healing needs to be done during the time your mother carried you to term — perhaps your mother experienced violence and did not want to be pregnant, or maybe she felt bad about herself as a female — you might want to do the exercise in the book *From Conception to Birth* in which you become pregnant with yourself. Ask spirit to place within your womb now the energy of your gestation. This exercise is done over nine days (one day representing each month of gestation) or over forty days (one day representing each week of your gestation). Or you can choose to do it for the entire nine months. In this exercise, you send love to your developing self every day, asking for your developing being to be healed. This healing process takes you through layers and layers of working with yourself.

Unexpected Results

Dr. Cathy: Energy ran through me in various ways as we went through that process, including the forty-week exercise.

Margaret: I apologize. I'm going to try keep it brief. I've always had this problem of arrogance and being dragged down. I never have the right words to explain it to myself. Then I had this whole download and finally got the words to explain it to myself.

Okay. That must have had something to do with sexuality since it happened during this type of healing session, so that's wonderful.

Margaret: I don't like the way females are treated by males. We either get super sick or super heavy, and then we're not attractive to them. That keeps them away and keeps us out of trouble. It's an ongoing thing. That was connected to sexuality. Then the arrogance thing, I could never figure it out, but I finally got the right words for it. I'm sure it's all connected.

Margaret is an example of how we don't know how a healing will affect us on a particular level. When I was doing hypnotherapy training, we traded sessions with each other during the internship. Things came up for healing and caused changes in my life that did not even seem connected to what happened. Anybody else?

Cleo: When Amiya was talking about the women having to be subservient to the men, I recalled something right after my husband died. I was having my life review with the Elohim and so forth. They told me that if I hadn't married Dom, my husband, that I would have never gotten married, because I did not want to be subservient to anybody. That must have been a force in my life.

Did you experience anything today?

Cleo: No, nothing.

Okay. And you're not someone who usually feels things anyway, are you?

Cleo: Well, it depends. Sometimes I do, but I did not today. And just to add about my relationship with Dom, we were partners; I wasn't even a tiny bit subservient.

That is wonderful.

Victoria: There was a lot of shame around my mother. My parents were Mormon and highly religious. My older sister was conceived out of wedlock, and my parents felt so much shame about it. They viewed their anniversary as a dark day. I didn't even know that anniversaries existed because they never celebrated it. There are five of us, and I know that she felt that shame for every birth.

You can remove that energy. Over the next few days, notice any changes about how you react and feel about yourself, about your marriage. Notice whether there are any changes with your relationship with your boys. Just notice.

Victoria: Okay.

CHAPTER THREE

Physical Exploration Is Natural

Amiya

Last time we took you on a journey to heal specific things that came from your birth mother and father and their impact on you during gestation. We did not work with issues that could occur if you were premature. That isn't often a sex or sexuality issue. If you wish to work with issues surrounding prematurity, please go to the book on healing, *From Conception to Birth*.

In this chapter, we will continue with the common issues affecting sex and sexuality, about things that are not traumatic, abusive, or have anything to do with molestation or physical or emotional abuse. Those topics will be explored later in the book.

An infant begins to explore his or her body, especially a little boy who finds his penis and enjoys pulling on it. A tremendous belief system surrounds what people call "playing with yourself." (We will use the technical term "masturbation.") Parents feel shame when their child does this. From the Judeo-Christian tradition, where does the wrongness of pleasuring the body come from? Even if you were not raised in the Judeo-Christian tradition but grew up in a predominately Judeo-Christian country, you absorbed many of these views and beliefs.

We're going to begin with exploring the body as an infant. Did you know that documented evidence, via ultrasound, shows that a little boy will play with his penis even before birth? There is nothing wrong with anything pleasurable you do for your body when done at the appropriate time or place. Most of you will not have memories of events for this first area of healing.

Connect with your healing team. Ask them, "Please locate any event when I was an infant or toddler in which I was punished, deterred, or shamed for physically exploring my body." We're going to go through the Basic plug-in, step-by-step. Ask your healing team (your encodement technicians will do this), "Please remove all artificial encodements placed on me by whoever tried to move my hand, slap my hand, or chastise me. Remove any encodements that came from someone else's shame about me exploring my body. Now repair any damaged or altered natural encodements that resulted from someone projecting shame on me for exploring my body." That is good.

Now we will work with any natural encodements deactivated at that time due to the shame. Know that you can deactivate an encodement if you feel it is unsafe, perhaps due to emotion. So if you wish, ask your healing team, "Please activate any encodements for bodily pleasure that were deactivated by whatever happened at that time." We are not going to force you. "Now please activate any encodements that need to be activated."

Now we will connect this with the energies of other lifetimes, using the Healing over Lifetimes plug-in. Ask your soul-healing angels, "For all these lifetimes, including this wound that is being healed, please find and bring back all the pieces of me that I lost in this incident; clean, repair, and heal all pieces; and fully integrate all pieces within me."

You might experience some sexual arousal due to the energy moving within you as this other energy is released. You might experience shame as you experience that sexual arousal. Yes, the sexual arousal is unusual, as you're doing something during what you could call a time of prayer, but shame is not usual. It is not normal. Ask your healing team, "Please locate the wound that is the source of that shame.

Please apply the Basic plug-in, the Healing over Lifetimes plug-in, and then the Remove Victim Consciousness plug-in, which is meant to remove any victim consciousness about the belief that it is wrong to have a body that experiences pleasure."

Replace Old Beliefs with New

Now, let's ask for the Belief plug-in. Some of you might not be familiar with the Belief plug-in. It removes all encodements holding in a belief that is contrary to the beliefs we place within you. Then we create and activate the encodements needed for these new beliefs. Command the following:

- "It is ordained by God for my body to have pleasure with touch." (Of course, we are speaking of touch related to mutual consent and delight.)
- "It is appropriate for my body to experience sexual arousal even at unexpected times." (That is just your body's expression.)

We're going to contradict ourselves. Some of you have sexual arousal at times of prayer because of the intimacy you experience in joining with spirit. You have a body, and your body is to be enjoyed. Think about it, women: Why would the Creator give you an organ solely for the purpose of pleasure if you were not supposed to use it?

We now call for your healing team to go through your energy system. They will use the Repair the Energy Field plug-in to balance and remove energies contrary to what we have been saying about the body. They will remove energies that contradict the beliefs we just installed, such as the energy contradicting the statement that it is wonderful for the body to be able to feel pleasure. Keep breathing gently as this happens.

We'll give you an aside. This will affect sexual arousal and how much you enjoy taking a shower or a bath, being outside, or anything that is tactile, such as clean sheets. These sensations of touch are part of sensuality. You will find they are heightened when you remove energies that prohibit enjoying physical pleasure. Not all physical pleasure is sexual.

Ask your healing team, "Please remove from my DNA" (and this is basically a miasma and not always in the genetic code) "what is contrary to what you have balanced." If you have imbalance within your DNA, your healing team will remove it and bring total balance to the DNA as it connects to your divine blueprint. "Remove from my DNA the fear and shame of sexual pleasure. Again, please use the Healing over Lifetimes plug-in for the same issue."

Now we will go specifically to the mitochondria of your cells that comes from the female line of DNA. It has been imprinted into women that it is shameful to enjoy the sexual act. We ask your healing team to remove this from the mitochondrial DNA. Then we ask that they apply the Healing over Lifetimes plug-in to this same intention. Now we ask them to use the Remove Victim Consciousness plug-in for the same intention and area. This removes the feeling that you are a victim of your body and how it responds, particularly when you do not wish your body to respond in that way. A man is familiar with this response, as he will get an erection at what he considers an inopportune time. That is just how the body responds. Women are the same, but it shows itself differently.

We're going to add one last thing, and then we'll use everything we just said as a plug-in to go even deeper. Let's remove the energy of authority figures, whether you're male or female. This can be feelings of objectification, being used, shamed, or seen as less than. It doesn't matter at which level. This can come from teachers, religious figures, or the parents of playmates (and as you get older, the playmates themselves). We ask for that energy to be totally removed from your energy field now. Good.

Heal Years of Sexual Experience

Now your healing team will apply everything we have done before and apply it to the years of your lifetime. We'll begin monthly for the first twelve months and apply the plug-in yearly. Just relax and open yourself to receiving the healing.

We ask your healing team to take everything we just gave them and use it as a plug-in. They will apply it to the first month of age, the second month, the third month, and the fourth month. (Yes, we're going rather quickly, but your healing team can keep up.) Then the fifth, sixth, seventh, eighth, ninth, tenth, eleventh, and twelfth months and the entire second year. If you wish to go back later and do each month within each year, please feel free to do that. We won't do that now because of time.

Now, we ask them to apply this to the third year and then the fourth, fifth, sixth, seventh, eighth, ninth, tenth, eleventh, twelfth, thirteenth, fourteenth (remember, we're referring to years), fifteenth, sixteenth, seventeenth, eighteenth, nineteenth, twentieth, twenty-first, twenty-second, twenty-third, twenty-fourth, twenty-fifth, twenty-sixth, twenty-seventh, twenty-eighth, twenty-ninth, and thirtieth.

Although you can continue by year, if you wish, we are stopping at thirty. That is usually the time period of sexual inquisitiveness and when you become comfortable with sexuality in a non-traumatic way. This happens developmentally, giving you a fairly good beginning in the knowledge of sex and sexuality. We will work with other issues later that interfere with the development of a healthy view of sex and sexuality.

We have two more things to deal with at this young age. First, apply everything we have already given you to a time when you were young. Perhaps you walked in on your parents while they were having sex. Ask your healing team, "Please remove any fears that might have resulted, especially if I thought it was violent. Please heal that. Now heal any wounds or shame that came later, when, as a young child, I played doctor."

This one we speak through has many other things jumping through her head, but we say this is enough for now, believe it or not. You really are not aware of all the changes occurring in you due to the work in this chapter.

CHAPTER FOUR

Heal the Phases of Sexual Development

Amiya and Dr. Cathy

Amiya: Healing occurs on all levels. As you heal yourself, as you open yourself to healing, you heal the world; you heal the planet. In fact, you heal the universe. Can you have that big of an influence on the universe? Of course. As you heal the planet, you raise its vibration, and that affects the vibration of the universe. Because the universe is infinite, it expands and expands.

One cell can cause problems in your body when it is out of balance. If one cell in your body — one organelle or one mitochondrion of the thousands of mitochondria in your cells — has a problem, that throws your whole body off balance. That is what oneness is — not the off-balance part but the connection of one to another. As you become more "you," your vibration rises, as does the vibration of the planet.

We have been talking about one of the most sacred aspects of your physical life, which is your sexuality. We will continue healing the ordinary trials you face as you grow and develop in your sexuality. Are you ready?

Heal the Fear from Your First Sexual Sensations

Connect with your healing team. Focus on the front of your heart center, as we're going to have you focus on your physical aspect more. Get a sense of your body. We gave you an assignment to see whether you notice any differences following the last healing. How do you feel physically — the sensations of water, clean sheets, going outside, the sun, cool air?

Let us go to the very first time, whether or not you remember it, your body experienced sensations you had not felt before. A little boy notices it much earlier than a girl, as he has a sexual organ outside himself. A woman has to find her organ for sexual sensations. Especially if you are a woman, when was the first time you discovered that a part of your body, when touched, produced strange feelings, strange physical sensations, and you didn't know what to do about it? Perhaps you asked a parent or someone else, and it was not received well, you were in fear of asking, or you felt embarrassed or shameful. Simply ask your healing team, "Please use the foundational plug-ins to heal that part of my lifetime if there is need." (What might have been casual observations for some of you could have caused discord in others.)

For men, remember the first time you had white fluid come out of your penis and it scared you. You didn't know what to do. It soiled your sheets, and you were embarrassed or ashamed. We ask your healing team to address that shame and heal the wound that caused that shame, that embarrassment.

For women, recall the first time blood came from you. Some of you were prepared, and some of you were not. Perhaps you were ashamed or embarrassed. You didn't know what to do. Ask your healing team, "Please bring healing to the shame and the embarrassment I felt from my first period."

For both physical genders, think about the first time you felt sexual passion. Perhaps it scared you and at the same time fascinated you. Perhaps you didn't know what to do with it and might have been embarrassed or ashamed because of the sensations or because of what you did afterward. All these little things contribute. Ask for that healing now. Good. Know that some of you might have had those sensations, but they do not need healing because you were not wounded or you addressed the healing at another time.

Let's go to the very first time you had a romantic interest in someone. It could be male or female, but you felt this pulling, which actually came from your hormones. You could have been afraid, scared, embarrassed, or ashamed. Whatever feelings you had, ask your healing team, "Please heal any wounds from my first romantic experiences using the foundational plug-ins."

We have asked your healing team to gather all those times people made comments, from when you were very young to now, about your body. These include any comments that you were pretty, handsome, ugly, or fat. Perhaps you were compared negatively with a family member or with someone else. They are gathering those painful feelings and the events associated with them. This one is remembering comments people made because of her weight. These all contribute to your sense of self, sexuality, and comfort level with your body. Your healing team will clear this with the foundational plug-ins.

Why the four foundational plug-ins? The first plug-in, the Basic plug-in, focuses on a particular event in this lifetime. The Healing over Lifetimes plug-in heals events similar in nature from other lifetimes, including this life, parallel lives, future lives, and past lives. Your healing team will use the Implant Removal plug-in to look for and remove the deeply congested energy of those wounds that seems almost like a hard, energetic knot. Then the Remove Victim Consciousness plug-in removes the victimization you felt or still feel.

Reconcile Your Rites of Passage Experiences

Now let's move through the ordinary rites of passage almost everyone experiences: the first time you wanted someone to kiss you or you wanted to kiss someone and it did not happen. Perhaps you were rebuffed. Ask your healing team, "Please bring healing to that using the Basic plug-in."

You might have felt confused by the feelings that came up the first time someone touched your body by your invitation or agreement. Ask your healing team, "Please heal that wound and wounds from similar events in this lifetime. Please balance them using the Basic plug-in." We don't want to leave out the first time you touched your own body out of curiosity or for expressions of pleasure and felt either embarrassment or shame. If that was present, ask your healing team, "Please use the four foundational plug-ins to heal wounds created from my sexual curiosity and expressions of pleasure."

Many of you are surprised at some of the things we are bringing up for healing. Here are more: Your healing team will use the four foundational plug-ins to heal any wounds that might have occurred the first time you witnessed nudity, the sex act on television, or any time you witnessed sex but did not participate in it. If this brought imbalance to you in any way, we ask your healing team to balance that now.

We're now going to one of the most tender challenges of your life, the first time you were in love and you either did not get together or the relationship ended. The first time you experienced, what you call, unrequited love or when you had a wonderful love relationship that dissolved and left you with a broken heart was painful. We ask your healing team to heal that event and all the smaller events that happened within it. We ask them to work with the encodements. We ask your healing team to bring back all the pieces of you that you sent away, and we ask them to clean, repair, heal, and then fully integrate them within you. There you go.

Now let's move on to heal the time when you wanted to be part of a group or friends with a particular person but it did not happen, and you felt less than. This might not seem to have anything to do with sexuality, but it is about your sense of who you are. Ask your healing team, "Please heal those events now using the Basic plug-in."

We ask your healing team to use the four foundational plug-ins if you need healing for the first time you had a sexual relationship with someone. For a woman especially, this could be the pain of the first time you had intercourse. It could be (we're talking about mutual desires and agreement to have sexual relations) that it was not all you thought it would be. We ask your healing team to bring healing to your disappointment and bring into alignment what can happen in delight and joy. We also ask them to use the Basic plug-in to bring healing to any embarrassment you might have had and to bring healing to anything that happened this first time that hurt you, even if inadvertent and unintentional, and resulted in your feeling less than or fearful.

Bring to mind a time, and it could be more than once, when you heard about the pain or abuse of another and it tore at your heart in some way. We ask for that pain within you to be healed through the Basic plug-in and for the cause of the pain to be healed using the four foundational plug-ins with emphasis on the Healing over Lifetimes plug-in.

Ask your healing team, "Please bring forward the consciousness of any time I felt sexually inadequate. Please use the four foundational plug-ins to heal that entire ball of energy." For those who have a penis, this could be the first time you made love with someone and your penis did not cooperate, you could not hold an erection, or you could not attain one. Ask your healing team, "Please use the foundational plug-ins to bring healing to the embarrassment and shame I felt for those events."

Bring to mind someone you were interested in or had dated and were told that you were not good enough or appropriate or that person was not good enough or appropriate. Ask for healing of that time using the four foundational plug-ins. Not all of you will have wounds related to this. If someone said a person was not good for you, you might have agreed and even been looking for an excuse not to be with him or her. If you were told you were not good enough to be with someone, ask for healing in that area.

If you are a woman, ask your healing team to heal the times when your body did not respond as you thought it should to make intercourse easier rather than painful, when your body did not lubricate as it should, or when you did not feel any excitement and wondered whether something was wrong with you. Ask for healing in that area using the four foundational plug-ins.

Explore Other Areas for Healing

Now we will touch on some areas we will explore in greater depth later in the book. Those of you who are not heterosexual, bring to mind the first time you discovered you were not attracted to the same people your friends were. You were attracted to women, if you were a woman, or you were attracted to men, if you were male. If you experienced shame or confusion, ask your healing team, "Please use the four foundational plug-ins to heal this experience as many times as it happened. Please heal those wounds that caused me to think that something was wrong with me."

Ask for healing, using the plug-ins, if you found yourself attracted to anyone, male or female, and others judged you, you wondered whether something was wrong with you, or you were affected in a painful way. Call your healing team to bring healing to you in this area.

If you have ever noticed that you did not feel you were the gender your body portrayed, we ask your healing team to bring healing to you now using the four foundational plug-ins. (We will explore this subject further later in the book.)

We ask for healing for those times when you who were told you must have children and you did not wish to have children. You might have wondered whether something was wrong with you, or you might have felt put down or less than. Ask your healing team, "Please use the four foundational plug-ins to heal this area."

We ask for healing if you have had many children and were criticized or made to feel shame because you wanted to have more children you could love, care for, and support in being who they are. If you wanted children but did not want to engage in the ritual of marriage or did not desire a partner and you were criticized and shamed for your decision, we ask your healing team to use the foundational plug-ins to bring healing.

We ask your healing team to gather within you all those times when someone said, "You can't do that because you're male," or "You cannot do that because you're female," and you did it anyway, and this left you with anger. Ask your healing team, "Please use the foundational plug-ins to heal this. Also heal all those times I was hurt, confused, or wounded in some way because I did something contrary to what society believed I should do as a female (or male)."

Now, healing teams, we ask you to look at the wonderful humans before you, the ones you have agreed to be here for and to support their healing. Look into their energy and find those wounds we have not mentioned that came from the growing-up process of discovering who they are sexually, their sexuality, and as sexual beings in every way. Please bring healing to them using the four foundational plug-ins. Fill them with love. Use the Belief plug-in to place within them the belief: "I am perfect as I am and as I grow and develop and change."

Earth Is a Learning School

Louise: Even though the topic is complex and affects everybody in different ways, these healings make me feel that I should just sit back and relax. I don't know if it's because of my age and I've experienced so much, but it's a pleasant, nice feeling.

Dr. Cathy: That's good. It takes great trust to sit back and relax while healing is occurring. It might be different when we move into more painful events later in the book. I'm experiencing changes in my energy, but I don't have the same angst I had when I was much younger.

Cleo: When Amiya said we would start a book on sexuality, I thought, "Oh, no. I'm not interested in that." But today, with the multitude of things she brought up, I thought to myself, "Gee, I don't remember that, but I am so grateful now to have this healing take place." This is a wonderful book that applies to everyone. I offered a little prayer of gratitude to Amiya and my healing team for all the healing.

Victoria: When Amiya asked us to think about when someone hurt us, I thought about the people I hurt. I hope my sense of knowing that I hurt them will help them as well.

Maybe Amiya was going to do this later, but let's do it now. From your heart source, ask your healing team, "Please find those times when I consciously hurt someone, even if I have forgotten about it. Please heal what caused me to do that. Heal the people I wounded without meaning to. Bring healing to them in any way they will allow. Thank you."

Victoria, did anything else come up?

Victoria: Just the guilt about that.

We can do some pretty crummy things as human beings. It's one of those times when you might think, "But that's not who I am. That's not who I want to be." You asked for healing of whatever caused the pain.

Victoria: Or what you did wasn't even mean. People just liked you and you didn't like them back.

Yes, in the same way.

Victoria: Yes. And then they didn't leave you alone. You were nice at the beginning, and then you had to be sort of mean to get rid of them.

That's a good point, and something to ask for healing. You had to do something that hurt their feelings for you to be free. Ask for healing for them even if they're not still alive. Then ask for healing for yourself.

Kristina: I felt some really deep wounds surface, especially the part about being rejected by another. It just really hit home. Then, of course, I started analyzing it as everybody was talking. I think it's something I can further investigate.

Michelle: Quite a bit of this didn't seem to apply to me. I wonder how much of that, if any, is denial. I don't want to have any connection with whatever it was.

I think some of it can be denial. Some of it can be things you've forgotten. Denial sounds like doing everything you can to not look at it. So it can be an unawareness. For people reading this book who are in their thirties or forties or who haven't done much healing work, the events might be right in their minds.

Sharon: We come to this Earth plane to learn lessons. If people don't push our buttons and cause trauma, we can't heal these lessons. That helps me be more compassionate to others and myself. We are here to learn and grow, and hopefully we can learn to grow without trauma.

Thank you, Sharon.

Margaret: After I married, the most important thing to me was getting approval. I took my husband to meet my friends, people at work, and even people I knew who I hadn't seen in years. They were all like, "Hey, this is cool; this is great." Having their approval of my happiness was wonderful. So approval can be really important to how people feel.

Good, thank you for sharing that.

Carolyn: I would like to add I feel that Earth is a school where we're learning all this. The more we open ourselves to spirit, the more that comes through and the more we learn to absorb it and go with the flow.

Okay, thank you.

CHAPTER FIVE

Accept Your Bodily Functions

Amiya

You might notice differences within you from the healing we have done over these first few chapters. These things you've healed might seem minor, but they are foundational. Your sense of yourself as a human being began with the love your parents gave you, the love of your birth mother. That is why it is important to heal from the moment of conception to your birth and immediately after.

We will now work with your sense of coming to know your body and all the first sensations you had as a young one. Your body's first sensation was being surrounded by fluid and then being filled with fluid. You had the sensation of the first time your body released a stool. As a little one, you had sensations as you began to explore your body. You explored the sensation of your mother's nipple or a bottle's nipple in your mouth. You already explored this in the womb as your senses developed and you sucked your thumb.

Your body — your wonderful, beautiful body — was born. Even if someone lovingly said, "But his face is all wrinkled and squinched up," or "You know, newborns really aren't very pretty," that was not what your mother and father saw. The first time your mother saw you (for almost all reading this book), she expressed wonder, even if she was also confused. Many mothers feel absolute joy. They forget everything that happened in the hours of labor.

That was your first experience of being acknowledged as who you are. But some of you did not have that experience of love. Even though this healing is in the other book, we will do it now. We ask your healing team to gather around you and search for the first time you were seen and if you received (even if you did not know the words) negative information about your body. Perhaps you did not have five fingers and five toes on each hand and foot. Maybe your nose wasn't quite in the right place. Maybe your color was strange; you were born a little blue.

Ask your healing team: "Please bring back all those pieces of me that I have lost. Clean, repair, and heal them, and then fully integrate them within me. Please remove all the encodements somebody placed on me who said my face was red and wrinkled, who did not laugh with joy (as many do), or who didn't appreciate my screaming. Please heal all the energy from people who said I was not perfect."

Heal Early Shame of Bodily Functions

Now we go to a time in your life that holds a great deal about how you feel about your body and how it functions. We believe it is called potty training. First, we ask your healing team to remove any encodements from any authority figure — parent or teacher or similar — who was frustrated or angry because you still wet your diaper, wet your pants, or wet your bed. Your healing team will use the four foundational plug-ins to remove any negativity that came to you from potty training. Some of you might feel your body relax in a place that you didn't know was not relaxed.

Ask your healing team, "Please remove the wounds and beliefs that something is wrong with my body because of this experience, that something is wrong with me because I could not manage my urine or stool as my family or someone else wished. Go to that first wound I experienced when I tried so hard to tell someone that I needed to go to the bathroom but didn't make it in time." You might not have been punished for that, but you felt embarrassed and ashamed. We ask for that healing now.

We go now to a time that you might or might not remember: the first time you felt embarrassed at someone seeing you nude. As a baby, you didn't notice. Then you became aware that not everybody shows their bodies, and you didn't want to see some people's bodies. This could have been a family member. It could have been when you were getting dressed or undressed even when you didn't care whether someone saw you when you were going to the bathroom. It could have been something different, or maybe it happened at another time during your life. Your healing team is bringing healing to the first time you felt embarrassed or ashamed when someone saw you nude and then the second time that happened and the third.

Many of you had experiences of your parents continuing to bathe you when you believed you could handle it yourself. You no longer wanted them to touch your body or clean your bottom. You felt ashamed and frustrated, and you thought they did not trust you or believe in your capabilities. Ask your healing team, "Please gather all those times and use the Basic plug-in and the Healing over Lifetimes plug-in to bring healing to those wounds, and please use the Remove Victim Consciousness plug-in to remove feelings of victimization." This might have been the beginning of you not being able to set physical boundaries with people. We now ask your healing team to find where energy is blocked from being suppressed and congested. We ask them to find those implants within the second chakra, front and back; third chakra, front and back; and first chakra.

You might have felt forced to reveal your body in gym class or in the dressing room and were traumatized. You attempted to act normal but did not feel normal. You might have been fascinated by the bodies of others when others your age did not appear fascinated by them, and you felt shame and confusion about yourself. Ask your healing team, "Please find the implants related to these wounds and gather those energies. Then use the Basic plug-in, the Healing over Lifetimes plug-in, and the Remove Victim Consciousness plug-in on each wound."

You likely walked in on someone who was nude or in some stage of undress, and you felt embarrassed or even ashamed. You could have walked into a bathroom at the wrong time or walked into a bedroom and seen one of your parents naked for the first time in a long time.

You might have been surprised or startled, or your parents' reaction might have produced shame or embarrassment in you. If you have any need of healing in this area (and this won't be the case for all of you), we ask your healing team to please take care of that with the four foundational plug-ins.

Heal Later Shame of Bodily Functions

Now we ask your healing team to gather any of the embarrassment or shame you felt because of the way your body functions. For boys, this is often erections. For girls, this is often when you have your period, your menses, and blood is on your clothes. We asked your healing team to apply the four foundational plug-ins.

Next we go to the first time you had a kiss with someone outside your family. If your feelings about that kiss caused you internal pain or artificial encodements, we ask for them to be removed. Perhaps those encodements pertain to your fear that you didn't kiss good enough or how slobbery and wet it might have been. You might have felt the kiss was forced on you, and you didn't like it. We also ask your healing team to heal any wounds related to you forcing a kiss on another. We ask your healing team to go to that time and bring any healing needed — healing in any sense of not being good enough or of being violated.

We now go to something that might not apply to you — bedwetting problems. Perhaps you wet the bed just once, and you felt much shame, especially if you had friends over or you were at a friend's. We ask for that to be healed now. If your bedwetting problem was ongoing, this goes back to not being able to control your body, your bodily fluids. We ask your healing team to remove every encodement of shame and embarrassment you felt. Your soul-healing angels will find and bring back every piece of you that you lost. They will clean, repair, and heal those pieces and fully integrate what you denied and sent away from yourself.

We now ask your healing team to remove others' shame about your bodily functions that was projected on to you. This could be from parents, babysitters, siblings, or friends. It could even be from a past or current partner.

We end this topic with the Belief plug-in to remove any old belief that is contrary to this new belief. It will remove the encodements of the old belief itself and install this new belief (many of you already know it): "My body is perfect as it is." Your healing team is doing this encodement work now.

In the next chapter, we will work with body image. We have some homework for you. To allow your consciousness and your subconscious to surface negative feelings about your body, please stand nude in front of a mirror and look at your body for a minute or so. We will ask for the healing of your feelings of the parts of your body, from your head to your toes, all down your body. Stand in front of the mirror while nude and really look at your body. This will, believe it or not, help in the healing by surfacing your feelings.

CHAPTER SIX

Appreciate Your Body

Amiya and Dr. Cathy

Amiya: Be in a place of gratitude no matter what is happening on your planet. You are not aware of the small threads extending outward in time. Gratitude changes the energy of tragedy. Even your Christian scriptures say to always give thanks and praise. That is part of the first ray of being in alignment with and accepting the will of God. Yes, there is a grand plan, and yes, humans change it. The Creator is always creating. Things can change. By reading this book, you work with healing, and you truly cocreate with the Creator to assist in anchoring those changes.

You were given an assignment to stand nude in front of the mirror. You might or might not have done this. We are working with your self-image related to your body. Your body is a borrowed structure that has a soul we call the body-soul. You borrow your body for life. You may not return it until you end this lifetime. You may make changes to it, and some of you make a lot of changes. You might have made changes using drugs, scalpels, diets, or exercises.

Some changes are easier or healthier than others. For example, it is not healthy to change your body to such an extent that it does not have the fat it needs to function. Appropriate fat does wonderful things; it provides energy for your body. Water is necessary, but if you decide to drink a couple gallons a day, you can overburden your body and drown it. Undergoing extreme plastic surgery can damage your body.

Whether you looked in the mirror or not, form an image now in your mind of you being totally nude. See the shape of your body that you're not happy with. You are bringing up energies about your body to heal. First, ask for healing of whatever is behind the fear, resistance, sadness, shame, or even contempt of your body. Ask for the wound beneath those feelings to be healed.

Remove Negative Feelings about Your Body

We will do the Basic plug-in a little differently today: We will start with the soul-healing process, which is usually at the end. Connect with your soul-healing team, your soul-healing angels. Picture your body as clearly as you can now, as it is. What feelings do you have for it? Say to your soul-healing team, "Dear soul-healing team, my body has served me despite what I have put it through. I want a good relationship with my body. Please find the wounds most responsible for all the negative feelings I have for it."

The beings in charge of the soul-healing angels are giving us more instructions to communicate to you. They say it would be faster to ask, "Soul-healing angels, please bring in front of me now all consciousness of the shame and revulsion I feel about my body." Ask your soul-healing angels, "Please find and bring back all the pieces of me related in any way to this energy I called forth from me body." Your soul-healing angels now ask you to draw Archangel Michael's Sword. As the energy of your soul pieces returns, ask for those pieces to be cleaned, repaired, and healed. Assist in this process by placing the Sword in the middle of the energy. It will transmute the shame, revulsion, anger, and despair.

We now ask your soul-healing angels to return all those pieces in order to return you to the way you were before you had any thought that something was wrong with your body. That brings you to a very young age, does it not? It might bring you to a time when you could pull your toes all the way to your mouth and enjoy them. There you go.

We ask your encodement team to please remove all artificial encodements that continue to hold in negative feelings about your body. You have fewer negative feelings now, but there are some. Please repair the damaged and altered natural encodements related to all that we are doing now. Deactivate the natural encodements you no longer need for your body. (You needed some when you were a child that you do not need now.) Ask that any encodement you might need to love your body be created and activated. They are integrating and harmonizing all those encodements now.

Next, we use the Belief plug-in to install the belief: "I love and appreciate my physical body." With the Belief plug-in, your healing team removes any encodements holding in the old beliefs, including any belief that is contrary to, "I love and appreciate my physical body." They now create or activate the encodements needed for the new belief and place those within you. From your heart, say aloud, "I love and appreciate my physical body."

Heal Feelings for Specific Body Parts

Now we will heal your feelings about various body parts. Let's begin with the head.

Head and face. Think about what you don't like about your head, including your ears, eyes, nose, face, cheek, chin, and skull. Bring all that to mind. Think: "I love and appreciate my physical body." Pull out Michael's Sword. Command: Come before me all the energy that is contrary to loving and appreciating any part of my head and face." Place the sword within that energy to transmute it.

Your soul-healing angels are now finding all the pieces of you that are missing and have anything to do with you not being able to love and appreciate your face and your head, including your hair (or lack thereof) and skin. Thank your face for the skin you have, no matter its condition. Give thanks for your eyes, nose, mouth, chin, cheeks, ears, skull, and hair. As you are being thankful, your soul-healing angels and encodement technicians are working with you. Energies release when you give gratitude. Say aloud, "Shame about any aspect of my face, I call you now. I don't need you anymore. You must leave. Leave now." Some of you might need to take a deep breath and blow it away.

Hair. Command, "Any shame or discomfort about my hair or lack of it, come before me now. I have no further need of you. Leave now." If you need to, use Michael's Sword to transmute that energy. Now give thanks for what you have.

Shoulders, neck, clavicle, upper part of chest and upper back. Call for any disparaging energy of that part of your body to come before you. Focus on it and say, "I have no need of you now. I am in a place of loving and appreciating my physical body in every way. All that is not in accord with that belief, leave now." If you need Michael's Sword, use it. If you have had problems with these areas of your body, you might feel anger. Allow it to come, and then tell it to leave.

Arms. Call forth any energy that is not love and appreciation for your arms. Again, tell that energy, "I have no need for you. Leave me now." If you need Michael's Sword, place the sword within the energy to transmute it. Declare, "For my arms, I offer you my deepest love and appreciation."

Breasts. Feelings about the breasts depend on your gender. Men don't want them. Some women often want more than they have while some want less. All this is based on society's view, which you have accepted. If you were a mother and used your breasts to nurse, recall what it was like to nurse your child. Recall what it was like for your child to be in your arms and nestled against your breast.

Whether you are male or female, call forth any energy about your breasts that are not love and appreciation. Speaking to the energy, say, "I have no further need of you. Leave me now." Even if you lost a breast to an accident or illness, give love and appreciation for the energy still present where your breast was. Ask your soul-healing angels, "Please remove any artificial encodements inhibiting the future functioning of my breasts, especially the lymph moving through them. Repair any damaged or altered natural encodements preventing the full functioning of my breasts. May that happen now. Please place within my breasts the energy of love and appreciation."

Upper abdomen. Follow the same process for your upper abdomen. Ask your soul-healing angels: "I call forth any energy within my abdominal area that is contrary to love and appreciation. I have no need of you. Leave me now." You might need to use Michael's Sword and ask to place the energy of love, appreciation, and gratitude in this area and in all parts of your body. You can keep repeating this for every part of your body.

Lower back. Focus on your lower back. Say, "I call forth all energy within my lower back that is contrary to love and appreciation. I do not need you anymore. Leave now." Use Michael's Sword as needed. Then say, "I now ask my healing team for the energy of love and appreciation to move into my back."

Lower abdomen. Just keep repeating the same command as you go: "I call forth any energy contrary to love and appreciation in my lower abdominal area." So many women who have had children sometimes look at the effects of carrying them and see the wrinkles and loose skin. Thank your skin. Place love and appreciation in that entire area of your body. See that love energy move in. Even if you've never had children and have wrinkles and loose skin as you age, offer appreciation and ask for love to fill that area.

Let's ask your healing team, "Please find the collection of wounds most responsible for me not liking any part of my body. Please use the Basic plug-in, Healing over Lifetimes plug-in, and Remove Victim Consciousness plug-in to remove any implants having any effect of holding in energy contrary to love and appreciation for my body."

Hips and upper legs. This area extends from your knees to your thighs and up to your hips. Again declare, "I call forth all energy from my legs and my hips that is contrary to love and appreciation. I do not need you anymore. Leave now." Then say, "Healing team, place within me the encodements for the love and appreciation of my hips and upper legs."

Buttocks. All people have opinions about butts, do they not? Say, "I call forth all the energy within my buttocks that is contrary to love and appreciation." You might need to use Michael's Sword. Then tell that energy: "I no longer need you. Leave me now." Say, "Healing team, place the energy and the encodements within my buttocks of love and appreciation."

Genitals. Whether you are male or female, call forth the energy of your genitals: "I call forth any energy within my genitals that is contrary to love and appreciation. I do not need you any longer. Leave me now." Then say, "Healing team, I ask for the energy and the encodements of love and appreciation to be within my genitals." (We will do more work on this when we get to other areas of healing.)

Knees and lower legs. Say, "I call forth any energy contrary to love and appreciation that is in my knees and lower legs. I do not need you any longer. Leave now." Then say, "Healing team, please place within my knees and lower legs the energy and encodements of love and appreciation."

(We neglected to tell you that when your healing team places the energy of love and appreciation within you, energies contrary to those leave.)

Ankles and feet. "I call forth all energy from my ankles and feet that are contrary to love and appreciation. I am no longer in need of you. Leave me now. Healing team, I ask that you infuse my ankles and feet with the energy and encodements of love and appreciation."

Skin. Now we will do one part as a whole — your skin. Think about whatever part of your body where you are not happy with your skin. Say the following: "I ask to speak to the consciousness of my skin. I call forth from you any energy contrary to love and appreciation that I have placed within my skin or allowed to come into me." Call forth that energy and declare, "You are not part of my life anymore. Leave now." Then say, "I call on my healing team to place within every molecule of my skin the energy and encodements of love and appreciation."

Fascia. The fascia is like another skin. Say, "Healing team, please remove all artificial encodements within my fascia." This will occur over time, because many low-vibration feelings are trapped within your fascia. Your healing team does not want to tax your energy field right now. In a few days, your healing team will remove most of the artificial encodements from the fascia in your body. They will repair damaged and altered natural encodements and install the encodements of love and appreciation. Now ask that your encodement system be completely harmonized.

Other people's attitudes: You have done a lot of work, and we'll do just a little more. Say, "I call forth from anywhere within my body anyone else's low vibration, negative concepts, and anything contrary to love and appreciation for my body. You are no longer part of my body. You're no longer welcome in my body, and you must leave." Of course, you do not have to use those exact words. Then say, “Healing team, wherever there is emptiness due to the low-vibration energy leaving, please fill it with love and appreciation.”

Deal with Physical Reactions

Margaret: I've been having a histamine reaction at the top of my head. It was very itchy, and I've tried different things to relieve it. It's really nice to have this whole setup of healing the skin. It's timely for me.

Dr. Cathy: Margaret, ask your healing team to please remove any artificial encodements holding in the allergic reaction.

Margaret: Okay, thank you.

Anybody else?

Carolyn: When we worked on the shoulders, I felt some energy move. My left shoulder has been losing some range of motion.

That's good. You might already be doing this, but I got a message to look on YouTube for range-of-motion exercises for the shoulders.

Louise: I have major physical-body issues. I do exercises throughout the week for my back and knees. When we worked on the back, the energy was wonderful. I felt great. And then when we came to the knees, I experienced more pain. So I don't know exactly what was going on.

The message that I get is to especially use the Basic plug-in on your knees.

Louise: Yes. My healing team is so busy when I call them.

They enjoy that. You're here helping them do their job.

CHAPTER SEVEN

Examine Your Physical Sensuality

Amiya and Dr. Cathy

Amiya: It seems that the more you learn, the more questions you have. That is exactly what scholars do. The more you learn, the more you know you have more to learn. It becomes overwhelming sometimes, does it not? We are working to keep this simple for you.

Yes, the topic is sexuality and sex. An integral part of sexuality and sex is sensuality. We have worked a bit with sensuality already, and we're going to work a bit more with it now. Some of these issues may seem unrelated to the topic or seem small and insignificant. Please trust us.

We want your body, this wonderful physical body of yours, to be fully integrated with this wonderful soul — you. The two have an amazing synergistic effect and can interact in this world in powerful and tremendous ways. The more grounded you are in your body, the more you can feel the sensations of this world. Think about that for a moment.

This world has many sensations. Take a moment to imagine the softest garment you have ever touched, the softest fur. If you have any blocks to physically feeling softness and textures, ask your healing team, "Please use the Basic plug-in to heal any wounds that cut off my sensations in the physical realm. Please use the Healing over Lifetimes plug-in." Sometimes the reason you cut off sensations is due to pain from other lifetimes.

Ask your healing team, "Please remove those energies, blocks, and artificial encodements. Then balance and repair the natural encodements that need to be balanced and repaired and activate inactive encodements so that my body has the sensations I need to fully enjoy this planet."

As you know, sensations are important for sexual expression through touch. They are important to enjoying aromas, flavors, sights, and sounds. You might feel some movement of energy within you as you ask for this healing. Now we're going to do different senses.

Enhance Your Senses

Let us go to the sense of smell. We're going to call this "right" smelling, meaning a rose will smell like a rose, fresh-mown grass will smell like fresh-mown grass, apples will smell like apples, and cinnamon will smell like cinnamon. So apple pie will not smell like peach cobbler. When you go into a field and smell the aromas of nature, you gather information. Animals know when something in that field does not belong. You can also learn to discriminate odors, but you will not be able to do this to the extent animals can, because they have many more scent receptors.

What does this have to do with sex and sexuality? You choose your partner with your sense of smell. Interesting, isn't it? Relationships can change due to this. A form of birth control can change a woman's sense of smell, and as long as she is on that birth control, her sense of smell is altered. When she and her partner decide to have children and she no longer takes the pill, her sense of smell changes. On this subconscious level, her partner no longer seems right to her. That is how important the sense of smell is.

We ask your healing team to align your senses. We'll do them all at once: smell, taste, touch, hearing, and sight. They're doing that now. You would like to know the difference between a raw potato and an apple, would you not? We're having your healing team make this connection between your physical senses and your physical connection to the one you make love to. This is where it comes together: sensuality, sexuality, and sex.

Your healing team is using the four foundational plug-ins to integrate all we've just done. You might be feeling sensations. If not, don't worry. All is being done according to plan, and that plan is to determine what you need. Now we ask your healing team to bring healing to you for any aversion to nature. They will use the four foundational plug-ins, the Basic plug-in, the Healing over Lifetimes, the Remove Victim Consciousness plug-in, and the Implant Removal plug-in, related to any fear of or aversion to nature.

Some of the major interferences in relationships (which we will discuss more in an upcoming book on relationships) are feelings of abandonment, rejection, or isolation. If you were punished as a child by being sent outside and isolated, you might have difficulty being in nature. We ask your healing team to use the four foundational plug-ins to heal the wound most responsible for feeling alone or isolated when outside.

Recover from Physical Discipline and Religious Ritual

If you were told you had to go outside and select a switch from a tree so that someone could use it to strike you in anger, that wound might have caused you to be adverse to the wonders of trees and their small branches. Ask your healing team, "Please remove all the artificial encodements established in such incidents that caused me to become adverse to the wonders of nature."

You didn't know that had anything to do with sex or sexuality, did you? You might have been struck on your bare bottom. You might have had your pants taken down to strike your bottom in anger. This can cause a great wound and shame, including body shame. If you experienced this, ask your healing team, "Please collect the shame, anger, and other feelings embedded in me due to these experiences and remove all their artificial encodements. Let the love from Source fill those wounded areas, especially those that interfere with my sense and joy of my body."

We will go more deeply into this in the book on relationships. Not everybody has experienced deep wounds in this area, but so many have experienced the wounds of spanking but not of sexual abuse. Now ask your healing team, "Please call forth from me any cellular memory of pain due to physical discipline."

If you are a man and were circumcised, circumcision occurs without anesthetic to numb the pain, as doctors erroneously believe that infants have not developed enough pain sensors to experience pain. This is not true; there is extreme pain. Call on your encodements team, "Please remove all artificial encodements from me due to circumcision. Repair the damaged and altered natural encodements that occurred due to circumcision."

Some who perform circumcisions are sadistic and enjoy causing pain to another. Others might get sexual gratification when performing the circumcision. Ask your healing team, "Please use the four foundational plug-ins to heal these energies that were transmitted to me. We ask them to place over the penis a diamond hologram in which the top point is a healthy penis with a healthy, loving respect for the penis. At the bottom is the heart's healing center, and at the right is the divine blueprint that contains the blueprint for the penis as it was meant to be, including sensations of pleasure. On the left point is the consciousness of your stem cells. This hologram will spin gently for the next forty-eight hours.

You might be a woman who underwent female circumcision. The intent of female circumcision is different from that of male circumcision. Male circumcision is done either for religious reasons or for health reasons. Female circumcision is done so the female cannot feel and therefore not be tempted to have sex with someone other than the man she is with. First, ask your healing team, "Please remove all artificial encodements produced by the event; repair the damaged and altered natural encodements; find and bring back all the pieces of me that were lost when circumcised; clean, repair, and heal all the pieces; and fully integrate them within me."

Of course, they will use the Healing over Lifetimes plug-in, because everyone reading this book has had this experience in some lifetime. For women, circumcision was done when a young girl was about eight or nine — sometimes a little younger or older. Your healing team will remove all the artificial encodements of terror and other negative feelings. They place the same type of healing hologram over the genital region. The top point is the fullness of the genitals — the woman's clitoris. The heart's healing center is at the bottom point, the divine blueprint is at the right point, and the consciousness of the stem cells is on the left point. For women, the hologram has another point to the front, which is the front of the second chakra and the back of the second chakra. Another point to the back represents the front and back of the third chakra.

We are also implementing the Healing over Lifetimes plug-in and removing the encodements containing feelings of denigration of yourself as a woman and that you were not to feel pleasure and only the pain of childbirth. Whether you are male or female, we ask for the fullness of Source's love to fill you. We place within you the following belief using the Belief plug-in: "I am whole and can feel joy and pleasure."

I think that's enough for now. We took you to an unusual place, did we not?

Bring the Body Back to Balance

Victoria: If we heal it, does that mean the feelings return? What are we healing, exactly?

Dr. Cathy: With female circumcision, we're removing all the pain, fear, and other energies that came into the woman. Women who have been circumcised are unable to enjoy intercourse in the same way women with a clitoris can. Children can die of this. Women can die from complications during childbirth.

Louise: My son was circumcised. We had the ceremony, called the Brit milah, at our home, with close family and friends present. The person who performed the circumcision, the milah, kept giving my son wine on a little rag in his mouth before the ceremony. My son slept through it, which I was very grateful for. It truly was a ceremony. My husband and I felt the sacredness of it.

The energy of that would be so different from the energy of a circumcision for a boy in a hospital.

Louise: Right. And that really does make a difference, I think. Later, you have to change the dressing, and my husband and I did this together. I felt, "Oh, my god," for my baby. I'm sure my son got that energy from me. It is a wound. So there is a mixture of energy — the sacredness but also the reality of healing the wound.

Margaret: Amiya talked about scent and other senses. I've never had a strong sense of smell, but other people in my family have very strong senses of smell. They can't get near certain things or people. They can even smell when someone has a disease. Not

having that strong sense of smell allows me to get close to people, and being a teacher with so many people around, that's a blessing.

Victoria: About getting the switch from outside, I assume there's a correlation between smelling trees or wood and the negative thing that happened to you.

I'm getting from Amiya that it has more to do with the tactile experience, like feeling the tree bark — you know, how sometimes it's fun to feel the textures.

Victoria: So how do you heal that?

Well, that's what we do when we use the different healing plug-ins. Each plug-in contains the Basic plug-in, which of course is the first plug-in. The plug-ins take care of balancing and healing the encodements system. It also brings back the energy of where the person dissociated.

Victoria: Okay, good.

Kristina: I just want to comment on my son's circumcision experience in the hospital. I did not want him to be circumcised, and the hospital staff knew that. I had to switch rooms, and while that was going on, they took my baby to the nursery and circumcised him. When I got him back, he was hysterical — screaming and holding his breath and sweating and shaking. I took off his diaper and it was soaked in blood. It was a huge trauma; I was so upset. He never really looked at me quite the same after that. He looked at me like, "How could you let them do this to me?" It still breaks my heart.

CHAPTER EIGHT

There Is Spirituality in Sexuality

Amiya

How are spirituality and sexuality related? You might have already guessed that it has to do with love: love energy, love essence. When the Creator created, decisions were made about how higher levels of consciousness would propagate. A microbe does not need another microbe to reproduce. A plant requires fertilization from another plant, but the two do not join. Most animals need to physically join to reproduce, whether the offspring come from eggs or are born from the body. (You might know that for some species — fish, for example — egg fertilization occurs outside the body.)

Four-legged animals react to scents, pheromones. The male knows the female is ready to be mounted so that fertilization can take place within her body. Some animals have what you could call small families. Some do not stay around in couples to protect their offspring. Other animals, such as wolves, protect their offspring in packs; group energy protects the young.

You might not realize that when the human species began, groups protected children. Early humans did not know that their passion and intercourse produced a child. They thought an essence was transmitted, but they didn't realize that physical joining brought that essence in. Groups protected the members of the clan or tribe until people slowly realized that the male transmitted his essence to the female.

As science evolved, you began to understand that what you call the sperm fertilized the egg. Society believed the male was responsible for beginning life because the seed of the male was very apparent. But the seed of the female was unknown. Only blood could be seen from the woman, and this produced fear in the male. People had no idea how bleeding, which in a male could mean the end of life, might be beneficial. This fear of monthly bleeding began the separation of women from men during menses, as people feared a woman's bleeding could cause harm to the male.

Women are a mystery to men, just as men are a mystery to women. The complexity of the woman's hormonal interactions with the lunar cycle (and research shows this) produces an opening through her encodements to a greater access to intuition. A woman's job, in a sense — in the aspect of producing children to continue creation — is to choose a proper partner who melds with her energy and can produce the healthiest child. In earlier times, children needed to be sturdy and physically healthy, as people did not know how to care for weak children. That is why, in many cases, fragile children were left to die. That sounds terrible now, does it not? (Of course, your society still does that in other ways.)

Morality Shifts over Time

The Creator knew that the evolution of time — and we're not using evolution as Darwin used it — provided for growth and development. Your encodement systems changed, and you began to see the production of children not just as a means of survival for the tribe or the clan but as a symbol of love between two people. Think about that: moving from the survival of the clan to a symbol of love between two people.

As you grew and evolved in your concept of love, you began to realize that the love you had one for another helped the tribe or the clan survive. Sexual relationships began to take place between one man with one woman, not one man with twenty women. Your Hebrew scriptures speak of one man and many women. Some figures you revere, such as King David or King Solomon, had harems. Why would that be permissible from a human moral standpoint?

Morality shifts. It flows back and forth, depending on who decides what is moral. So in the times of King David and King Solomon, in places where harems existed (and some still exist), people practiced different sexual morality than people in the Western world. Many times the male chose the female because of her beauty, because of her body. Why were there harems? Go back to the need to keep humanity going. How many men are needed to impregnate 100 women? One man could increase the ability of the tribe, clan, or family to be strong in numbers. Only those who had more money and goods could support more women and the children they produced.

Of course, that view changed. From the very beginning of your Judeo-Christian scriptures, the woman was thought of as being less than. Generally, she could only produce one child a year, unless she gave birth to more than one at a time. Mothers needed protection and children needed care. Both were seen as weak because men were stronger and could produce more progeny. Thus, men were seen to be of greater importance.

How does all this apply to sexual abuse? Spiritual abuse occurs any time someone is not acknowledged in their sacredness. When you are not acknowledged in your sacredness, a conflict develops between who you think you are and who someone else thinks you are. When love is involved in a sexual relationship — and the amount or quality of love is on a continuum from lust to the ultimate love in which you would give your life for someone even if you never joined together sexually — you bring the spiritual and the physical together.

Your Creator/All That Is/Love Itself did not create with another being. Your Creator allowed creation to spring forth from Its love. That is how oneness developed. How can oneness be separate and, in a sense, not separate? From the springing forth, a thread of golden energy connects you and every soul to the Creator. You never lose that energy connection. You might, in the human realm, seem to be physically separate, but you never are. Energy from the Creator connects directly to your heart chakra.

The Creator knew that in the evolution of humanity and your relationships, the physical union of one to another would be a symbol and a truth of coming back into oneness. The physical union produced life from that oneness. As consciousness and awareness grew, you expressed your love for another — wanting to share that love, affection, and deep caring, one to another — through the physical act. The result was a union of bodies in love. Think about that: the body and the love. In this union, in this love, individuals did not know where one ended and the other began.

Love and Attraction Vary in Expression

In society — whether the animal kingdom, the fish kingdom, or the human kingdom — there have always been differences in how beings express love one to another. There have always been gays and lesbians. There have always been polyamorous relationships, where people love and have sexual relations with anyone they feel affection for. They express love to another as long as the other is in agreement. Agreement is crucial.

Love is generated and produced by the mutual exchange of love. The more you love another and the more the other returns that love, with or without a physical relationship, the greater the love energy between you. At first, the attraction produces energy within your hormones. Hormones produce the desire to come together and create progeny. Yes, even if two males or two females come together, you have the desire to produce more, which is why people in same-sex relationships have the desire to have children and make them one with their hearts, whether from their seed or from adoption.

Love shared perpetuates love, whether in friendship or a romantic relationship that hopefully becomes a friendship. When you bring together the various types of love, you produce an image of the love of the Creator. Of course, in your human form, you are not able to love as infinitely as the Creator, but you can feel love more and more each day.

The Creator enjoys variety. Think of all the different animals you know. Consider the differences in the animals you in North America don't see except in zoos or circuses: elephants, giraffes, zebras, kangaroos, and more. Different parts of the country have variety. Think about the hippopotamus, the anteater, or the skunk.

Think about your variety of fruits: pomegranates, avocados, tomatoes, bananas, dragon fruit. Variety is life-giving. It stimulates the senses and the awareness of human creativity: If the Creator can create such a wide variety of fruits, vegetables, and animals, what can you create with your art, science, and architecture?

All Creation Is Sacred

You have a variety of attractions: male to male, female to female, female to male, male to female. Some people are more attracted in a sexual way to those of their own gender than to other genders, with whom they want to share their love, physically, one with another. Why would anything that the Creator creates be wrong? No matter what happens when the sperm and egg come together, the result is still the Creator's creation, and the Creator loves that creation even if it only lives for a few weeks once conception occurs. The Creator still loves that creation.

Just because something is not the norm does not mean there is anything wrong with it. Is there anything wrong with a cat who is not black, tabby, or calico? Is there anything wrong with a cat that has grown so large that it runs around in the jungle? Is there anything wrong with an elephant or a hippopotamus because it does not look like a dog or a cat? The variety of Creator's creations brings excitement to life.

The same is true for your variety of sexual attraction. The key to that attraction, regarding human creativity, is the love that results. You were created thus. When you were an adolescent, you had sexual attraction and the desire to touch your body and to have someone touch your body and to touch others. You had the desire to join. It might have been one gender to another that would produce a child. It might have been the same gender together to produce more love. These are simply different ways to produce more love. These are different ways to come into this life to experience a love relationship that is different but no less sacred than the love relationship of a man and a woman.

Damage occurs when people are not accepted as they are in the love they give to another and with whom they desire to share their love. Let's take a heterosexual relationship. You might have been told that the one you were attracted to in high school was not the right one for you. You might have been told you were too young. (But if you had lived several hundred years ago, you might have been the perfect age. Some time ago, it was more important for the woman to become pregnant to keep the species going.) You might have been told such things as, "No, they are the wrong race. They're from the wrong country. They're from the wrong socioeconomic background. Your love is not right."

Religions and their rules state what is correct and incorrect. Many rules are based on what enhances human relations. Other rules, the values of different people, are based on control. The "rule" that romantic relationships must be heterosexual comes from the need to have children. Relationships of man to man and woman to woman, which could not produce children biologically, became an abomination. The relationship was useless unless there was progeny.

Producing love, one for another, is not useless. The love you produce that moves out into the world is never useless; it is never wrong. Notice that we said "love one to another." That love requires mutuality, one with another, sharing that love with each other is then shared with the entire world. Anything that produces a mutual sharing of love that synergistically increases the love on the planet and goes out into the world is never — we say it again — *never* an abomination. It does not matter, as long as there is mutual agreement for love relationships with each other.

When you are not accepted because of who you love and that love is called an abomination, other feelings interfere with the joyful and pure development of love, which is a denial of the oneness of the Creator. Denying who you are in your sacredness causes a split between you and your sense of sacredness with the Creator. This causes pain. We will work with healing that area, the denial by others of your sacredness and people violating your sacredness, later in this book. As more and more of you are healed, the planet will come to accept all people and who they choose to love in mutual agreement.

Then there are those who come into life in one body and feel they are not that particular gender. They decide to live their chosen gender. You call them transgender people. It is an anomaly, but it is not an abomination. Researchers are studying how this happens scientifically. We simply suggest that you have a choice to live your life as you feel called to live it; you only need to accept that life. The genitalia of an individual and how one wants to live should not matter.

How does it affect your life if you do not know someone who was born female decides to live as a man? What if someone was born male and wants to live as a woman? How does someone you do not know who decides to have a love relationship with someone of the same gender affect you? It does not. It has no impact on you except for your attitudes and beliefs.

The healing work we will take you through in this next part of the book is for those who have been damaged by the rejection of who they are. We will also work with healing those who do the rejecting and have such rigid views of how people should love and act, causing separation in the oneness where there is no separation. They also have great wounds.

All creation is sacred. All creation is wondrous and filled with love. Get ready for the next adventure in discovering what needs to be healed within you.

CHAPTER NINE

Understand the Nature of Sexual Attraction

Amiya and Dr. Cathy

Amiya: Have you noticed any differences in yourself and your sexuality or your sense of your sexuality since you began reading this book? Have you noticed whether you pay more attention to what you see — the lights and colors — or how things feel? If you have a partner or a spouse, have you noticed any differences in physical sensations, even hugs and holding hands, and what it feels like to have someone acknowledge you and all the beauty that you are?

Before we get started with this chapter's message, we will balance a belief. Beliefs determine how you respond or react in life; they contribute to your worldview. If you believe the world is safe, you will see elements of safety. If you believe the world is dangerous, you'll see danger. If you believe it crucial that no trash be on the ground anywhere around you, you'll notice trash. If you believe that the most important thing you see when you walk are flowers, you will notice flowers. If you believe something is inherently wrong with you, you will find things that are wrong with you. If you believe you are an inherently good, wonderful, and beloved individual, you will discover those wonderful things about you, and when you discover things you consider not as wonderful, you will know these are things to release.

If you have struggled with your sexuality, we're going to bring healing to issues of gender expression, gender identification, and sexual preference. This one was asked, "Are there more transgender people than there were before, or are we just more accepting of people identifying themselves this way?" There are more transgender people because they are being allowed to say more.

We'll begin our healing for those of you who first realized you were attracted to someone of the same gender. Remember what we said in the last session: Everyone is beloved. We also said that when you are not recognized and accepted for who you are, you cannot be fully who you are. You are limited in your full expression of self because of fear. We also discussed how the Creator enjoys variety. Variety occurs in many ways: animals, plants, trees, fish, birds, sexuality, gender identification, who you love. The Creator does not judge how you express your love as long as it is an expression of love and an acceptance of that expression of love. You judge how you love and who you love.

This one read up on this topic when she was a social worker. Your research shows that few people are completely heterosexual or homosexual ("hetero" meaning opposite, "homo" meaning the same). Most people are somewhere on a continuum. Some of your young ones today call themselves polyamorous; they love and share sexual relations with whomever they wish. You have friends of the same gender and there's no problem in your society, is there? But that is not the case with expressions of love toward another. Why do you think this is a hot-button issue for people?

As we mentioned in the last chapter, it goes back to how the species continues. If everyone is in relationships with people of the same gender, far fewer babies will be born. You will always find a way for the species to have babies, but the species would not be propagated as fully. Also, what is most often seen in humanity is usually considered the norm and what is acceptable. People equate "most often" or "usual" with it being the way it is supposed to happen.

In nature, when more storms occur in a season than normal, you might wonder why, but you accept them. You manage the repercussions of the storms. You do not call the storms evil. You accept them as they are and prepare for them. But when it comes to love, why are some of you threatened by someone who loves differently than you do even when that love has no effect on you whatsoever?

Same-Sex Relationships Make Some People Uneasy

Ask yourself: "Do I feel threatened by people's choice of who they love? Does it make me feel uneasy?" We're speaking now of mutual love relationships, not a choice to love someone in a sexual manner who freely wants to love you in a sexual manner. If someone of your gender you consider a good friend came to you and wanted to express his or her love physically with you, what would your reaction be? How would you respond? Consider that. This is a serious question.

If you say, "Well, I'm just not interested," that's an appropriate answer. It contains no angst, fear, or intent of injury. It is simply, "I'm not interested in that type of relationship with you." If you are heterosexual, this is no different from someone of the other gender wanting to have a physical relationship with you, but you're just not interested in having one with that person. As long as the other person respects that, you can still be friends.

But if you feel the smallest sense of revulsion because a good friend of the same gender wants to kiss or touch you in a romantic way solely because this person is the same gender, you have a wound. The other might feel rejected, which is that person's wound, and that wound is complicated due to your sense of revulsion of this being someone of the same gender.

Let's begin the healing here. Connect with your healing team. Ask them, "Please find that wound within me that, on some level, identifies the other person's request as being abnormal and separates me. Please use the Basic plug-in to heal that wound. Please also use the Healing over Lifetimes plug-in to heal any sense of unrequited love from another lifetime." This is an important plug-in in this area. It is possible you and the one who asked for a sexual or romantic relationship shared such a relationship in another lifetime. You could have been different genders or the same gender; it does not matter. When you use the Healing over Lifetimes plug-in, you are asking that the energies you brought in with you be healed.

Now we move to healing any wounds that occurred because you

were, or are, attracted to someone of the same gender. Ask your healing team, "Please find the wound, if there is one, that I don't remember due to my age or suppression in which I was first physically attracted to someone of my gender and was confused by your reaction or someone else's reaction. Please find that wound and use the Basic plug-in to bring healing. Then use the Healing over Lifetimes plug-in and the Remove Victim Consciousness plug-in, if needed."

Think about any time you might have felt uneasy or even repulsed when you heard about someone who loved someone of the same gender. Ask your healing team, "Please find this wound even if I do not remember and use the four foundational plug-ins." If you remember the incident, recall it again to see whether your feelings have changed and whether you are now in a place of acceptance. If you are not in complete acceptance, ask your soul-healing angels, who are part of your healing team, "Please find and bring back all the missing pieces of me that make it difficult to accept others in same-sex relationships just as I would accept others in heterosexual relationships."

Ask that those pieces be cleaned, repaired, and healed. Ask that they be fully integrated within you, and then say, "Thank you," of course. Your soul-healing angels light up with thank-yous because your gratitude flows out to the universe and is returned to you.

That is a simple process for healing this area. Any time you feel discomfort or even revulsion about someone else's choice of a sexual partner, as long as both (or all) parties agree, then you have a wound that needs to be healed. Ask your healing team to heal that wound. Healing this area will not change your sexual orientation, who you are attracted to. It will allow you to feel joy and appreciation for anyone who loves anyone else.

Heal Your Disapproval and Shame

Let's use an analogy related to food. Let's say you are at a buffet where every type of food is before you. You have a choice of many vegetables. This one we speak through would turn up her nose at Brussels sprouts. She's tried them in different ways and still doesn't like them. Do you feel a discomfort with her or revolted by her because she does not like Brussels sprouts and you do? Does that make you uncomfortable? She loves sautéed spinach, spinach salad, and creamed spinach. Let's say you don't. Do you feel discomfort or revolted by her because she likes spinach and you don't? Her taste buds dislike Brussels sprouts and enjoy spinach. That does not affect what your taste buds enjoy.

Who someone loves does not affect who you love unless that someone tries to choose who you want to love. If you feel revolted by or disapprove of a mutually agreed on love relationship, you are the one who needs healing.

If you are attracted to a love relationship contrary to the norm (the norm being heterosexual), you might need healing — not because of who you are attracted to but because of others' reactions to who you are attracted to. Perhaps you have heard people talk negatively about those who choose to be lesbian, gay, or bisexual. You chose who you would be sexually attracted to before you incarnated. You are born with the capacity of sexual attraction to one or both genders. You choose who to be in a relationship with. That choice is also determined before you incarnate but has more flexibility than who you are sexually attracted to.

Let's do some healing if you are attracted to your gender and have been shamed by society for your attraction. We ask your healing team to identify the wound that produced the shame and to use the Basic plug-in to heal that wound.

If you plan to eventually use these tools with others, know that the shame in this area can begin at a very young age, depending on the situation in which the shame began. Shame can result from religions and family members who believe same-sex attraction is an abomination, and that person can then take on that belief. Great healing is needed for the individual's relationships with self, family, society, and the Creator.

Command Your Discomfort to Leave

Before our next chapter, examine yourself. Ask, "Do I have any revulsion, discomfort, or antipathy toward someone who has chosen to love someone of the gender I would not choose?" Can you celebrate the love relationship of your child no matter the gender of that person? Can you have the same delight for your child as you would have for another child who found a person of the opposite sex to love and marry? Seriously consider and examine this. If you have difficulty in this area, you might have simply absorbed this energy. Your healing is as important as it is for those who need healing because of their homosexual orientation. It's important for you to release your judgments about people who love each other mutually.

Let us begin healing in this area. You will do some commanding and releasing. Call forth from your body all your discomfort, on any level, with anyone who loves someone differently than you do. If you are heterosexual and have been raised with the belief that it is the only way to love and that something is inherently wrong with those who are homosexual, call forth that energy now. You might not even be aware it is within you. Command that energy to come out of you now. Thank that energy, and tell it you do not need it any longer. Command it to leave now. Take a deep breath in and blow it out.

Ask your healing team: "If a wound within me still holds in feelings against someone who loves differently than I would, find and heal that wound using the Basic plug-in. Now use the Healing over Lifetimes plug-in and now the Remove Victim Consciousness plug-in."

Now that they have healed that wound, call again for any energy within you that contains any discomfort, no matter how small, of people of the same gender loving each other, making love to each other, having a family with each other, or living together in happiness. Ask it to come forth now, and say, "Thank you. I do not need you anymore. Leave now." Take a deep breath and then exhale.

Now connect with your encodement technicians in your healing team. Ask them, "Please deactivate within me any encodements I acquired from any social or spiritual institution that relationships between a man and a man or a woman and a woman are wrong or against society. Please deactivate every one of those encodements no matter when I acquired them, even if I brought them with me into this incarnation."

Ask your healing team, "Please activate within me all inactive encodements that are in full alignment with sexually loving one to another, no matter what gender, as long as it is freely and mutually agreed on." One more time, call forth any energy within you that contains any discomfort, no matter how small, of a man loving a man or a woman loving a woman. Say, "Thank you. Leave now. I do not need you anymore." Breathe it out. Good. If anything comes up over the next few days, do this same work; use the plug-ins.

Carolyn: Do past-life experiences have an influence?

Dr. Cathy: Yes. You can choose to bring energies from other lifetimes into this lifetime. You might have had a heterosexual love relationship with someone in a past life, and then you come to this life and you are both the same gender. That past-life love relationship can have an influence in this lifetime.

CHAPTER TEN

Accept Your Sexual Orientation

Amiya and Dr. Cathy

Amiya: Not everyone has this issue we're about to work on, but awareness of it has increased worldwide. The issue is accepting yourself if you are attracted to someone of the same gender and are interested in a love relationship. As you know, the majority of people on this planet are attracted to those of the opposite sex. In this way, the human race can continue. Others are attracted to people of their own gender to share deep love with each other. Some of them have children and others do not. Either way, they contribute their love for each other to the world. People forget this powerful contribution.

As we work with this today, imagine yourself in a large circle. Within this circle, we call for those of you who have felt less than, maligned, rejected, and ostracized and those of you who were told you were wrong, terrible, and acting against God's law because you love someone of your gender and express that love physically.

We say again that any love relationship expressed physically with mutual and mature agreement is of the highest order. It doesn't matter who is involved. We call for every person on planet Earth who is attracted to a physical love relationship with someone of the same gender to join us in the center of our group to absorb the love we have for you. We will work with your healing team to bring you healing. We do this because there is great unrest in the world in this area, and we want you to know you are precious, wonderful, and beloved. You are perfect as you are.

We will now work with your healing team to help balance you. We ask you simply to move into your heart and give agreement to what is being done. Relax and absorb the love coming to you.

If you are on the outside of the circle because you do not have this particular challenge, your job is to open your heart and send love to bring peace. Since you in the outside circle are working as healing facilitators, call on your healing guides. Remember that your healing guides guide you in what to do with healing. Send love to those you love who are in the circle. Even if you are reading this book a hundred years from now, you are all here.

Heal Early Experiences

Healing guides, please connect with the healing teams of those we are working with. We first ask for the release of all energy that either parent brought into the pregnancy of their sexual-orientation issues and concerns about who they should love. Some people attracted to their own gender enter heterosexual relationships that produce children because they do not want to appear different. That energy can enter the ovum from the sperm. Healing team, we now ask you to remove from the ovum, the sperm, and the initial fertilized egg any energy that is contrary to the full acceptance of the physical relationship on a heterosexual level. Going deeper, we ask to remove any shame from the parents that entered the ovum, sperm, and fertilized egg that they did not believe they were being true to themselves regarding their choice of sexual partner. For those in the outer circle, if this applies to you, the healing will occur to you as well.

If one or more of your birth parents were not comfortable with being who they were sexually, that energy might have transmitted to you as a heterosexual or homosexual. We ask your healing team to remove all artificial encodements that entered you from the time just before conception to birth from either birth parent. Your birth parents did not intend the energy to move into you, but it is there. Remove all those artificial encodements now, and repair any damaged and altered natural encodements from the point when the sperm and the egg joined to the point of birth.

This is now happening for the first month of gestation, the second month, and then the third, fourth, fifth, sixth, seventh, eighth, and ninth months. Allow that energy to settle. Next, see the image of whoever you wish to hold — you, this wonderful child — as the Belief plug-in is used to install this belief within you: "I am perfect just the way I am." (We will come back to parental influences at another time.)

Now we go to the very first time that you who are gay, lesbian, or bisexual knew you were attracted to someone of the same gender and the first time you heard that was wrong or were made to feel that you were wrong. Using the Basic plug-in, we ask that energy to be removed from you now. As it is removed, a new belief takes its place at an even deeper level: "I am perfect just the way I am."

We move to the first time you felt attracted to someone of the same gender and were confused by your attraction. We ask your healing team to use the Basic plug-in to bring healing to that experience. (Here's a hint: All this work we're doing will become its own plug-in, and we will do it over time. We just want to let you know where we're going with this [see the Just Done plug-in in the appendix].)

We go now to the first time you experienced a person attracted to someone of the same gender, and that person was berated, made fun of, and bullied. That energy entered you and triggered feelings in you. You did not acknowledge your sexual orientation and felt shame about your feelings and not standing up for the person being bullied. This is a complex experience. Your healing team knows how to work with it. They will use the Basic plug-in for your inner reactions to what you saw and heard and then for any feelings of cowardice or shame you might have had for not standing up for that individual.

Your healing team will use the Remove Victim Consciousness to remove the encodements of any energies you took on from either the perpetrator or the one being bullied. We ask your healing team to use the Basic plug-in to remove all those energies. Now they will use the Healing over Lifetimes plug-in to identify and release those energies from other lifetimes. You had lives in which you were heterosexual but felt shame or a lack of courage because you did not stand up for someone who was being bullied.

Now we ask your healing team to go to each chakra, in the order needed, to remove any implants of that energy. Just allow this to happen. We ask your healing team to use the Repair the Energy Field plug-in to repair the entire energy field — chakras, aura, meridians, and all hidden structures — from this incident and to replace all the energy removed with the belief: "I am perfect just the way I am." Take as long as you need. You might want to put this book down for a moment and allow the balancing to occur.

Heal through Age Eighty

Everything we have just done is a plug-in. We laughingly call it the Just Done plug-in [see the appendix]. Your healing team took all the instructions we gave them and used it for that one incident. Now we ask them to apply it to the following ages, beginning at age three. We ask for the Just Done plug-in to be applied to anything within the age of three, four, five, six, seven, eight, nine, and ten.

We add to this plug-in the removal of any shame, guilt, or fear from the first time you touched someone of your gender in a sexual way, in an exploratory way. This might have occurred as early as nine or ten years of age, maybe younger. We ask your healing team to use the Basic plug-in, the Healing over Lifetimes plug-in, and the Remove Victim Consciousness plug-in to repair the energy field and then use the Belief plug-in to the belief "I am perfect just the way I am." We do all this for ages ten, eleven, twelve, thirteen, fourteen, fifteen, and sixteen.

You might feel the need to pause as you go through the ages most difficult for you. Know that there is no time, and all this is being healed. Simply allow it to happen. We now move to age seventeen, eighteen, nineteen, twenty, twenty-one, twenty-two, twenty-three, twenty-four, twenty-five, twenty-six (yes, we're going to continue, year by year; if you are in the outer circle, continue sending love and acceptance), twenty-seven, twenty-eight, twenty-nine, and thirty.

If you are experiencing healing — if you find tightness in your chest or abdomen or anywhere in your body, even on the second chakra or any chakra — focus on that area and ask that whatever wound is responsible for that tightness be healed now using the four foundational plug-ins. Now, we continue with ages thirty-one, thirty-two, thirty-three, thirty-four, thirty-five, thirty-six, thirty-seven, thirty-eight (yes, we know we are going quickly, but healing is happening), thirty-nine, and forty.

People who are heterosexual might not realize that many people attracted in a sexual manner to people of their own gender often hide their feelings, even at older ages. So we will continue everything your healing team has been doing. Again those in the outer ring, your job is to send love and acceptance. We continue with years forty-one, forty-two, forty-three, forty-four, forty-five, forty-six, forty-seven, forty-eight, forty-nine, fifty, fifty-one, fifty-two, fifty-three, fifty-four, fifty-five, fifty-six, fifty-seven, fifty-eight, fifty-nine, and sixty.

Some of you on the outer ring might be wondering to what age we are going. We're going to eighty, because so many have suffered the pain of not being accepted for loving who they love. We continue with years sixty-one, sixty-two, sixty-three, sixty-four, sixty-five, sixty-six, sixty-seven, sixty-eight, sixty-nine, seventy, seventy-one, seventy-two, seventy-three, seventy-four, seventy-five, seventy-six, seventy-seven, seventy-eight, seventy-nine, and eighty. Apply the entire plug-in to all the years lived beyond eighty. Allow that energy to settle. You might want to pause in your reading and come back later, or you can continue if you like.

Heal Relationship Issues

Now let's go to the first time you entered a committed love relationship with someone of your gender and you hid the relationship. You might have lived in that relationship for years and never publicly admitted it. People might have thought this was a good friend or a roommate you shared a room with for years and years. You did not say, "This is who I love." Your healing teams take all that energy and pain of not being accepted and of not being able to declare, "This is who I love."

We call on Archangel Michael with his Sword to dissolve that energy within you now and transmute the fear of coming out publicly, saying, "This is who I love." We ask that energy to be transmuted to the highest level of pure love that you shared with each other. Those in the outer circle, send to everyone in the inner circle: "We love you as deeply as you love the one you love." Repeat this.

We ask your healing team to apply that to any messages, events, and energies you received from your family, church, school, media, friends (including those you knew were not your friends), strangers on the street, and places worked or volunteered. We include jokes said by those who did not know who you loved and the hurtful things said by friends or family that wounded you.

Now we ask your healing team to gather all your regrets of not taking the risk to love who you wanted to love. We ask that those regrets be transmuted to love with Michael's Sword. We ask that the knowledge and wisdom from those regrets be fully incorporated within your encodement system.

We now ask your healing team to gather the incidents you experienced of physical trauma and violence because of who you loved — along with your pain, fear, and shame — and transmute them into complete love using Michael's Sword. We ask them to add the belief: "I am perfect the way I am."

Now your healing team will gather from you the energy of the complex feelings you had when you read or heard about those who had violence perpetrated against them because of who they loved. Again, we ask that the energy be transmuted to the highest level of pure love with the Sword of Michael, and add the belief "I am perfect the way I am."

If you are in the center of these two circles, you might be tired and need some time to collect yourself. If something comes up from within, simply ask your healing team to use the Just Done plug-in and apply it to that feeling. Allow the love you are to shine into this world. Those of you on the outer circle who assisted in this healing, may the love of the inner circle and the love of the outer circle join together in acceptance and cover the entire planet. Now we add everything we have just done to the Just Done plug-in.

Heal Wounds from Negative Perception

Dr. Cathy: That was pretty powerful. Anybody have any comments or questions?

Louise: I placed myself both in the outer and inner circles, because although it didn't apply to me directly in this lifetime, I'm quite sure it applied to me in other lifetimes. When you said something about the second chakra, I felt a tightness there. I felt a release as well.

Thank you for sharing that, Louise. Anyone else?

Carolyn: I had a sad memory come up. When I was forty-nine, I was supposed to die, and my sisters put me in a nursing home. A woman was there who nobody wanted to interact with. I spoke to her once, and one of the nursing staff came over later and warned me to stay away from her because she was a lesbian. When her partner died, she ended up having to go into a residential nursing home and suffered greatly for it, just because she was gay.

Yes, those are the wounds we're working to heal.

CHAPTER ELEVEN

Release the Shame of Sexuality

Dr. Cathy and Amiya

Dr. Cathy: Amma says it's time to activate all dormant encodements related to the heart source. So go into your heart source and ask your healing team, "Please activate all dormant encodements related to my heart source." Now she's asking us to use St. Germain's meditation, so connect with St. Germain and connect with your soul self within your healing team. (All your healing team is present.) Request the violet-flame energy to come into your *sushumna* at the exact vibration needed for you. Just allow it to come down at its own pace, at its own spin. Let all that wonderful violet-flame energy pool at the base of your spine, in the little reservoir located below the entryway of the three channels that move upward with the kundalini.

Now ask your healing team to assist you. "Please bring that violet-flame energy up the central channel and the channels along the sides of my first chakra." The ones along the sides outline the chakra and then cross at the top of the chakra. Now the *sushumna*, the central channel, comes up at the same time as the other two cross at the top of the first chakra. Now the energies of the *ida* and *pingala* continue up and outline your chakra on the opposite sides. The *ida* and *pingala* meet at the top of the second chakra, cross, and then move up the opposite sides of the third chakra. Just let it come up.

The violet flame moves up into the third chakra, outlining it. The *ida* and *pingala* cross at the top of the third chakra and continue up to the fourth chakra, the heart chakra. Again, the energies of the *ida* and *pingala* cross at the top of the fourth chakra and outline the opposite side of the fifth chakra, crossing at the top of the fifth chakra. This continues with the sixth and seventh chakras.

St. Germain is adding something different. He wants us to bring all the energy back down the *sushumna* and the *ida* and *pingala*. You can ask for more violet flame, if you wish. St. Germain, your soul self, and those assisting you govern the amount and frequency of the violet-flame energy running through these channels.

The energy comes down the *sushumna* and moves through the *ida* and *pingala*, outlining both sides of the chakras and then crosses at the bottoms of the chakras before moving around the opposite sides of the next lower chakra. The three channels of energy move downward together from your seventh chakra to your sixth, fifth, fourth, third (mine is going a little faster), second, and first. Now let all that energy rest.

As you go against the natural direction of the *ida* and the *pingala*, you remove congested energy caught deep within the sides of the channels. Think of a scrub brush rubbing against the grain of a fabric to get all the dirt out. Going up, you go against the grain for one of them, and coming down you go against the grain for the other. Of course, you go back and forth with the mid channel. If you feel called to practice this — such as helping those who are crossing over, healing, or working with the fairies — as you bring in more energy and clear the channels, it allows for fuller expansion and exploration of the energies you're working with.

Release Shame from Your Genetic Line

Amiya: You are learning much and healing much. In this chapter, we will heal the energies of shame and the emotional and energetic abuse from others' actions, reactions, words, and thoughts toward you. We'll heal physical abuse later. People who have felt attracted to someone of their gender have experienced that energy, and it is present whether you know it or not. The only way that energy is not present is if you had absolutely no shame, guilt, anger, or rebellion within you as you explored your attraction to someone of the same gender. That leaves very few of you without shame or guilt. Some people might say, "Well, I wasn't affected by it," but they're angry. Their anger is a sign they were affected.

Connect with your healing team. Archangel Golden is with us to help direct this process. She asks you to call forth the consciousness of your genetic line, so set your intention to move into your familial genetic line. We'll begin with your male genetic line from your biological father. This time, we're going to have you move through your genetic line from your Merkabah. Your Merkabah is your heart source. Feel yourself in the Merkabah, moving into the actual double helix related to your father's line. This makes you seem very tiny, does it not?

First, sit in your Merkabah and acclimate with the energy of your DNA. We'll be using a plug-in each place you come to as you roam around in the DNA of your father's line. Stop any place that contains shame about any aspect of mutually agreed on sexual relations and release that energy. ("Mutually agreed on" means people have the ability to make the decision to be in a sexual relationship freely for themselves. Children do not have that ability.) An area might contain shame, guilt, fear, revulsion, rage, and anger about someone whose love relationship or attraction is for one gender or bisexual.

State: "I am the Sword." Turn your Merkabah into Archangel Michael's Sword. Are you ready for your trip? You might feel twists and turns as the double helix twists and turns. First, go to the energy that came in for your generation — all encodements of shame, anger, fear, revulsion, rage, and any other low-vibration feelings projected on to you related to those feelings that came from the DNA are removed. Any altered or damaged natural encodements are repaired. The encodements related to giving you joy and delight and self-acceptance no matter who you love are activated.

The encodements from this shame (and all the other emotions we mentioned) that came from religious institutions are removed. Almost everyone has at least some shame about sexuality from religious institutions. (This will go faster later when we put this all into one plug-in.) Now we remove all the artificial encodements and repair damaged and altered natural encodements that came from educational and social institutions. (That's a large category, correct?) Now we remove all the artificial encodements and repair damaged and altered natural encodements that came from governmental institutions and then any other place the energies might have come from, such as individuals, groups, or institutions. With this particular plug-in, we add the Remove Victim Consciousness plug-in and the Healing over Lifetimes plug-in. Yes, we're going to other lifetimes — past, present, future, and parallel — so this healing energy will spread outward. We're going deeply within.

We're adding one more thing to this plug-in: The intention to go into every particle of a cell within your body, to all the little organelles and mitochondria, for instance. This is where cellular memory is held. This is our Release Shame about Sexuality plug-in [see appendix].

Heal Generational Energy

What we just did was for your generation. Let's now move your healing Merkabah to your father's generation. Just imagine your Merkabah sitting there, and remember, it is also Michael's Sword removing that energy. Go back to your grandfather's generation, and remove that energy. In certain places, you'll find more balance because some members of your ancestry were attracted to people of the same gender and dealt with their shame and guilt.

Let's move to the first great-grandfather, second great-grandfather, third great-grandfather, and fourth great-grandfather. Can you feel the energy of healing spread throughout the generations? Now we'll do your fifth, sixth, seventh, eighth, ninth, tenth, eleventh, twelfth, thirteenth, fourteenth, fifteenth, sixteenth, seventeenth, eighteenth, nineteenth, and twentieth great-grandfather.

From your twentieth great-grandfather, we're going on a little trip. Continue backward in your father's line to the beginning of the shame, anger, fear, and revulsion of anyone who was attracted to the same gender at any time, as far back in time as needed, to the very source of this energy in your family line. Set that intention. With your Merkabah, you're transmuting the generational energy of your family. When it feels complete, you and your Merkabah come back to the entry point of your DNA where you started.

Now do exactly the same thing with the female line. You've already completed the healing with your generation. Now move your Merkabah to your mother's generation. You are Michael's Sword, transmuting the energy as we identified in the plug-in for this process. Ready? Move from your mother to your grandmother, first great-grandmother, and your second, third, fourth, and fifth grandmothers. Do you notice any changes within you? Then go to your sixth, seventh, eighth, ninth, and tenth grandmothers.

Don't worry if you feel we're moving too fast, as this all happens outside of time. Go to your eleventh, twelfth, thirteenth, fourteenth, fifteenth, sixteenth, seventeenth, eighteenth, nineteenth, and twentieth great-grandmothers. From the twentieth great-grandmother, set your intention to take your Merkabah, which is also Michael's Sword. With our plug-in, set your intention to travel backward in time along your mother's line to the source of any shame, revulsion, guilt, or fear of being attracted to someone of your gender. Go on your travels right now. When finished, come to the beginning of your DNA.

Now slide out of your DNA. Be conscious and aware of your body. You can remain in your Merkabah or just be in your heart source. You have done a generational healing, healing your feelings about yourself — if you have been attracted to someone of your gender and felt guilty about it — and removing the energies of people who are angry, vile, or rageful toward those who are attracted to people of their own gender.

The anger some people have toward those who are attracted to their own gender comes from all the sources we've mentioned, including religions, society, governments, school, and your fear of yourself. When you release that anger, that energy, and take away that shame, you experience no reaction to anyone else, no matter who they are. That is what we wanted to give you today.

Uplift the Planet

***Louise:** When we entered on my father's side, the energy was really dark and negative. It really surprised me. We kept going back and back, and when we finally got to the source of it, I was like, "Oh, there you are," and the energy changed; it cleared. All that*

darkness left. On my mother's side, I didn't have any of that negative energy. It was good, overall.

Dr. Cathy: My experience was very similar — very strong on my father's side. There was some on my mother's side, but it was more of the "I wish you weren't, but I love you" kind of energy. Anybody else have a similar experience?

Cleo: I had no experience, which is no surprise, since I rarely have those experiences. But I know from other sources on my paternal grandfather's side, at least back to ancient Greece, that they were awful people. I'm going to trust that in the now moment, whatever healing was required took place. So thank you, Amiya.

Good, thank you. Anybody else?

Margaret: I didn't get any of the feelings Louise had. But I was thinking how cool that our family was getting a double healing through my sister. Our generations got a double healing. I thought we must be very powerful that we have two of us to do this. I have a question. Are we healing individual people, or are we just healing the generational energy that's been carried throughout time?

It's actually the same thing. As we heal the generational energy, we also heal other people.

Margaret: Okay. So through this exercise, we're actually healing the entire planet.

Yes.

Cleo: Then does this exercise have any influence on the collective consciousness?

Yes, it does. It helps to release and relieve all that energy. I'm getting some new information now: It releases energy from those who have passed on. They no longer gather that energy. Those living might still experience the energy in the world. Tracings in their brains are still active. When people have a release of energy from the past, they have a greater opportunity to choose a different way of reacting or responding. Imprinting within the brain can be such that you need an act of will to change the tracing.

Cleo: And those people who were affected before die and come back. Does the energy pick up again?

When they come back, they have different life plans. They might have made different choices about what they're going to experience. They might or might not bring in that energy.

Cleo: The more we can heal the collective consciousness, the greater service we are to Gaia and Earth, because Earth is resetting.

Yes.

Mimi: I didn't feel anything and was more of an observer. I felt what was happening was a positive thing. Then it made me wonder: You go back generationally with your parents in this life, but then you come back to a different life with a different generational line that hasn't been healed.

Correct. You're right.

Mimi: So it's complicated, for sure.

Michelle: I have no idea if this applies, but before we got started, it came to me very clearly that this is also for the homeless.

Okay. Thank you.

Michelle: Can it be applied any possible way you think? Because that seems really odd.

I think many people are homeless because they have been rejected by their families.

Michelle: I guess my question is if a group of people could receive any of this without being aware.

Amiya just told me that whenever we do any of these exercises, we put out the intention for it to go into the planet and everyone here. You can do that for any healing. Thank you.

CHAPTER TWELVE

You Are Perfect as You Are

Amiya and Dr. Cathy

Amiya: We have done much work with healing, very intensive work, and we have much more to do. Our message for you today is short. Do not think that because you have healing to do in your life that you are not perfect. Do not think you are imperfect. You are exactly who you are meant to be at this moment in time.

You have lived thousands of lifetimes. People try to figure out how many lifetimes they have left. Here's a little secret: No one truly knows except God Almighty, the Creator. People think of lifetimes in the humanoid form. You began your lifetime as a spark of light, as a tongue of flame, but you wish to think of coming from the Creator. In so many cases, people see the Creator as the Father energy. You can think of sparks, tongues of fire, and being a penetrating force of father energy from the human sense. But that creative energy comes to rest in the fertile ground of the love of the Creator, which is the feminine energy, is it not?

When you come to this planet, you forget almost everything about who you truly are. You get tired of doing the healing work, of sludging through the mud, you could say. But as you sludge, you are perfect. It does not matter what has happened to you in your life or what low-vibration energies you have absorbed. You are perfect.

Yes, a spiritual evolution occurs. But let's put it a different way: A continual upgrading, changing, and raising of your vibration occurs. We're using these human terms, but we look at it differently from where we are. Often, what you see is the change of your color, the color of your light that comes from you. It does not matter what color your light is. That does not determine how much you are loved. We realize this is difficult to understand, believe, and accept from your human form, that every being and every source of energy that springs from the Creator is loved as dearly as the next. Even though some have gifts that you wish you had, those gifts, those attributes, the ways you express your light, have nothing to do with how much you are loved.

When you return home to us and review your life, you do not stand there in fear. When you return Home to stay, you have come to know again who you are. Perhaps you have heard people talk about the tunnel and how you have a life review led by a beautiful being. Those of the Christian tradition usually experience Yeshua. Those of the Buddhist tradition usually experienced Buddha. Those of the Jewish tradition, the Hebrew tradition, usually experience Moses, Abraham, or Elijah. The experience of who takes you on your life review and what you did has nothing to do with the love you are and who you are on the other side. It has to do with what you are comfortable with on Earth.

Those in a near-death experience go through what they need to experience as part of their life plans, and then they return to Earth. People read these experiences and think that's what life review is. It is not. When you are there for a visit, your life review is different.

You Are More than Your Pain

The way you move from Home to Earth is the tunnel of unknowing. The direction toward Home is the tunnel of knowing, of remembering. The fears of your lifetime drop away. The encodements of who you truly are activate in totality. When you come to your life review, you do not wonder whether you're a sheep or a goat, whether you were in the Christian tradition, or whether you are one of the 144,000, as in other traditions. All that is not who you truly are. All the beliefs you acquired to live that human life and that are not truth fall from you.

What remains is your essence, the power and presence of God in all its glory. You know in the depths of every part of you, within every encodement, that you are love. You are not love incarnate anymore, because you are not incarnated. You are love, and you know you are loved. When you have your life review, it is like sitting in a movie theater (not exactly but this is a good metaphor for you). You sit in a movie theater and remember the plan you had before you left, because it is right in front of you. You look at how it played out, and for you advanced souls reading this book, you look at the changes you made. The lives of souls who don't have as much experience as you, the newer souls, are planned much more meticulously than yours.

With your experience, you have potentials and options. You can probably think now in your life of what happened when you tried to decide between this option and another option or one of five options. Those of you with many aptitudes in the human realm have many options for how you can live your life on this planet. When you are at your end-of-life review, it is like examining a wonderfully delicious book that, with its twists and turns of plot points, was written with such poetry and elegance. Along with your council, your guides, you see how they interacted with you at each point of your life. It is not just your life review. It is also the life review of your angels and guides who contracted to be with you. Isn't that interesting?

You have no fear at this time. You are there in joy. You all laugh and applaud, and you applaud your supporting cast. The soul selves of those still on Earth when you came Home join in this review. The energies of the soul selves who passed on, like parents or children who died before you, join you. It is a huge movie theater, and the movie shown on the screen is your life. Each individual enjoys watching how they contributed their part, which is also how you contributed to their experience. To use a human analogy, those of you who enjoy popcorn will have your popcorn (buttered or not), and those who like soft drinks (although we have a different type of elixir here) will choose your favorites as you watch.

We tell you this because we have been working with you in these past two books on pain, which can be indescribable in the human realm. It hurts, does it not? It opens your heart or, by your choice, closes your heart. The pain you experience at any one time is not the end of that experience; it is the beginning. All is designed, in this long, circuitous route of being human, to open your heart and for you to come to realize the amazing glory that you are. You volunteered to come here to love, to be a beacon of light. You knew that in the human realm, being a beacon often comes from great pain. It is the human way of opening the heart and remembering who you are. It is a paradox.

The Planet Needs Your Light

Can a being come to this planet and have great light without having problems or going through pain? They are here, and they are called angels. They are your guides, some of whom experienced great pain when they were in the physical. For humans to understand light, you must experience not having light. When you slog through these things, know that your pain is not who you are. Your experience of how people treat you is not who you are. Who you are is what you cannot see or sense. The guides surrounding you with love cannot be seen.

Many people ask, "How many angels and guides do I have on my team?" They might list three, four, five, six, or seven. Yes, those might be the ones who speak to you the most and give you the most support by speaking to your heart. But you are surrounded by hundreds who love you. When you feel most alone, you are surrounded by more love energy than you ever knew. You are supported and loved.

We place this at this point in the book because Amma spoke to us and said, "My healing friends, my precious children are beginning to think they are only their wounds because we work so much with healing. They are not their wounds. They are more precious than they could ever know or imagine until they come Home. So let's remind them, even if they can't get in touch with that feeling of love and magnificence."

That is what we wanted to share with you right now at this point in your journey. We know you might not have read the first book, so you are not aware of all the healing that took place there. Very soon we'll go into the depths of healing sexual issues. We've been dealing with the surface issues that affect most people. We want to remind you, before you continue on this journey, that you are perfect. No matter what happened to you, you are not that pain. The actions done to you do not determine who you are. It was simply a plot point, a device, if you would, as you come to understand more of humanity, so your light can shine more into this world. The planet needs your light. It is your love; it is your joy.

We are here. Amma is here. Abba is here. Yeshua, Melchizedek, Metatron, Kathumi, and St. Germain are here. When the names of loved ones pop into your head, you might think, "Where did that come from? Why did I think of them?" It is because they have visited you and wanted to remind you they are present. So, perfect example of love, perfect being of love, remember always who you are even as we work with you in healing on the human realm.

Spirit Brings an Uplifting Message

Dr. Cathy: It feels like they came in just for me because I've been having a tough time lately. So if you don't think this applied to you, that might be why.

Cleo: I thought that was the most beautiful, wonderful, uplifting message I've ever heard. I want to listen to it over and over.

Good. Thank you. Anybody else?

Carolyn: That was really good and profound. Thank you.

Cleo: When she was talking at length about life review, I was reminded when Dom, my husband, passed. I ended up having a life review that I didn't ask for or expect. That was when Amma said to consider my life with Dom as a past life and to move forward. It was a very different life review than what she described, but it was perfect for the moment, and of course, the Elohim were present. What more could I ask for?

True. Wonderful.

CHAPTER THIRTEEN

The Challenges of Gender Identification

Amiya

You are perfect the way you are. You are love. You are called to shine light on this world. You are called to be and to recognize the love that you are. You live in a world and a society that has a very difficult time with what they might call the "strangeness" of how people present themselves.

We're talking now about the gender of who you're attracted to. That continues to be a struggle for many in this world who still believe that being attracted to someone of the same gender is abhorrent. Some have killed or attempted to kill others because of this belief. This engenders shame and fear that can result in people fearing to know who they are. This situation has gotten better in many countries.

We will now talk about something that is becoming more well-known: gender identity. Your young ones are much more open to this than you older ones. They are not as limited by beliefs about others. They are more open to exploring their sexuality and gender. You see this in the language they use, such as saying they are nonbinary; they do not claim to be male or female. Most people have the genitalia of one or the other; however, some people are born with both male and female genitalia. Your medical community calls these people hermaphrodites.

Some say that something went wrong in the gestational process of transgender people. We say this is simply a difference, and nothing is wrong with people who are confused about their gender. In fact, the most confused people are usually those who believe being trans is evil or wrong. Just because people are not in accord with the norm does not make them wrong.

Understand the Spiritual Aspects of Gender

Before we go into healing, which we will do in the next chapter, let us talk about this from the spiritual level. Many of your indigenous tribes knew about transgenderism and accepted it. In these societies, transgender people were thought to have great power because they had access to both male and female energies.

Eons ago, before the time of the Judeo-Christian story of Adam and Eve, people did not have two genders. Have you considered that the story of Adam and Eve was actually a story of people no longer being androgynous? Logically, other people had to be living at the time of that story, unless the sons had sex with their mother. The Creator wants diversity. You do not get diversity when three men have intercourse with one woman. All the children would have the same genetics. So think about the story of Adam and Eve, which is mixed with the creation story. Think of it as a story of when males and females came into being. Interesting, is it not? Diversity is wonderful; males are wonderful, and females are wonderful. The two genders bring so much to this planet.

If you are born with an abundance of masculine energy but are physically female, you might doubt what gender you are. So here is a question for you: Is gender really important for anything other than procreation? You have two genders for procreation, do you not? You are not like certain fish who can change gender. There really is no other purpose needed for two genders other than procreation. You need eggs and sperm and a way for them to come together, but as your science has discovered, these can be brought together without the benefit of the sexual act.

Men and women have both masculine and feminine energies to different degrees. In a relationship, a female partner might have more masculine energy than her male partner. The same can be true in same-gender or non-declared-gender relationships. And depending on the situation, who exhibits the most masculine or feminine energy can change.

Let us go back to what we have said many times: You planned your lifetime on Earth. If you are transsexual, you planned to investigate what it was like to be uncertain about your gender, just as others planned to investigate who they were sexually attracted to. Just because you are different in something as foundational as gender does not mean you are different from others, except in certain characteristics.

What is your job if you do not question your gender? Your job is to love those who do. Your job is to support them and say, "All things are within the realm of possibility," when someone says something negative about others questioning their gender. You do not have to argue.

Gender identity questions can be due to past-life influences. One hypothesis is that a soul who strongly identified as either male or female in a previous life returned too quickly and was born the opposite gender. That can contribute to a person's confusion. Doing past-life regressions can assist you, as a transgender person, to become clearer about what you want. It can also help clarify any energies keeping you from moving on or living your life as your preferred gender.

Accept and Love People as They Are

The way to live your life is to accept people as they are. Let's take something very simple, such as being a parent. Perhaps one of your children wants to be an artist, and one wants to be an engineer. It is not uncommon for families to discourage the artist from becoming an artist. As parents, your job is to nurture your children, give guidance the best you know how, and accept them as they are. It is much more difficult when it comes to gender identification and gender attraction, because you are going counter to the norm.

People fear things that are different. But just because you are not aware of something does not mean it is not there. Before you learned of black holes, just because you didn't know of them did not mean they didn't exist. Just because someone is not aware that eating a particular food is possible doesn't mean other people do not eat it. We go back to where we started with this book. Anything done with mutual consent and with love is within the space of love.

Love those in society who struggle. Those struggles would not exist if all people were accepted by society. Love people as they are. Listen to them. Do not tell them what to do unless they ask your opinion and you are knowledgeable. Be there to listen — also to comment lovingly and with acceptance but more so to listen. That is how you give support.

Not all people (especially the very young) who believe they are transgender are indeed transgender. Some come in and realize that one gender has certain benefits than the other gender does.

Someone can identify as one gender and still have the bodily functions of the other gender. A male cannot give physical birth if he is born male, but someone who identifies as male and has the reproductive system of a female can give birth as a male. It can be mind-bending, can it not? More and more will become known about this as your scientists open up about it and as people open their minds. Scientists know much more about gender, genetics, and the X and Y chromosomes than is commonly known.

In the next chapter, we will help people heal wounds from not being accepted as they are. We will work to resolve past-life influences that can contribute to gender confusion. We will work to heal those who are confused about their gender. We will work to heal difficulties people have who are unfamiliar with these differences. And we will work to heal those who insist someone should be the way they prefer.

If you become confused any time you hear of or read about people struggling with their gender identification, we suggest that you ask your healing team to assist you in healing any wounds or confusion by aligning your encodement system to be more open to what happens in life.

CHAPTER FOURTEEN

Clear Sexual Trauma

Amiya

In this chapter, we begin to heal the more traumatic aspects of sex and sexuality in your life. Before we go into the deep trauma, we will start with a simple clearing for everyone. First, it's important to realize that your sexuality and spirituality are complementary. By that, we mean your spirituality is who you are as a spiritual being. Your spirituality is that part of you that transcends this third-dimensional world and can tap into and experience Spirit, All That Is, Love Itself, us, any of the masters, and any of the beings you have known and loved here who have moved on and are now here with us in the fullness of themselves.

It also assists you to connect with each other in sacred ways. This connection does not have to be sexual; it is your auras joining with each other. When you're with someone having tea or coffee and sharing each other's energies and words, you move toward each other and join together. Imagine your energies holding hands and connecting on a deep level. That is the spiritual aspect.

Your sexuality is your physical aspect. It also connects with you spiritually. You cannot separate the two. When you do something you believe has brought you shame on a sexual level or you feel wounded or dirty because of something someone has done to you, it affects you spiritually. When you decide to engage in any physical activity from the goodness of your heart, even if others say it is wrong, there is nothing wrong with that. You could say that the only "wrong" is that you feel shame about it.

Sexuality is much more than your physical interactions on a sexual level. It is how you present yourself as a male or a female — not necessarily male or female in body but rather your masculine nature and your feminine nature. Your sexuality is involved in how you care for the planet. It is involved with how you relate to your children and how your children relate to you. It is involved in every aspect of your life, just as your spirituality is involved in every aspect of your life.

Separate the idea that sexuality is just about the act of making love, the act of having sex, or the physical responses in your body. Sexuality brings together all the different aspects of you, including your love of self. You feel deserving of being loved, which connects with spirituality. You feel deserving of loving others. We say it again: What connects to spirituality are those basic beliefs of feeling deserving, being loved, being loving, and loving self. That opens your ability to express love one to another. Sometimes that is physical, but it is not necessarily sexual. It could be a hug, a kiss on the cheek, holding hands, or a pat on the shoulder.

Spirituality and sexuality negatively influence each other when love or desire becomes convoluted. Your body might respond, or you might misinterpret signals. This is the very beginning of working with abuse issues. First, connect with your healing team. Ask them, "Please gather all the energies I produced or that invaded me from another, such as when someone looked at me in an objectifying way. Please remove all those artificial encodements. Find the wounds that allowed that energy to come into me and use the Basic plug-in to heal the energy of all those wounds."

This one is seeing an interesting image. It's as if the wound has opened up, and within it, she sees the pain and the changes made in your encodements system. Ask your healing team to go inside that wound, which has connections on many levels. This is where the other plug-ins come in. Ask your healing team, "Please use the Remove Victim Consciousness plug-in for each of those wounds. Trace that victim consciousness back through the lifetimes of my soul using the Healing over Lifetimes plug-in. Now use the Implant Removal plug-in for each area within this opened wound in my energy field, especially in my chakras and subchakras, and release and remove that energy."

Instead of working with the DNA as we have in the past, let's develop another plug-in — the Heal Genetic and Generational Experiences plug-in [see appendix]. We've done this work before. This time, we're making it into a plug-in. So in each of those stopping places, you're going to use the four foundational plug-ins. We'll do this through the familial line.

Heal the Female Line

This will be a little different. First, we'll go through your mother's line (your mother, your mother's mother, your mother's mother's mother, and so on). In addition, we'll go back through your father's female line as well as each grandfather's female line. This will be on the mother's side as well (her father's mother, grandfather's mother, and so on). Do you see how we're moving the healing out to even more generations? The Healing over Lifetimes plug-in will intersect at certain places: You might have been your great-great-great-grandfather or your great great-great-grandmother. Just allow that to occur. You might or might not feel it happening.

Again, we are working with removing the energies of the times you felt objectified because of your gender, sexual orientation, or gender identification. This will apply to each person in your family line. For some of you, the objectification will move through socioeconomic classes. For example, some in the upper class believe they can do whatever they wish sexually, speak however they wish, or objectify whoever is of a lower socioeconomic class. We apply this plug-in to that as well.

This will make you ready for healing such things as rape. We are clearing some of the energy so that you can go even deeper when we approach these other experiences. Just allow your energy to adjust. Remember, the last step of all the plug-ins is to harmonize your energy field.

We'll now work with wounds you might have inherited. We use the word "inherited" loosely here because it is not necessarily a genetic inheritance. It could have occurred when you were raised by someone other than a birth parent. This applies to adoptees and foster children. You might have spent a great deal of time with particular families other than your own. Maybe this was your second family, especially when you were young.

Heal Objectification Experiences

We ask now that your healing team gather all the energies from this family in which you might have felt objectified. We're going to use the same plug-in we used earlier. You might say, "But wait, how do we heal backward in time when it is not my genetic family?" We ask for this healing through the plug-in to go backward in time to the families of these people you are focusing on. We ask that healing to occur as much as individual members of the family allow. In a way, we're doing spiritual lovefare work. Again, it can only happen as much as others allow. You make the request and allow that energy to move through their genetic line.

We'll use the same plug-in in these different ways: school systems or educational systems. Did you ever feel objectified? Did you experience incidents of what we now call sexual harassment? Call that up. You might have absolutely none or some. Ask your healing team to apply the same plug-in to you and to the perpetrator. (Let's see how you can help facilitate healing throughout the planet in this area.)

Let us do the same for religious institutions. Call forth any energies where you felt objectified, as a sexual object, by members of religious institutions or by the actions and beliefs of the system as a whole. Remember, sexuality is broader than just sexual acts, such as women being considered subservient to men in a religious area. It can also apply, as this one has experienced, in the Catholic Church. Only priests can perform sacred rituals after women do all the preparatory work. Women do not get to celebrate in the same way as priests. There is that struggle on a gender basis that includes sexuality. Now ask your healing team, "Please apply the Heal Genetic and Generational plug-in to all experiences I've encountered of sexual harassment and gender bias and to those who were the perpetrators of such as much as they will allow."

Now we will apply the plug-in to work situations. Gather the energy of feeling objectified or used because of your gender or sexuality. (Gender is a part of sexuality.) Again, apply the plug-in to the perpetrators as much as they allow.

This Work Affects the Greater Good

Let us move to society as a whole, for lack of a specific designation or category. This would be situations in which somebody made a lewd comment to you or treated you as a servant, expecting you to walk through the door, smile, and act a certain way for them. Ask for this plug-in for yourself and for the perpetrators. Good.

Now, some more spiritual lovefare. It is impossible to heal yourself without having an impact on the world, on society as a whole. Ask the wonderful healing teams across your planet, "Please assist me in gathering the energy of objectification around the world and please apply this plug-in." See yourselves gathered in a circle around this huge ball of energy. As the healing teams work according to your request, as much as each individual allows, use Michael's Sword. Declare, "I am the Sword." Place the Sword within this energy to transmute the energy. Now ask for Spirit — God, Amma, Abba, whatever name you use — ask that all the places within you that are now empty due to the healing and removal of the congestion be filled with love.

Good. Now you are ready. After one additional message, we will begin working with the more difficult areas of trauma, of woundedness, involving you in sexual areas and sexuality. Even though this might not apply to you in this lifetime, you have generational work to do. You have soul-level work to do that extends through lifetimes. We will also work to clear this on your planet.

CHAPTER FIFTEEN

Give Thanks

Amiya and Dr. Cathy

Amiya: We are going to do work with the DNA. The DNA is a type of fractal. That is why, when cells reproduce, the DNA remains the same until something enters it — and thus enters the cells — that changes it. The DNA is in its pure form when it matches the divine blueprint. Other energies come in that alter the DNA. This altering occurs because you made a decision before you came into this incarnation to experience certain things in your life. As you expand in your spiritual growth and development, it is important not to be angry with that part of you, your soul self (higher self), for what you chose for this life and what you've experienced.

Instead of anger, frustration, or regret, rejoice and be in gratitude, always. Being in a state of gratitude to praise God, to praise Source, for all that happens in your life, even if you do not understand it, is an important part of spiritual growth and development. It is an important part of healing. Say, "Thank you," even if it's, "Thank you for the experience of my father invading my room and raping me, as I now have the experience of learning how to overcome these wounds. I have learned how to have compassion for myself and others, perhaps to learn compassion even for my father."

People on a different spiritual path might not understand. "Thank you for my husband dying." "Thank you for my child dying." These are terrible things. What you give thanks for is the gift of life and love received from them. You're not thanking them for dying. You're thanking them for the gift of life. This might seem unusual, even antithetical (if that is the word for it). You contain a paradox of being able to thank Source, All That Is, Love Itself, for everything that happens. When you do that, it prevents changes in the DNA that can pass down, if you're young enough to have children, to subsequent generations.

An interesting thing happens with DNA. This one read about an experiment in which scientists wanted to discover whether an individual's enzymes change when the enzymes are no longer together. To do this, they had someone spit in a cup. How about that? They divided that split into two parts and separated them by feet, then yards, and then by miles. Then they changed the enzymes in only one of the samples and did nothing to the other. They measured both and found that the sample that had nothing done to it changed based on what had happened to the altered half. Why? Because both samples were energetically connected.

Gratitude Changes the DNA

Let's apply this to your DNA. Your children's DNA, even your grandchildren's, changes when you ask for your DNA to be healed. That seems impossible, does it not? It is impossible from your view of physics in the mechanical sense. But when you get to what is known as quantum physics, it is not in the least impossible. It is no more impossible for that to happen than for you to connect with a loved one when that person is in another city or on the other side of the world. You know this if you are a parent; you often know when something happens to your child. This connection is beyond most people's understanding.

The fractal nature of the DNA is not yet seen with the equipment your scientists currently use, no matter how amazing the technology. Even greater magnification will allow you to discover the fractal nature of the DNA. You'll see the fractal nature of replication as a cell separates into two and the DNA replicates with one set for each cell.

If you are in a place of gratitude, even for the worst things that have happened to you, a change occurs in the energy of your body that brings in gratitude. You realize that growth has occurred or can occur if you allow it. In a way, this is where the phrase "I look for the silver lining" comes from. What is the silver lining in the terrible things that happen to you? You might be thinking, "But why does this have to happen?" The simple answer is that this was your plan, and you are expanding.

A deeper answer to this is beyond your understanding at this point in your life. When you struggle with what you call the "horrors of the world," you often ask, "Why does it have to be this way? How can the horrors be stopped?" The "why it has to be" is to allow you to make a choice to be part of stopping that sort of behavior. Eons ago, the DNA of other forces entered the human DNA and brought in a darkness that has hidden the light of how you were originally created. The only way to change that is not to be caught up in the darkness, to rise above the darkness.

You have heard that you cannot change a situation from the same energy with which it was created (a paraphrase of Albert Einstein). Darkness was not created from gratitude. Darkness was created from control. Absorb these words. When anyone attempts to control another, it is darkness. Yes, there are levels of darkness. Levels of the deep, deep dark seem impenetrable. This is what some of you might call evil. Some darkness is like a cloud — anxiety, depression, fear. Despair is a deep darkness, as it is the loss of all hope.

When you can, go into the back of your heart source into your sacred space. From there, offer gratitude for whatever is evolving in your life from the negative thing that happened. As you work to heal the trauma in your life, part of healing is to accept that this was part of your plan and to be in gratitude that your plan unfolded. All events in your life — the joys and difficulties, even the extreme difficulties — make you who you are now. These things are within your life.

Practice Gratitude

If you are willing, take a pen and paper, and list all that you have learned from the most difficult events of your life. This one is remembering something her brother said as he held on to his mother immediately after his son died: "I am so glad I had him because I never knew I could love that much." We do not mean that you should minimize some of these things you have had to overcome (and you might have had to overcome some horrendous things) and say, "No, the pain is not there." You admit your pain and feelings that are there. At the same time, you look at what you have learned, such as opening your heart to be able to have more compassion for others.

When you are in gratitude, you are grateful that your life is unfolding as needed and that you are learning and experiencing your evolvement. In your gratitude, you admit you do not know the purpose. You would rather it not have happened, you do not know the purpose, but you are grateful because you trust the Source, the Creator, All That Is. The greatest act of trust, the greatest act of living out the first ray of the will of God, is to be in gratitude for what has happened.

We say this to you now because you might soon experience more disturbances in the United States and around the world. More things are coming into the light. Whatever comes, even if you think it could not be happening, go into a place of gratitude that it is being revealed. Even if something turns out not to be true, the plan for the planet has a purpose and an alignment.

Your gratitude penetrates the darkness that surrounds certain elements of your DNA. It penetrates the darkness that surrounds some of your family line. We challenge you to practice gratitude every time you can, at least by your words or thoughts, even when you do not feel grateful and even the times you say with gritted teeth, "I do not understand. I trust you. I give thanks for what is happening because you have helped me in these areas." Then list those areas. If you are a parent, you can list your children. You can list your wealth. You can list how you have grown. You are moving from "I don't know how to offer gratitude" to "I will be in gratitude." Then recall those things you are grateful for, even if they are no longer with you at this time.

Again, when you are in a place of gratitude, you inject energy into your DNA that can dissolve the darkness, the stuckness of that situation. Because of the energetic connection you have with those you love, it will transmit to those who have your DNA.

It is time to practice gratitude. What is one thing in your life you have not been able to release? You do not have to get into the emotion of it, but what is one thing? In whatever words you want to use, say, "I don't understand, but I trust that you are well aware of the plan that we made, and I thank you for the unfolding of that plan. I am in gratitude for the unfolding." This brings more light into the situation. Be in gratitude at the beginning of difficulties. That is when you remember what you are grateful for. List every person you love and who loves you. Look around the room you are in and give thanks for whatever you are thankful for. If you are not thankful for an object in your room, it might be time to release it to someone else.

Be Grateful Even for Deep Wounds

Since this book is about healing issues surrounding sexuality, bring to mind a wound in that area of your life. It does not need to be a wound of being raped or abused in some way. It could be a wound of embarrassment. Bring that to mind and offer thanks. If you cannot do it from your heart, do so from your mind and connect to your heart simultaneously. You can say, "I am willing to become willing to be in gratitude, and I am grateful you are here to assist me to become willing."

Why is it important to bring this up now? Because we are going to start talking about healing deep wounds. We will talk about healing things that might not have happened to you or to those you know and love personally but things you've heard about on the radio, seen on television, or read about in newspapers. You might have even seen fictional events in movies or on television or read things in novels that horrified you. What you have seen or read happened to someone, and you are wounded by that pain since you feel pain through your compassion. You are horrified that a human being can do that to someone else.

Give thanks for what you have become aware of and for the people involved and what they have done to teach you. Whatever you are to learn or experience, offer thanks for the victim and the perpetrator. Offer thanks for being angry about what has happened. Offer thanks for being unsure that this could ever be from God. As we go through these things, they might be difficult for you to read, especially if some form has happened to you or to someone you love. We want you to have this other part of healing — thanksgiving, praise, gratefulness — for what is. That is the first ray. As you work in these areas, you will also be working with the fourth ray of ascension and the third ray of wisdom. It is all there.

We will begin the more difficult parts in the next chapter. If you are reading this, you likely have compassion and empathy for others. What you read can be painful. Be in gratitude that you feel those emotions. Be in gratitude that your brain works in such a way that you are connected to people. You can be in gratitude that you are not like those who did the abuse. You can even be in gratitude that it did not happen to you. You can be in gratitude that you experienced pain from reading or hearing about someone else's pain. Thank them for what they went through, and send them love from your heart.

If you do not understand what we are saying, be in gratitude for that. It is a paradox on the human level that you will understand when you leave your body and come Home. We are in gratitude for you: what you do, what you have done, what you experience, your questions, your resistance, and your absolute glorious love.

We want you to take from this chapter the message to reflexively say words or phrases having to do with gratitude. This one is remembering how she always used to say, "Praise the Lord." Praise God, from whom all blessings come, and know that many of those blessings are hidden in something you might not want to see.

Detach from the Pain

Dr. Cathy: Well, that is not what I was expecting. I thought we were going right into the healing today.

Cleo: At the end, she was talking about those of us who are empathetic and feel compassion for what's going on. I've noticed recently that I am deeply troubled and have more compassion for things going on than ever before, such as COVID. I can barely watch TV when these things come on. I don't understand what's happening with me, why my compassion seems to be expanding.

Carolyn: I think everybody is going through this. For me, it's like a growth thing. It's allowed me to become more aware in order to be in gratitude.

Cleo: For sure.

What came to me as you were speaking, Cleo, was the statement,

"The more you heal, the more your heart opens to what is happening in the world." There comes a point in a progression of growth that, as you heal, you become more aware of others. Then when you move into that place of gratitude, you can detach from the pain. You detach from the pain, but you don't detach from the people.

Cleo: Detachment is the element that seems to be missing for me or needs to grow more. We talk about having eyes that see the seen and unseen. I see the suffering in what's going on, and I don't want to see it.

When I watch the detective shows I enjoy, I find myself being more affected by them. I've been asking that love be sent to those in reality who are experiencing similar events and that love break open the hearts of perpetrators. I've been moved into a greater sense of prayer, which I've found rather fascinating, to be honest with you.

Cleo: It's kind of the same thing when I watch the news and see things happening. My first reaction is of compassion. I send compassion and love. I flow love to them.

Amiya is saying to me to thank them for the work they are doing that has brought you to this place of greater compassion. Every time you experience these things, compassion increases. Every time you find yourself being compassionate for someone you couldn't have been compassionate for five minutes ago or ten years ago, you have grown. This can be described by one of my favorite quotes from scripture, where God says, "I will take your heart of stone to give you a heart of flesh."

Cleo: I say a similar affirmation: "I am the open heart of love of God I Am."

There's that story about a man on a park bench who looked down and saw a butterfly struggling to get out of a chrysalis. In his compassion for the butterfly's pain, he reached down and opened the chrysalis. But in so doing, he killed the butterfly because the struggle of getting out of the chrysalis strengthens a butterfly's wings and moves fluid down where it needs to go. In some way, our experience is the process of moving out of the chrysalis into who we truly are, whether you want to call it ascension. It is impossible to see that from our level. That's where trust comes in.

Sharon: And faith.

Elaine: I thought this was amazing. There were times when she could have said, "Elaine, this is for you." What I find particularly gratifying, or I'm extremely grateful for, is that

the healing we do for ourselves positively affects our children, grandchildren, and ultimately, anyone we touch. Gratitude is a big one.

When she talked about the death of a husband, I thought of you.

Elaine: In fact, I thought about him this morning when I meditated. He passed away from cancer. There's all this information now about alternative treatments, and I was wishing that I had done more research or done other things at that time. But it was his soul's choice as to when and how he departed.

Cleo: Elaine, I had a similar experience. My husband also died of cancer. Out of forty-five years of marriage, at least twenty or twenty-five of them were cancer years. He had every intervention that was available in that moment. When the end came, it was really awful.

CHAPTER SIXTEEN

Heal the First Encounters of Sexual Abuse

Amiya and Dr. Cathy

Amiya: We are not going to gloss over people's wounds regarding sex. We are going to talk about sexual abuse in its many forms. This could trigger memories for you. It could bring up memories not from this incarnation but from another incarnation. It could bring up familial memories that go back generations.

It is important that you be in your heart source as you read this material, so we will take you through those steps now. First, focus on the front of your heart center in the middle of your chest. Put your hand on the center of your chest, and with your awareness, move underneath your hand to deep within your heart center. As you read this material and live your life, try to at least be in your heart center.

Now move into the back of your heart center, which is opposite the front of your heart center. Move deeply into the back. If you go deep enough, you will go through a passageway that expands into a big room. This is your sacred space. We recommend that you stay in your sacred space as we do this work.

Move into the front of your third eye, your brow chakra. Allow your energy to go deep within that chakra to where it connects with the pranic tube. Now go deep into the back of the brow chakra and connect with the pranic tube.

Connect your heart chakra with your third eye. Imagine a beam of energy that goes from your heart to your third eye. Feel what happens to your body with that connection. It brings your heart brain and your physical brain together, the energies of your heart and third eye. Now send that beam of energy straight up to the center of the universe. Have no worries about where that is; it knows where to go. Then send that beam of energy straight down into the center of Earth.

Now command: "Heart source, expand to the farthest reaches of my aura." Now say, "Chakras, spin, and spin as fast as is good for me."

Any time we work with you and you feel difficult emotions, connect with your healing team. Ask them to implement the four foundational plug-ins for whatever wound was triggered within you.

Now call your healing team to be with you. If you are not aware of your healing team, know that everyone has one. Your healing team consists of your soul self, what many call the higher self, your bodysoul, which is the actual soul of your body (you are borrowing the body), your encodement technicians and the soul-healing angels who work with you. You might have others with you. People have various beings on their healing teams. You may also invite whomever you wish.

As you go through this process, you are firmly grounded and centered. You are surrounded by the love in your heart source. No matter what happened to you, you were continually within the womb of Amma.

As you know, you chose to experience these things. You might wonder why. You will rediscover the why when you have finished this life and leave your body. Know that the ultimate reason was from love: your love for yourself and your love for other souls participating in your life.

Now we are going to begin with your very first experience of sexual abuse. We're going to do this from a time we have touched on already in the book *Healing from Conception to Birth*. This section begins the healing of sexual abuse that occurred in this lifetime.

Heal Conception by Rape

Take a deep breath. Be sure you're in your heart source. The first place you might have experienced sexual abuse is being conceived by rape. Let us define rape for you. Rape is when there is sexual intercourse not agreed on by both partners. Yes, a male can be raped. A man's body can respond in rape just as a woman's body can respond. The key is that sexual intercourse is agreed on by both partners.

Rape at this early stage goes into the energy of the sperm and the ovum available for conception. That energy combines within the fertilized ovum. This results in dual energies entering the fertilization process. Ask your healing team to do what we suggest, whether or not you know about your conception. Notice what happens as we use the four foundational plug-ins. (Remember that one is the Healing over Lifetimes plug-in that will heal the many lifetimes of your soul.)

We now focus on the sperm. We ask your healing team to look at the energy within the sperm, and if there is any energy of rape — sexual power over someone else — we ask first that the wound within the male that caused him to do this or left him open to do this (yes, he had a choice) be healed. This is the wound that left him open to this choice of exercising power over a woman and does not involve love. We ask for that man to be healed. (That is your biological father if you were conceived by rape.)

Ask your healing team, "Please apply the four foundational plug-ins to the sperm that contained rape energy." Remember, these are the Basic plug-in, the Healing over Lifetimes plug-in, the Remove Victim Consciousness plug-in, and the Implant Removal plug-in. Ask your healing team, "Please specifically apply the Implant Removal plug-in to the energy of the male contained within the sperm that invaded the DNA by the action of rape as well as the pain of what happened to him when he was wounded."

Now we go to the ovum. Ask your healing team, "Please move back in time and find the ovum that will soon receive the sperm. The energies that enter at the time of the rape include terror, confusion, fear, self-doubt, and powerlessness. Tell your healing team, "Please surround and fill that ovum with love. Please surround my mother and fill her with love. On all levels of this action of rape in which she was invaded, abused, and nullified as a human being, please apply the four foundational plug-ins."

Heal the Fertilized Ovum

We now go to the fertilized ovum. Call forth the consciousness of the DNA of that fertilized ovum, and ask your healing team, "Please use the Heal the DNA plug-in to remove any energies of rape." This can be more than the act itself, such as all the feelings that came from the male and the female.

We are going to do something a little bit different with the ovum but still to the DNA. Remember, when the ovum is fertilized, it is just one cell. Then it becomes two, then four, and then eight. We are at the very beginning, when the sperm and ovum join. It is one cell. From this point, from this very beginning of life, ask your healing team, "Please apply the Remove Victim Consciousness plug-in to remove victim consciousness from the very depths of the two strands of DNA, male and the female."

This will be interesting, because two types of victim consciousness are involved. One is the victim consciousness of the perpetrator, in which he (or she) believes there was no choice; the person felt driven to do this. Your healing team removes that victim consciousness. Now they remove the victim consciousness from the person who was raped. (This is usually from a female, but it can be from a male if he was violated in such a way.) Now they remove that energy from the DNA of this new being created from this event, which is you.

Earlier, we removed energies from the DNA back through lifetimes. We're going to do that again. For the abuser, call forth the energy of that DNA going back generationally as far as needed to remove that perpetrator energy, the energy in which other people are seen as objects, as tools for their emotions. Ask your healing team, "Please heal this now."

Now call forth the energy and consciousness of the victim's DNA going back generations, male and female. This can encompass hundreds of people, thousands of people, depending on when the victim consciousness begins. Ask your healing team, "Please remove from this DNA the sense of being a victim and being powerless over anything having to do with sexual issues, including sexual assault. Now remove perpetrator energy from within that DNA. I command that this occurs now, the complete healing of the DNA and the release of all perpetrator and victim energy in sexual issues."

We now move back to the perpetrator, because we have not yet removed his (or her) victim energy. Say, "Healing team, remove all victim energy from the DNA of the perpetrator back as many generations as needed. Do so now." One last time, regarding the DNA as a whole of the individual who was conceived by rape, ask your healing team, "Please fill with love those spaces in which victim consciousness energy and perpetrator energy were removed."

Now consider what we did as a plug-in. We ask your healing team to take everything we just did and remove any sexual violence that took place during the nine months of gestation. Remember, a woman can be raped by her husband or her partner, and the energy and feelings of the violence can enter the developing child. Ask your healing team, "Please take the process of healing for everything we just did and apply it to the first month of gestation, the second month of gestation, and the fourth month, fifth month, sixth month, seventh month, eighth month, and the ninth month of gestation."

We used that particular plug-in in relation to sexual violence at the time you were in the womb, but that was not necessarily sexual violence perpetrated on your mother. She could have heard about sexual violence from someone else, watched it in a movie or on a television show, or read about it, or memories of earlier sexual victimization of women — other women or herself — might have come up. The energies that can also enter you as the developing child were also removed.

We are going to add soul-healing. Ask your soul-healing angels, "Please find and bring back to me any missing pieces. Clean, repair, and heal those pieces, and fully integrate them within me. Thank you soul-healing angels and encodement team, my entire healing team."

Your healing teams are saying, "That's enough for today." We forget what it is like to be in a body because we never have been in one.

Stay Within Your Heart Source

Dr. Cathy: One thing I received during this channeling is that many women have sex because they think it's their marital duty, not because they really want to. They feel degraded and objectified in some way. They feel powerless and believe something is wrong with them because they don't want to have sex or they don't have any power.

Does anybody have anything they'd like to say or ask? Is everybody okay?

Michelle: We have taken both the victim and the perpetrator roles through our lifetimes, and it is horrifying.

That's to be released and healed. When you continue to feel the horror from the situation, know that there's more to heal. And it can be very hard. Intense energy came in as I facilitated this. We might do this in shorter segments so that we are able to handle it all.

Michelle: I hope, at the conclusion, that we can have some hope that humans will change the way we are.

I truly believe healing is happening. That's why all this stuff is coming up. It doesn't seem like healing is happening, but it has to be revealed before it can be healed. For example, we have to recognize that sex trafficking is real and much more prevalent than we realize.

Michelle: I really wish they would make it more known, not just every now and then. I don't know that it's taken seriously. I think we people who are more awake and working toward ascension have an understanding of what is happening. Those who are asleep just don't know. They have to wake up, somehow, and that is complex.

It is complex. Also, how much can we handle at one time? Racial conflict is coming out. The great divide between Liberals and Conservatives is more apparent. Violence is increasing between those who disagree. More horrors are being committed than are reported against people for their gender identification, sexual orientation, or the color of their skin. Then there is sexual abuse and sex trafficking. How much can we handle at one time before people shut down? That's where the heart source comes in. That's where we have to stay within the heart source. I've become very aware that I have to be in my heart source to have the courage to stand up even when it's against what some call "microaggressions." I want to stand up against those if I'm present.

Louise: As we started, I felt a dark energy I wasn't expecting. It doesn't matter where it started, but I know it's been healed. I'm grateful for that. Then, as you said it, it came to me that women felt they were obligated to have sex regardless if they wanted to or not because of both church and society — the obligation based on women as chattel.

A thought came to me when you mentioned the dark energy. Remember that any time you start feeling darkness, say, "I am the Sword." That puts you in the place to immediately transmute that energy. So thank you for saying that, Louise.

Cleo: I am very grateful I have this opportunity to clear the DNA of these things in my maternal and paternal ancestral lines, all the way back. I have recently started working on family trees again because more information has become available. Now I see things back into the 1600s. These people had eight children, twenty children. I feel my ancestors are calling out to me to heal them. I don't know whether that's my imagination, but I'm glad to do it, no matter what.

Thank you for sharing that.

Margaret: A lot of this seems to revolve around being powerless and unworthy but basically about not having power. Because why would you want to have power over somebody unless you didn't feel that you have power? You prove to yourself you have power by stepping on people.

Exactly.

Margaret: For centuries, people lived in isolation in very narrow circumstances with very little awareness and lacking a sense of power. So people take various steps to try to give themselves a sense of power even though they don't feel they actually have it. That's a big issue and has caused a lot of these abuses.

Brenda: As we go through this clearing and are all connected to the grid, does it help humanity clear this so that they don't have to do all this, or does each individual have to go through this clearing?

I believe we are helping to clear humanity. We're going back through generations. I think of myself and my family in Texas. I'm a sixth-generation Texan. I remember hearing one great-aunt say that her father had slaves. I'm pretty sure the other side had slaves, but I'm not positive. Whoever had slaves and used them for sexual purposes, what we do can also bring healing in that area. In addition, everybody on this planet has a choice to accept that healing. Amiya is saying that whatever healing occurs lightens the load on the planet.

Mimi: I found great joy in the concept that other places where we incarnate do not have this darkness or feeling that people need to perpetrate ill on other people. I trust that eventually this planet will rise up and have those beautiful frequencies as well.

When you said that, I got this image that if we feel overwhelmed by what comes up within us, we can tap into the energy of a lifetime in which we weren't involved with this current energy, and we will experience true reverence for what love is and the reverence of the individual.

Margaret: That brings up what I've read from many different channels, that this planet was set up to see how far we could go into darkness and still rectify it into love. So the deeper we go into darkness, the more we have to find where we are capable of loving those who have done horrible things. Our love expands. Then this planet is a shining beacon to the rest of the universe of how much we can actually love.

CHAPTER SEVENTEEN

Heal Sexual Abuse in Infancy

Amiya and Dr. Cathy

Amiya: As we proceed with our healing, it is important to know that you have accepted the responsibility, on a soul level, to anchor the healing for the planet. You know that, but we want you to recognize the truth of what you are doing — that as you read this book and receive healing for yourself, you play an integral role in healing the planet.

When you expand your heart source to the tips of your fingers, to the outer limits of, let's say, the seventh layer of your aura or beyond and you walk around this wonderful planet, you walk into other people's energy. Your love enters their auras. That is why it's so important to stay in your heart source. You do not want to take on another person's low-vibration energy. If you wish, you might also stay in the energy of being the Sword of Michael to transmute energy as you move about Earth. The goal of this spiritual life is to walk on this planet and leave behind love, peace, joy, and gratitude wherever you go. No matter who walks into your energy, that is what they experience.

We move today into the healing of sexual abuse during infancy. It might seem unreal to you that children can possibly be abused sexually in infancy and how people can do that. It comes from the perpetrator's wounds, pain, and abuse. We're going to work with three areas related to infancy (through age two).

We have said that we won't hold anything back in this book. If you get triggered, if painful feelings arise as we take you through this healing process, be sure you are in your heart source. Ask immediately for your healing team to tap into the wound that was triggered and use the four foundational plug-ins. Because you have chosen to do this service for the planet, you will tap into the energies of others who have been abused in the ways we speak of. You can choose not to hold this energy, if you wish, and just listen and not channel this energy for the planet. But if you continue to channel this energy, you will feel that energy in a particular way. You might be horrified by these events we share for healing because they are not within your realm of awareness or ever happened to you.

The first area we will work with is where someone molests an infant with their finger or another object on the genitals. This includes fingers going into the vagina of the little girl and rubbing her clitoris to see what will happen. For the little boy, it includes rubbing his penis to see what will happen. For both, it can involve the anal area, usually penetration by a finger or an object.

The second area is penetration that causes physical damage to the infant. This damage can be permanent, because someone makes the decision to penetrate them with their penis or an object that causes great damage or even death. If she survives, the female might be unable to bear children of her own. This can also involve satanic ritual abuse or ritual abuse that is not satanic.

The third area of sexual abuse in infancy is the child witnessing or being within the energy of sexual abuse of someone else, including one of the parents or someone else who is present. Those are the three areas we will work with in this chapter.

Heal Abuse from Molestation

Anchor into your heart source. Set your intention, if you wish, to bring healing to all on this planet who have experienced sexual abuse, whether they remember it or not. We ask that we be allowed to call in the energy of any child on the planet who suffered such, whether that individual is still a child or 120 years old.

Connect with your healing team. You might also connect with those known as the Guardians of the Planet if you are working with the energy of the entire planet. (They are included when we call your healing team.)

If you have had this experience, even if you are not aware of it, ask your healing team, "Please remove all artificial encodements that came from being molested in some way as an infant." This includes your genitals or anal area being manipulated in some way. "Remove the artificial encodements of all inappropriate energy from the perpetrator."

Ask your healing team, "Please repair any damaged and altered natural encodements that came from abuse as an infant or for the ones I hold the energy for. I ask that this healing spread throughout the planet. Please use the Heal the DNA plug-in to heal any DNA changes that occurred because of the abuse."

Now ask your healing team, "Please apply the Healing over Lifetimes plug-in to me" (or someone you have in mind). This also applies to all on the planet who are willing to release and be healed of the energy of being used as a sexual object while an infant. Ask your soul-healing team, "Please find and bring back to me" (or to whoever you are holding in your mind and heart) "all pieces that were lost." This one wants us to say, "In psychology, this is called dissociation. This can happen with an infant, where you leave your body in some way. When you leave your body, you leave it unprotected."

Ask your healing angels, "Please clean, repair, and heal all those pieces and return them to me" (or to the individual you are holding in your mind and heart) "and to all those on this planet willing to accept them. Fully integrate these pieces within."

Now ask your encodements team, "Please reactivate, if needed, any encodements for love, the ability to love, and the ability to receive love that might have been deactivated by these actions. And fill with love any empty spaces in the healed DNA."

Using the Belief plug-in, we place within you the belief: "I am a pure, innocent, love-filled child of God." Now we ask Love Itself, All

That Is, to fill you, the individual you have in mind, or others on the planet with all the love that you or they needed at that time but did not receive.

Heal Abuse from Penetration

Now we move to the infant who had severe damage due to penetration by a penis or other object. We address their healing team, and the Guardians of the Planet, that we be able to call in your energy or the energy of any child on this planet who has suffered such, whether that child is still a child or 120 years old. We ask that all artificial encodements of anger, control, lust, or fear that come from the perpetrator be removed from you and anyone you hold the energy for. Repair the damaged and altered natural encodements, and activate any natural encodements that were deactivated or need to be activated for the acceptance of love and the ability to love.

We ask your healing team to use the Heal the DNA plug-in to remove any hint of this abuse from the DNA. We ask that love fill the space of all that is removed. Apply the Curse Removal plug-in to remove any curses placed on you or on any child you are holding in your mind.

Use the Belief plug-in to place this belief in your system, your subconscious mind: "I am the beautiful, innocent, undefiled child of God." We ask for this to occur through any lifetime that is brought to your memory or the energy of any lifetime within you or those you hold this energy for.

Now we move to the energy of ritual abuse. This is usually done in a group and sometimes can be satanic. A ritual of some sort is involved, and dark energy is associated with such abuse. Say, "I am the Sword." Call on the angels you work with from Michael's or Metatron's band. Ask these angels, "Please protect me from the darkness that surrounds this type of abuse in which a group intends to completely objectify an infant."

Again, say, "I am the Sword." Healing team, for anyone who has declared, "I am the Sword" and anyone who has had this abuse happen to them, we ask that the energy of Michael's Sword and the energy of your love completely break through the energies of anyone who has been ritually abused. As this is being done, we ask you, healing team, to use the Implant Removal plug-in to go through the energy of the individual and remove all implants and structures placed within this child. Of course, we ask that this be done safely for the child.

Now please implement the Curse Removal plug-in to break any curses placed on this child and any child you hold in your mind. We now call on Metatron, Yeshua, and others who have walked on this planet and worked to remove energies of darkness to stand before them and call forth any dark spirit that came into the child or the individual who is now an adult. Call them forth and tell them they have a chance now to return to the light, and tell them whether or not they make that choice, they must leave the individual now.

Heal Witnessing Abuse

As an infant, if you or someone you hold in your mind and heart witnessed the sexual abuse of someone else, such as a sibling or a parent, we call on your healing team to remove the energy of pain, anger, and defilement from this experience even if you do not remember it.

We call forth the consciousness of the DNA of this infant and that any sexual abuse or other abuse be removed completely from the consciousness of the DNA. We ask that any energy of abuse, artificial encodements, curses, and damaged and altered natural encodements be repaired. In all the places where this energy of abuse was removed, we place love and send love from our hearts to all who suffered.

For all groups we have spoken for by calling for healing, we now take our sword and ask Michael to use his Sword to sever from them the energy of the perpetrator so that energy is completely dissolved and no longer active. Further strengthen that belief with the Belief plug-in: "I am innocent. I am clear. I am undefiled. I am love, I am loved, and I do love."

Just so you know, if you have any perpetrator energy within you, we will spend time working with perpetrators at a later time, as they too need healing.

This was intense, and it will continue to be intense through the rest of the book. Now, for all groups we have already spoken to and done healing for, we gather the energy and ask that the Remove Victim Consciousness plug-in be fully activated. We ask that that plug-in be activated within any person reading this, as the fear from others can invade you.

This Is a Difficult but Rewarding Journey

Michelle: That was extremely difficult.

Dr. Cathy: It was, wasn't it?

Michelle: It was hard to keep my personal feelings out of it and stay in my heart source.

It was. You might have noticed that at times I kind of got lost in it, as I was focusing on that healing and energy also. I've had female clients who cannot have children because of the abuse done to them. So remember that if difficult feelings and thoughts come up, immediately go into your heart source and ask your healing team to please implement the four foundational plug-ins to heal the wound that was triggered. Anybody else?

Carolyn: This was very profound. I had a past life in which I was sexually abused, and it was ritualistic. Even though I couldn't speak as a baby, I remember the darkness and the fear I felt. That is all gone. I could actually feel that leave as we went through the process. In this life, I was sexually abused at the age of nine and went through years of therapy dealing with it. I think one of the blessings that allowed me to sit through this without blubbering was the fact that I had placed myself in group therapy with other people, men and women, who had been sexually abused, and I listened to the horrors of their lives. So this was a real blessing. Thank you.

You're welcome. Also remember that you worked with trauma in the last book, and that healing could have given you support in this.

CHAPTER EIGHTEEN

Release the Energy from Satanic Ritual Abuse

Amiya and Dr. Cathy

Amiya: You are experiencing much as you read this book, including things you might not have consciously known about in this wonderful world of yours. Please connect with your healing team. We ask them to clear any artificial encodements that have activated in you from what you have read in these chapters. We're speaking particularly about information on healing sexuality. Now we ask your healing team to heal the wounds most active at this moment and producing fear, and we ask them to please remove the artificial encodements of those wounds, repair the damaged and altered natural encodements, and activate any inactive encodements of peace, love, and joy.

One of the wonderful saints on this side of the veil just suggested to activate within you the belief that "this too shall pass." Some of you are worried that the pain will not pass in this lifetime. This lifetime, for you, is a blink of the eye. It seems long, but when you leave, you will be surprised what a short time it actually was.

Now we call on your soul-healing angels to find and bring back to you the pieces of you that are missing — and have been missing for a long time — in the areas of sex and sexuality and any pieces you might have lost recently due to the difficulty of facing and addressing these issues. We ask them to clean, repair, and heal all pieces and fully integrate them within you. Now, of course, we ask for the four foundational plug-ins. Finally, we're going to do one more pass of the Remove Victim Consciousness plug-in. That is wonderful. You are most wonderful beings.

Continued Abuse Forms Energetic Structures

We have discussed among ourselves whether to give you this information now or later. We recognize people of light have difficulty hearing about and working with this topic, but it will come up at different times as we do this work, and we want you to be prepared. We are talking about satanic ritual abuse.

Satanic ritual abuse is evil in its darkest form. This evil is the full denial of the specialness of the human being. It is the belief that you need to sacrifice a human being to the "gods" so that the people doing the sacrificing can receive what they want. All That Is, Love Itself, requires no sacrifice of any life form. You have no need to appease Love Itself, because Love Itself does not need to be appeased. You do not need to give something to Love Itself because Love Itself has absolutely no lack.

We're going to share certain things to understand about what happens with energy in an abuse ritual, whether it is satanic or not. It is similar to what can happen in rituals in which people make curses. A curse that includes a ritual has much more power than a curse given spontaneously. A spontaneous curse is "Go to hell," or "Damn you" — that type of thing. People performing rituals can go into the center of themselves and bring in objects, living objects, such as trees, plants, and flowers. They write things on paper that they burn in a fire. In those rituals, every step increases the power of the energy of the curse.

There are people who regularly practice satanic ritual. It's the form of the abuse that gives them power. (We understand you might find this very difficult to read and understand.) There is power in the woman, right? Only the woman can produce life. The male can begin life from his seed. It's the woman who gives her egg to be fertilized by the seed and holds that in her womb, allowing life to begin. The woman gives her body to nurture that fertilized ovum, and she grows that being within her. Only the woman has that power. Men have feared this power in women because they don't understand it.

In satanic ritual abuse (and this one is learning something new even though she has worked with people who have been victims of this), some women participate, and the men attempt to take the power of giving life by its opposite — taking life. Certain things happen. It is not unusual for a child, as long as she has begun her menses, to be impregnated and aborted many times. Each time this happens, an energetic structure forms within the female, similar to the energy of curses your healing team removes. The more often this happens to an individual, and it happens to some women for years, the stronger that energetic structure becomes.

Aborted Souls Can Become Trapped

If you were not in your heart source, be sure you are now. If you wish, you can facilitate with others the work we are doing in this book. But even if you hold them in your heart and work with them in this way, it does not remove the structures; it removes the energy around the structures. People who have the structures require much prayer and focused attention, so somebody needs to be present supporting them who is aware of what is happening.

Let us use the example of a woman who has been repeatedly impregnated and the child is aborted each time. You notice we say "the child" is aborted. The developing child has a soul. That is crucial in this group of people. It is possible, within the structure, that the soul of the child who was aborted becomes trapped. That sounds horrible, does it not?

When you become aware of women who have been victimized very much against their will, your job will sometimes involve releasing the soul of a child that was trapped within a structure. You might wonder what we do when the structure is released. One of the best supporters to call on is Mother Mary, as children leap into her arms, and she is there for them.

As much as what we are saying might offend you, know that love surrounds those who have had these things done to them. Again, it is difficult to understand why these things happen. They were not in the plan for how the world would progress, but an evil emerged. Libraries of books discuss this, but we will not go into that now. Know that each soul that has been captured within a structure has a guardian. The evil is the denial of life and love. Life is produced by the Creator; love is given by the Creator.

When you hear us talk about removing certain energies that have to do with satanic ritual abuse, the healing teams working with these people know much more than you or even this one we speak through about how to release this energy. It can be done, but you need more than the words, "Please remove the artificial encodements." It is much more complex than that.

Yes, these things can be healed and changed without you. But when you focus on someone you are working with, you connect through your heart source with the energy and love of the planet for her children who walk upon her. That includes the microbes within the soil and the tallest trees — all life. You connect to that and then to the center of the universe. You bring in love continually and fill the empty spaces with love so that there is no space left for another structure of darkness.

As you can imagine, some people have a difficult time letting go of these things that happen to them. Some break away. Victim consciousness is strong. Amma gave you the Remove Victim Consciousness plug-in. It's important to realize that people in the spiritual, psychological, self-help, and mental-health realms regard being a victim as a negative, as something shameful. "Oh," they say, "she's just being a victim." That energy of "just being a victim" keeps that person from wanting to grow, develop, and expand. Release yourself of any knowing of that. Release yourself from any shame you might have when you realize you feel like a victim. These are strong energies. When you meet someone who seems to be trapped in victim consciousness, that is a sign that what happened to them was difficult and contained a lack of love.

Some victims of satanic ritual abuse are stolen from their families. Some are given by their families as sacrificial victims. You would be amazed by who is involved with this. They might be deacons or members of a church, members of governmental forces, judges, police officers, or other people in power. You might hear conspiracy theories that everybody in government is involved in these things. That is not true. These things are hidden, and when they come out, they are made to seem so horrifying (and they are horrifying) and widespread that people pull back and put their heads in the sand. What better way to not know something is there than not to see it? Working with healing sexuality, we cannot avoid these things that have happened to people.

Share Love with Abuse Sufferers

Another kind of ritual abuse does not call in the name of the one that people say is the evilest in the world and has no love. People with mental health disorders might perform rituals. It is still devastating, but it does not make the same structures within a woman as satanic ritual abuse. Many rituals of sexual abuse involve torture, but not so much with the idea of capturing the soul of an infant child.

We do not wish to focus on these things. It is important for you to be aware these things are happening on this planet if you are to work with healing in the area of sexuality. We hope that some who have undergone these things will find hope within this book. We work with everyone in this book. Although you might not know how to release the structures, we do.

Some on this planet, such as the one we speak through, have learned how to release the structures. It takes much time and care so you are not fooled into what can happen. It is crucial to be grounded in the planet and, using the word in a different way, grounded in spirit in order to know who you are. If you work with someone who has undergone any kind of sexual abuse, you might, at times, want to turn away from their pain because it hurts you and you can't begin to imagine how it has hurt them.

It takes great courage to face these things, learned scholar. You might not feel the call to work individually with those who have undergone such terrors. We ask, however, that you call forth the consciousness of those who have experienced such. Bring in love from above and below, connecting with all the angels, saints, guides, and masters you know and work with. Focus that love on that energy to fill them with love and light.

If you want to be a witness of healing, we ask you to again feel that connection of your heart source into the center of the planet. Now feel that connection to the center of the universe. As you breathe, inhaling deeply, bring in the energy from above and below. Allow it to meet in your heart at that place where the front and the back of the heart chakra come together, the place of interdimensionality. As you exhale, send that energy out through your pranic tube so that it moves into each chakra. Do that several times.

Now call forth the energy of those who are suffering from such abuse. Surround the energy. Don't get into the energy, but surround it. As you breathe out and then breathe in the energy from above and below, let it come through your heart and circulate through all your chakras. Breathe out into the energy of those who need to know there is love. They are not alone.

Interpret Dream Messages

Louise: Every night before we have one of our sessions, I communicate with my healing team and request that any healing that needs to be done should be done during the classes. I woke up this morning with a dream in which I was basically used and abused. I didn't know where it came from, as that did not occur in this lifetime. But then, as soon as Amiya started speaking, I felt, "Oh." I was bringing that energy to my consciousness to be released and healed today. So I appreciate that.

Dr. Cathy: Thank you very much.

Margaret: Say a naïve healer in some other lifetime attempted to heal one of these structures. Could that healer get captured and pulled into the evil, or does that not happen? Could those entities come out and grab healers and make them part of what happens, or is that just a fantasy from like movies and TV?

That's pretty much a fantasy from movies and TV, as long as you're in your heart. What I get is that the greater danger is that somebody naïve would not realize that a structure contains traps. When I was working with one of these individuals and my healing guides were telling me how to do it, I had to be aware of a hook or a pin that could collapse the person's energy field if I pulled it. So the danger is really to the other person.

Cleo: This morning, as I was waking up, I saw with my closed eyes that I was releasing a sky full of dark, black energy. I said to myself, "Is this my darkness or darkness in the collective consciousness?" I didn't get an answer, but I could see it releasing and leaving. I thought, "Well, I don't care whose energy it is as long as it goes."

I think you and Louise were in that same place of being told what we would work with today. I didn't know Amiya was going to talk about this today. We chatted a little bit, and I was wondering whether we should wait until later, but they decided to talk about it today. So you and Louise were prepared for this message.

CHAPTER NINETEEN

Send Support for Others

Dr. Cathy and Amiya

Dr. Cathy: Today's check-in with participants evolved into Amiya's message. Many participants were struggling with the heaviness of this topic, a feeling you might share as you read this material.

Louise: I wonder whether there must be a higher group of angelic evangelists we can call on to work with the planet. I know they can't do anything unless we ask.

Amiya is whispering in my ear that this might be a question-and-answer sort of day, since the group here is a microcosm of the people who will be reading the book. Amiya is telling me: "Know there is a higher level of being, not just angelic energy, working with people who are being ritually abused sexually. You made a comment, 'I know they can't do anything unless we ask.' The victims of sexual ritual abuse are asking. Those in agony are asking. They might not know specific names to call on, but they ask for help until they give up asking. Many come to a point where they don't believe in goodness or God because of what has happened."

Amiya is showing me when this issue of evil came in from another galaxy eons ago. (I'm calling it "evil" even though some people don't believe evil exists. I could also say those who are without love or those who are into control and power.) Another group of wonderful beings, consisting of what some call the Galactic Command and angelic beings, came together to eliminate this evil. One of the ways this occurs is for it to become known.

A tremendously sad energy is coming into me as I talk. Many have written about this over the years. Much of the original writing was true, but the truth has since been distorted. That's my personal view because of what I'm seeing of the energy and how I interpret it. There is a system of child trafficking. I've done much studying of this over the years. If you choose to study it, know it's imperative to stay in your heart source. It's easy to become overwhelmed and then not want to believe it's true.

This is why Amma rarely talks about it. She knows we human beings and that we have a tendency to get caught up in the horror of these things. She focuses on the remedy: Stay in your heart, at minimum. The best protection and remedy is staying in your heart source. Be aware of what is happening, but do not get caught up in the energy of fear, as it takes you away from who you truly are and keeps you from the very simple remedy of staying in your heart. Also, some energies feed on fear. Every time you're in fear, you feed those who don't want you to access the love that you are. That is one reason Amma doesn't talk about it much — not that it's not real but because people go into fear so easily.

Help Those in the Trenches

Amiya: Accept that these things happen. Also accept that some will deny they were perpetrators and call the accusations conspiracies. Within your world, not just within your country, you believe that only certain people deserve power. Anything can happen to those who do not deserve power, and they cannot have what those who feel deserving of power can have. One example is "redlining," in which people of certain races or socioeconomic backgrounds cannot get loans. What you call a "glass ceiling" keeps some people from rising above certain positions in life. People are denied jobs or education because of their skin color, religion, socioeconomic background, or sexual orientation.

You know these things. You call them political. When you get to things such as sexuality, sex, satanic ritual abuse, and other ritual abuse, those seem to affect you more deeply. The fact of people in power trying to keep others enslaved in some way is just as difficult and terrible, except the connection to sex and spirituality that we've talked about and how they're bonded together, is not there. The truth is that they are.

You are not called to battle everything at the same time or to take an active role in everything at the same time. That would be overwhelming. Now we will contradict ourselves. You are called to do that by being in your heart source, connecting with the energies above and below, and bringing that energy through you and into the world.

This one was saying earlier that people do not recognize how important being in your heart source and sending love is. People do not recognize the power that you contain within you, of being able to pull in creative energy from the universe. Send that energy out with the intention that it go wherever it needs to go. When you hear about these horrible things — the ritual abuse, the souls of infants being trapped within a structure due to this abuse — very few people are called to release those souls.

Do what you are called to do, which is to send the energy needed to support those who release those souls. Let's say people are unjustly trapped in a prison. If you know their captors are not giving them enough food and you can give them food, would you not do so? Would you not go in and slide the food and water underneath their door so that they have physical sustenance?

When sending love to those who are in battle (yes, it is spiritual lovefare, but they see it as a battle in the trenches), they need the food of the love you send. They need you every day to give them that food of love that comes through you that you bring in from above and below. The reason they need your food is because as the love comes in from above and below you — mixed with your intention, energy, love, and care — it adds the human element and comes together so that they do not feel alone, at least not on a soul level.

After you leave this world, you'll discover how much is involved in a more detailed way. You can have discussions with your council and others' councils about why this is so. Do not let that need to know interfere with giving the food-of-love sustenance to those working in this area. If you were called to work in this area, you already have been doing this. It takes great energy, wisdom, and knowledge, and the people who work in this area have been gathering that wisdom and knowledge for most of their lifetimes.

Send Your Love to Those Who Are Struggling

You have been studying how to be in a place of love. You have been studying how to send that love to others, your family, friends, and yourself. You know, with spiritual lovefare, how to go out with the Sword of Michael and clear energy. Your job is to do that. Your job is to be the provider of the food of love for nourishment. Do not, and let us repeat, *do not* minimize the importance of what you are called to do.

Bring together all your knowledge, the love you know how to access, and the healing work you have been trained in for decades. Now is the time. You can still do your particular healing modality or modalities, because you have that training. What you have actually been trained in is how to access the energy, love, and creative force within this planet. You might want to call it grace. You know how to do that. It does not matter how you learned. Your job now is to feed that energy and love to those who need it. (Some don't know that they need it, but they do.)

Here are some options of how you can do this. (We are not going to tell you how to do it, just who to send it to.) You know how to connect above and below, bring energy in, and send it to others. But how do you disperse the knowledge?

We're going to go from the macrocosm to the microcosm. Ask for and connect with all the spiritual beings you work with. (You have many more you're not aware of.) Ask to send that love energy to the darkness surrounding this planet. Send your love energy to break through the darkness that crept in eons ago. You can do that. (That is the macrocosm.) Send that energy with the intention of giving support to those tremendous beings who are holding the energy of love and protecting this planet.

You can send energy to a country or to a group of people who are struggling with the racial divide, for instance. You could choose to send energy to people of color, to people of a different religion who are struggling. You could send it to their consciousnesses. By sending them that love, you help to neutralize fear, anger, shame, bitterness, and despair.

You could choose to send it to those who are caught in enslavement or sex trafficking. Enslavement is not just sex trafficking. There are also children and young men and women who have been sold or stolen to work. They have a little mattress to sleep on and are given just enough food to stay alive. You can surround them with love energy. You can choose to send love energy specifically to all who have been sexually abused on the planet. That is a large number of people — more than half the population. You can send energy to those who have been victims of any type of ritual abuse. You can send that love energy to those who have been victims of satanic ritual abuse. Notice that we went from the broader realm to the victims.

It takes an individual of high vibration who truly knows that you all are one to be able to send love energy to perpetrators, to send love energy to the masterminds behind these tremendous systems that steal children. Do you think you could be someone who stays out of judgment to send love energy, creative energy, to someone who has tortured, even killed, a child? It takes a very advanced being to minister to those people who might seem to you to be without a soul. Perpetrators are not connected to their souls.

Know that You Are Helping

Yes, send love energy to those who have been victimized. Send love energy to those who are attempting to end these practices even if they don't know about spiritual lovefare. If you can send love to perpetrators, fully from your heart and without judgment, anger, bitterness, or the desire for vengeance, you can help break through the shell of darkness and the shell of low vibration encasing them and hiding their golden hearts. Remember, every person has a golden structure within their hearts — every person. It is hidden in those who perpetuate such acts on the innocent. The things you have heard about sex trafficking and capturing, abusing, and harming children are true. This happens in many areas. It happens particularly to those who are lower in the power structure.

Don't try to understand why. Just accept it. How many of you know how the carburetor works in your car? Do you not just turn the car on and go? You do not need to know unless you are called from the depths of your being the details of what is happening. You are called to provide the food, the sustenance of love. Do not think that is not enough. Yes, call on other angels and masters and bring these forces together. The more people who call on them, the more who come with that love energy and the more you provide what is needed to change the darkness.

The cries of the suffering do not go unanswered. But those who have heard cannot demolish what is happening unless the beings of the species who created these things take action. They cannot change what humans have created because of the laws of the universe. Yes, call on them, but remember your role. You are of the beings of the species who created these things. Call on your spiritual support team.

Stay in your heart source. Spend time daily, every other day, weekly, monthly, however you want to do it, recognizing these things:

- You are all one.
- You all came from love.
- You all have that golden center in your hearts even though some people's are hidden by what has happened to them.

Some people are born without the brain capacity (not the intellectual capacity) to be empathetic. Your scientists are working on how to change that. Parts of the brain need additional blood flow that enlivens the creative energy within the brain that activates the encodements for compassion, empathy, and caring. These discoveries are happening. This is hope. This knowledge is coming to you.

Struggling to understand is useless in many areas. There is no way to understand these things we have spoken about. If you are attempting to understand, you are not working to change the actual machinery, as it were, of what is happening, and this does no good. You can learn the mechanics and engineering of the automobile, but only if you are going to change how the engine works does that knowledge do anything. For most, all you want to do is get the car to move. You are the one who knows how to channel love and send it out. You are the one who can facilitate change with your knowledge of the heart source and energy.

Every Person Is Love Incarnate

Margaret: This is also about respecting and recognizing that all people are God and respecting that they know, at some level, what they're doing. Can you speak on that, or have I just said it?

You've said it. On some level, they know what they do. On a conscious level, they know not what they do. When Master Yeshua said, "Forgive them, for they know not what they do," he was talking about their conscious and even subconscious levels. It is the level known as the superconscious — that part that helps you connect to your I Am presence even when you do not know it is there — that knows.

Most humans forget because they are very deep into the level of not knowing. They do not know how to reach into their hearts and find who they are. Doing this work requires exactly what you said: to know that each person is Love Incarnate. All people have that golden center within their hearts and are beloved. They might not be loved by a human, but they are beloved by the one who created them. They are beloved by the angels and saints who surround them even if they do not listen to them.

Participant: Do we work with a light (and I use the frequency of love), or are we working with the DNA?

That depends on different things. You can ask to help work with the DNA, but you need (and we're speaking here of the mechanics of healing in the human) to bring in the energy needed to clear what is within the aura, as the heaviness within the aura affects the DNA as well. When that is clear, you can work with the DNA. Does that make sense?

Participant: Yes, it does. I was just wondering, with the frequency that strong, if it would automatically move into that space. So, yeah, it does make sense.

Let us use another analogy. You know the concept "as above, so below." Let's look at microbes and using antibiotics to get rid of an infection. If the antibiotic gets rid of the bacteria but you still eat meat infected with bacteria, the antibiotics are pretty much useless. In essence, the DNA is affected by the darkness surrounding or within the person. So you clear that congestion first, and then the DNA is not continually reinfected.

Participant: That's a good analogy. Oh, this is heavy.

It is very heavy. We promised you at the beginning of this book that we would hold nothing back.

Cleo: Amiya, today you explained very specifically how we can direct our love. I know I'm part of spiritual lovefare, and I want to send love, but I never knew to send it out specifically in the many ways you described. That is very helpful to me.

Louise: It occurred to me this week that one of the main reasons for the timing of bringing the violet flame to clear the kundalini channels was because of the work required in this area. Could you comment on that?

Other than to say that you are very insightful? When you do this work, when you hear what is happening, you need to do self-care. What happens if you feel called to bring water and food to the prisoner but you never eat or drink? Soon no one will be there to bring water and food. As you work to clear others, use the tools. Clearing the kundalini channels is one of them. That was very insightful, but then that is who you are. We thank you for hanging in there.

CHAPTER TWENTY

Heal Sexual Abuse, Ages One to Three

Amiya

Wonderful love surrounds you as we bring healing to these very difficult sexual events. It's challenging for anyone in any incarnation to deal with wounds of this nature, no matter which dimension you are in. We are speaking about sexual abuse that also affects you on a deep spiritual level. Sexuality and spirituality are wound together so beautifully.

We are working to heal at the deepest levels. We began with the infant up to age one. We are now going to go from age one to age three, often known as the toddler stage. We're going to do two different healings. The first healing is for instances when no sexual abuse was intended, such as when a doctor, parent, or caretaker needed to address a diaper rash, irritation, or some other problem with the genitals. For example, little boys have great fun playing with that wonderful appendage of theirs and can sometimes hurt themselves. Depending on the child, he can feel insulted or self-conscious when someone checks to be sure all is fine or applies cream to an irritation.

Double-check that you're in your heart source. We call forth the energy of those who, from the ages of one to three, felt they were violated in some way. It does not matter whether the caretaker — such as a doctor, mother, or father — intended any violation; it is what the child perceives. Healing is based on what the individual perceives, not the intention of others. You have probably run into a good-meaning person who said something very painful and then said, "Oh, I didn't mean that." (This is different from what you call gaslighting, when someone means you harm but tells you the problem is yours when you object. They might say, "You're just too sensitive," or they deny your feelings.) Here, we accept someone's belief that what happened to them should not have happened.

To bring some perspective, a child might have felt insulted and dominated because her mother took her hand out of the cookie jar. This is similar, except for the fact that the misperception could have gone deeply into her on a soul level, into her dissociated and "send-away" parts. Despite the intention, she was injured on a deep level. This depended on many factors over which the caretaker had little or no control.

Heal Unintended Abuse

Let us do healing now. Again, be sure you are within your heart source. Connect with your healing team. Because we are asking you to facilitate healing, connect with your healing guides. (This one we speak through connects with her healing guides when doing any healing.) Feel the energy of this wonderful group of beings who are here to assist you in facilitating healing. Some of them are on your healing team, but others are not.

Call in the consciousness of those who felt they were molested or defiled between the ages of one and three. We bring in the consciousnesses of all who felt this way even if there was no intent of abuse. The effect on the children was the same, as it was their perception. The intent was to care for the children, and no perpetrator energy needs to be released. (Children who were intentionally abused contain perpetrator energy.)

You are doing this as a group healing. Even if you are reading this years later, you are all gathered together. Remember, there is no time.

Into this consciousness of the energy of all who felt sexually abused from the ages of one to three, we requested that you bring in the intraplanetary (meaning from Earth) consciousness of this energy. As something we have not done before, we ask you all in the group of healing facilitators to focus on this consciousness and ask for its heart to be revealed. This consciousness has a beating heart. It is not a physical heart, but its energy is made up of each individual heart that connects and makes up the consciousness.

Connect with the wonderful heart energy of those who have come to be healed with your beam of energy from your heart. You are gathered together in what is known as the healing-lecture room. Within this room, surrounded by the angels of both Archangel Raphael's band and Archangel Michael's band, is a central pilar. This pilar holds the energy of more loving beings than you can imagine who are here to assist. Connect to this pillar with a beam of energy from your heart. There is now one group energy of healing and love. You are connected to a heavenly host. You are never alone when doing healing work.

We are going to do this in a different order than usual. Call in the soul-healing angels. The soul-healing angels are from the healing team of each individual who makes up this group consciousness that has come here to receive healing. Even people who have no belief in this have healing teams. The soul-healing angels are always present with them as part of their healing teams. Ask them now, "Soul-healing angels, please find and bring back to each person in this consciousness who felt violated — even though that was not the intention, no matter how old they are now — the aspects of them, those pieces of their souls, they sent away and disassociated from." Include yourself in this, if needed. Ask the soul-healing angels, "Please clean, repair, and heal all the pieces and then fully integrate them within each person."

Ask the encodement technicians, "Please remove from this group energy any artificial encodements that all those who felt violated or molested from the age of one to three (no matter how old they are now) acquired at that time. Please repair the damaged and altered natural encodements, and please reactivate any encodements that were deactivated at that time and are needed for sexual and spiritual health. Please activate any natural encodements that were not activated because of what happened but should have been activated."

Notice the difference in what we did in the last two steps. One was natural encodements that became deactivated due to what happened, and the other was natural encodements that should have been activated but were not because of what happened.

Next, ask the healing teams, "Please find any implants that occurred or were activated at that time. Use the Implant Removal plug-in for any implants that were activated within any of the seven chakras, no matter where the implant is."

Now we're speaking directly to the consciousnesses of those who were not intentionally abused, as in the case of a doctor or caretaker needing to take care of the genitals of the individual due to some problem: "Healing team, please clear any negativity of the bonding between the child and this individual. Remove that low-vibration energy, distrust, or shame." Very good.

Heal Intended Abuse

For those who were intentionally molested, defiled, or injured, we ask that the bond of negativity between the individual and the perpetrator be replaced with love. We sever the bond with Michael's Sword.

You might find it interesting that we replaced the bond with love but still severed the bond. An artificial bonding between the two exists — not from the abused but from the perpetrator. We severed the bond between the perpetrator and individual so that no low-vibration energy would be left. If you sever a bond close to the body, a part of that cord still exists in the body. We want it all replaced with love. (You might not have realized you can use the Implant Removal plug-in to remove any residuals left in the body when you sever bonds or cords.)

Now, this will be fun. Stand in front of the consciousness you have been working with. Imagine this energy, metaphorically, in the shape of an individual. Place one hand just in front of the physical heart, the golden heart. Place your other hand just above the heart chakra. Ask the healing teams to clear any congestion from the golden structure within the physical heart. Now connect the energy of the golden structure within the heart to the heart chakra. This opens the channels from the heart chakra to the heart.

With one hand still over, but not touching, that golden structure of the physical heart, move the hand that was over the heart chakra to the second chakra. Ask your healing team, "Please clear the energy of the sacral chakra of any energy acquired during the abuse."

By the way, to show you the different ways this clearing can be done, if someone is standing in front of you physically, you do not need to work with a particular age. You can form the intention to remove energy from any sexual abuse at any time in his or her life.

Be in what we call "allow" mode, holding one hand over the second chakra and the other over the golden structure in the physical heart. You are a conduit of energy, allowing the connection between the two to occur. Don't send or force energy, but simply allow that connection to occur. If you're working with an individual, you'll find some will balance that connection quickly. When working with a group energy such as this, the connection will often be slower due to the different vibrations of those in the group. The more people with higher vibrations facilitating healing and bringing balance to the group energy, the faster it will be. You are combining your energy of the group with the energy of those in the central pillar of the healing-lecture room.

Check to be sure you're in your heart source. Check especially that your connection to the energy above and below is strong. You're not using your own energy for this. You are simply being a conduit for this amazing energy. You are cocreating with Source.

Notice that something is starting to happen. For those of you who cannot see these things, a light being generated from the core of this consciousness is erupting from within. You might call it a big bang. The energy from the second chakra and the golden structure within the physical heart are now almost totally connected within the individual people in this group consciousness.

Now move your hand from the second chakra to just over the heart chakra. Again, you are not moving your hand within the heart chakra; you are holding it over the heart chakra. Move into allow mode while bringing energy into you from your connection to the center of the Earth and the center of the universe. Because your intention of love and clarity is to connect the heart chakra with the golden structure, this wonderful circuit occurs, balancing the two areas.

You might notice darker spirits appearing as you raise the vibration. We will take care of those darker spirits who were created by

Love Itself and give them the option to return to love. We call on the heavenly hosts whose jobs are to gather these beings. You will find that two or three are from Archangel Michael's band, and the rest are from Archangel Raphael's band.

We now ask the wonderful angels present to go through this consciousness and locate each darker spirit who is trying to hide but has been revealed by this process. Gather them and take them to a place where they can be given the opportunity to raise their vibrations and rejoin the light. Hold the space for these heavenly hosts as they move through the group consciousness and collect these beings. Breathe.

Set your intention on those spaces once filled with pain and darkness. Fill them with love and light. Send your blessings to each individual within this group consciousness you have been working with. Disconnect from the heart of the group, just as you would disconnect if you were working individually.

Thank your healing guides and your healing team if they were involved with any healing for you. Come back to your body. It is your body. And that is complete.

CHAPTER TWENTY-ONE

Heal Sexual Abuse, Ages Three to Seven

Amiya and Dr. Cathy

Amiya: We have completed working with the toddler stage and will do one smaller segment from the ages of three to seven. We are being careful in these particular ages because the brain is forming rapidly. As the brain grows and certain things happen to an individual at certain ages, some very difficult problems can develop as an adult due to that interference with the brain.

This one is recalling research that showed the brains of children under the age of five do not develop correctly if the children fear for their lives. Such adults can respond to minor aggravations as if their lives are in danger. If you wonder why people would beat their children for spilling milk, it is because of what is going on with the brain.

In this chapter, we will work with the brain of the young child up to the age of seven. It never hurts to put people in the healing group who might not need healing. We don't want to leave anyone out, do we?

We did much work for those from the ages of one to three in the last chapter. You can repeat the same work with someone who was sexually abused from ages three to seven. Today, we are going to work specifically with the brain at this tender age of development. Yes, this can occur from inside the womb until the age of seven.

Tell your healing team that you're working with the resolution of problems within the brain that occurred because of sexual abuse. You might even be specific and say, "My understanding is that this goes to about age seven, but if it occurs later in this individual we're working with, say to age eight, please include all this information to age eight." We will do a later chapter on the development of the brain up to when the prefrontal cortex is developed. The prefrontal cortex is not nearly developed at this age. That usually occurs between the ages of twenty-one and twenty-five. Rarely does it occur earlier than twenty-one, but it can occur in some cases around twenty.

Begin to Heal the Brain

Now we will work with the brains of these young ones, especially those between the ages of three and seven. Imagine the brain is in front of you. You know what it roughly looks like even if you do not know all the parts. That's good. Let us do what we did before. Call forth the consciousness of the brain energy of the ages of three to seven, and include the proviso that anyone who needs this work and is outside this range is included.

We are doing this as we did last time with everyone in the world. If you know specific people, work just with them. It takes a great deal of energy to work with the consciousnesses of everyone in the world. You will need to repeat it often because of your energy and the energy of all gathered. We implore you to not get discouraged.

If you know of one or more people who have been abused in this way, please call forth the consciousnesses of their brains. If you were abused, call forth your brain consciousness. If you don't have someone specific to work with, then work with the consciousness of the planet. As we have said before, sexual abuse is much more prevalent than you know.

Since we know that many of you reading this are working with the consciousness of the planet, call on the angelic realms and especially those of Hilarion's fifth ray, the ray of healing, to join you. Feel, see, or sense yourself gathered around this energy, this consciousness. Double-check to be sure you are in your heart source.

Again, we are working with the consciousnesses of the brains of those who were sexually abused at a young age. We ask all their healing teams to connect with us. Now we call a special group of angels and encodement technicians. These specialists work with the nervous system, including the brain, nerves, and spinal cord. We call for the specialists who also work with the endocrine system.

You didn't know there are specialists. These specialists are very different from those in your medical field who only work on, say, the knees, hips, or nervous system. We called for those who work with the neurological and endocrine systems. In your medical professions, those two fields rarely overlap, and each requires extensive knowledge. But in the angelic and spiritual realms, these beings can tap into infinite knowledge of both areas. They know exactly how things interact, such as the importance of the endocrine system and how it interacts with the brain. You have an endocrine system and neurotransmitters. You have a limbic brain and an endocrine system. These all work together. We will work in both of these areas now.

Double-check that you're in your heart source. Good.

Now we go to the consciousness of the brains and endocrine systems of the little ones. Remember, we are speaking of being abused. Those who come into the consciousness could be of any age at this time. If the consciousnesses of everyone on the planet are too difficult for you to conceive of and work with, you can ask for the consciousnesses of everyone in your city, neighborhood, or home. Bring these consciousnesses into your hands. Hold your hands open and allow the consciousnesses of the brains, endocrine systems, and all you are working with to rest there. Your hands represent all those gathered who are assisting in this healing.

During the last session, I had you imagine or see the heart center of the consciousness. This time it is the brain. Let me remind you that the heart is also an endocrine gland. Hold that energy in your hands. Now say, "Chakras spin," speaking to your chakras. Feel energy come in, front and back, above and below, from every chakra. Form the intention that the energy you're bringing in, the love you're bringing in, moves gently from your heart. In other words, don't breathe it out forcefully. Gently move the energy from your heart to this consciousness of the brain, the neurological system. Hold this energy for a couple of minutes. When you're holding energy like this, you might need to bring yourself back. Simply say, "Heart source," and form the connections.

Work with the Nervous System and Endocrine System

Now let me tell you what you have done. You have sent heart energy to the brain, which has a similar effect on the brain as connecting your third eye and heart chakra. Interesting, is it not? You have sent pure love energy, not a perversion of what is called love, to those who have been abused. You have loosened energies. Now ask the healing teams of all those who are in this consciousness to please remove all artificial encodements related in any way to sexual abuse of each individual within this consciousness. You can also sneak in the request to remove any artificial encodements from their nervous systems and endocrine systems.

This one we speak through has noticed her hands becoming hotter as we ask for certain things and the energy moves through. Again, you want to continually check your heart-source connection. Your chakras have probably settled down a bit in their spin. If you feel the need, instead of saying, "Chakras spin at the speed that is safe for me," say, "Chakras spin at the optimum level of energy to bring in the energy needed for this process" (or this healing or however you want to say it).

Now request: "Healing teams, please repair any damaged or altered natural encodements within their nervous systems or endocrine systems." Each time you make a request — whether you're working with this planetary consciousness, which is a huge consciousness, or an individual — you need to continually check yourself, especially if you have some difficulty with focus. If that happens, bring yourself back.

Now request: "Healing teams, we ask for the nervous system to be connected to its divine blueprint. And we ask for this particular hologram to be established over each individual. The hologram begins with a diamond shape. At the top is the neurological system, at the bottom is the heart's healing center, to the right are the stem cells, and to the left is the divine blueprint. We add one other area, which is the endocrine system connected to the heart's healing center."

Next request: "Healing team of each individual involved who is accepting this energy, we ask you to determine, for that individual, how often the hologram should spin and how long it should spin."

Again request: "Healing teams, as this is occurring, we ask you to remove every artificial encodement holding the nervous system and the endocrine system in imbalance. We ask for the release of any damaged or altered encodements keeping the hypothalamic-pituitary-adrenal [HPA] axis frozen in a state of fear. Over the consciousness of the HPA axis, we place another hologram with that particular axis at the top of the hologram and then the others as usual."

We're going to do something different. When the pituitary gland is involved, it also involves the hormone known as oxytocin, the bonding hormone. Oxytocin is found in the uterus of the female and within everyone's hearts. We are placing the heart chakra within that hologram. Simply see a heart in the center of the hologram. You can't see this one we speak through, but she is still holding the brain, nervous system, and endocrine system in her hands.

Now we ask the healing teams to use the Implant Removal plug-in to remove from each individual the implants that came from any type of sexual abuse at this age, first from every lobe of the cerebral cortex. Each healing team will remove the implants in an order that is appropriate for the individual. Multiple implants could be in different lobes.

Hold the energy for a couple of minutes. Again, check your heart source; be sure energy is coming in. Remain as clear as possible so that you don't get tired or cause harm. Good.

Remove Implants

Now request: "Healing teams, we ask you to go to every area within the limbic brain, the emotional brain, and search for and remove all implants." These are energetic implants (I can talk to you as they're doing this) that come from the perpetrators. Again, each time you make a request, check your heart source, your connections. These implants, by the way, hold a great deal of fear. They can become activated when someone who has been abused has sexual relations with someone they love.

Using whatever terminology you wish, call on God, All That Is, Love Itself, Source, the Creator, and fill every place in which an implant was removed with your love and your joy. As they're doing this, we ask for whatever needs to be done to free the pituitary gland, physical heart, uterus, and any place oxytocin is produced. Free them so this bonding hormone can assist in connecting with someone heart to heart.

Now we will make several requests. "Healing teams, we ask you to use whatever energies, whatever plug-ins that have been developed, anything within all the books in this Encyclopedia of Healing series, any healing that is needed for the nervous system and for each endocrine gland that has been affected by abuse. Replace any energy of abuse with the energy of unconditional love."

"Healing teams, we ask for the removal of any energy of the perpetrator from the individual. Replace any of that energy with love."

"Healing teams, we ask for the removal of any shame the individual who was abused is experiencing or has experienced. We ask that that shame be replaced with the absolute delight of the Creator, the energy of love, and the energy of delight for the individual by the Creator."

"Healing teams, we ask you to remove any implants of fear, shame, and guilt in any place within the endocrine system, even those the medical community don't know about, and replace them with unconditional love."

Hold this energy in your hand, this consciousness — whether it is one person, two people, or a billion people — as long as you can feel and experience the energy from your hands. You may, of course, hold that energy as long as you wish. If it is time for you to go, gently disconnect with love from the energy, which we will do now.

With your intention of disconnecting (though the energy will not be leaving you) and your continued expression of love, give thanks to all the healing teams and soul-healing angels. You might notice your hands relax a bit as you gently disconnect. If you are not sure that you are disconnected, use Michael's Sword, or you can use your hand

and bring it down in front of you to your torso. You do not need to continually send energy to everyone. There you go.

Tremendous Healing Has Begun

There are several things we would like you to know. First, you have begun a tremendous healing process across your planet. When you work with group energies, you are never alone, even if you forget to call in other beings to work with you. We suggest that you form your own healing-lecture room with your angelic realm surrounding it. The central pillar contains everyone who is needed, and you can call in the consciousness of that group energy if you wish. Again, you can do this work with the consciousness of the planet, or you can work with the consciousness of your city, block, or family, if you know a lot of sexual abuse is there. So you can limit it.

If you work professionally, as you call it, or you do an exchange of energy in any way, when you work with one person, work with the energy of the family as a whole. If one person has been sexually abused by a member of the family, other members of the family have almost always been sexually abused. The perpetrator could have been sexually abused. You can work with the entire family this way.

As you work with this process, notice what works best for you. We are always here with you. Be at peace. Be at love. We thank you for the service you have given.

There Is a Bond Between Victim and Perpetrator

Mimi: Are souls still coming in who have a life plan that they want to be sexually abused?

Dr. Cathy: What I'm hearing from Amiya is that nobody wants to be sexually abused, but they offer it. Wait, Amiya is going to answer this question.

Amiya: It is difficult to be clear when talking about such a difficult topic. To answer your question, more souls are coming in to be of service to the planet by allowing themselves to be involved in either sex trafficking or sexual abuse for the sole purpose of bringing that consciousness up until people decide to release the energy from the planet. After that, fewer people will come in with that particular life plan.

Mimi: Hopefully, no one will eventually come in with that life plan.

Yes, this will happen as your planet ascends. In ascension, people will still have that physical relationship on a sexual level of making love, as you say, but it will come from the heart. Yes, the second chakra is involved, but abuse occurs only with the second chakra and does not move up into the third chakra or the heart. Energetically, there is that progression.

Perpetrators of sexual abuse have two active chakras: the first and the second. Not even the third is active. You might think, "Well, isn't the third their sense of personal power?" Your sense of personal power is an internal energy. With perpetrators of any abuse, only the second chakra — power over the outside world, including money and sex — is active at the times of sexual abuse. It doesn't matter who does the sexual abuse, whether it's a family member, government official, or church official; only those two chakras are active.

As healing occurs, you're able to free perpetrators. You work with every perpetrator on the planet because every perpetrator has been sexually abused. Did that help?

Mimi: Yes.

Michelle: When we were clearing the rage and hate, those emotions came in from the victims and from the perpetrators?

Yes. That is a very important thing you noticed. When that hate and rage move from the victim to the perpetrator, it keeps the victim bound to the perpetrator. When you held the consciousness in your hands for those several minutes at the beginning, you helped loosen that energy that went from the perpetrator to the victim and from the victim to the perpetrator.

If you work individually in this area, you will find that people who feel that anger and rage toward someone recover more easily because it eliminates shame and fear. The difficulty comes because people with that rage and anger have not had their third chakras (inner power) and heart chakras activated. Not all, but some can become perpetrators; they focus that energy outward. How someone becomes a perpetrator is actually very complex. We will go into that later.

Michelle: Thank you.

Anyone else?

Cleo: Amiya, you said we can heal the consciousness of sexual abuse whether it's local or global. I have been contemplating a move to Maryland to be closer to my son and grandkids. I know that was a slave state, and horrendous things happened there. If I made a move like that, could I do anything to help that situation?

What you have just learned will help the situation there. Let us talk about the complexities of that. It is not just slave states, the legal slave states of the United States; non-legal slavery also comes from sex trafficking and forced labor. The areas that had legal slavery are in great need for the Curse Removal plug-in to release slavery itself. When people saw their loved ones beaten and their backs shredded by whips or when they saw someone being raped or knew a loved one was raped, curses were often placed on the land and on the people associated with the perpetuation of slavery.

If you know that your family owned slaves, it is important to remove curses placed on them. When working with slave owners — and this also occurs with sexual abuse — the precious people enslaved or abused are not seen as people; they are seen as objects. The energy of seeing people as objects rather than as living, breathing, heart-centered beings, needs to be removed from the DNA.

You Can Add Plug-Ins to the Basic Four

Cleo: You often mention the Curse Removal plug-in. I have been thinking that perhaps we should add it to our foundational plug-ins, making it five instead of four.

You can definitely add that; anyone can add anything to their foundational plug-ins. When you have that desire, you can say, "Healing team, when I speak of the five foundational plug-ins, they include ..." Some of you might even require more.

When this one does her healing work with groups and individuals, she uses foundational balances. Two plug-ins you should not add to the foundational plug-ins are the Heal the DNA plug-in and the Clear the Gaps in the Aura plug-in. You have many other choices for foundational plug-ins. Choose which ones work best for you in particular situations. The reason we chose these four is that everyone needs them. Not everyone receives the kinds of curses you are talking about. But if you ask for one to be used and it is not needed, the only thing that happens is it is not used, correct? So those are the four key plug-ins.

When you work with someone on a long-term basis clearing these major issues — victim consciousness, implants, and so on — then you move to areas deeper within. This is where you can add plug-ins you use every day. Then it would be good to use the Heal the DNA and the Clear the Gaps in the Aura plug-ins.

Cleo: Sometimes I remember them but not often.

You have been introduced to the hologram. There is a hologram known as the Hologram of Love that contains every hologram and plug-in within it. We go through these step-by-step because you humans believe everything should be complex. The only action you need is to be within your heart, holding that energy, holding the intention of the one you wish to send energy to, and allow that energy of love to move toward them. This is what you did at the beginning of this session.

You could begin to loosen congested energies, thought forms, and plug-ins. Nobody in that energy you worked with today consciously gave assent to what was happening. When you work with group energy and individual members know what is happening, they give their conscious assent, and the energy is able to penetrate much faster.

CHAPTER TWENTY-TWO

Address the Effects of Sexual Abuse

Amiya and Dr. Cathy

Amiya: We're going to talk about what happens with the throat chakra and how sexual abuse can affect your ability to live and proclaim who you are, meaning living and proclaiming your truth. As you know, some people do not live the truth of who they are for many reasons.

As we have said before, sexual abuse is also spiritual abuse. A change takes place within the spiritual energies that connect who you believe you were when you came into this incarnation. Changes occur with the vulnerability of your heart, your ability to speak your truth, and your ability to bring in energy from spirit and the planet.

Changes do not occur because spirit does not talk to you or the universal energy is not present. They occur because you form a protective barrier in order not to be hurt again. The changes are for inner protection, the type of which varies depending on the circumstances of the abuse. One type is when you are abused by someone unknown to you and unknown to anyone you know. This happens in situations such as sex trafficking where no one in the family had anything to do with the trafficking.

Another type of sexual abuse can occur when others know it is happening to you. In other words, the other parent, another adult, or even another child knows the abuse is happening and does nothing to stop it. You could say there is that knowledge in sex trafficking where others know about it, but we're speaking of people who know about it and could stop it. When you are caught up in sex trafficking, you are captured by people whose purpose is to objectify you, to use you only for money or work. A helplessness occurs.

When you are in a home or a school where somebody knows or suspects and does nothing, a different type of injury occurs. It is a nuance, you could say. We're going to talk about what happens when it is in the home or a school or when the person is surrounded by people who could help if they know and have the courage to help.

Trust Is Damaged

When you are involved in a sexually abusive situation with someone who is supposed to love you and protect you, you lose all trust in authority figures and love. We said, "You lose all trust," but some do not lose all trust; they lose a great deal of trust. It wounds deep in the heart and psyche. When you grow up with people telling you there is love and you believe there is love and then they abuse you or do nothing to prevent the abuse, this damages your ability to trust.

Even as an adult, when you begin to understand these circumstances through your intellect and know others are there who can help you, such as a therapist or a partner, there is so much damage to your trust that it is difficult for you to reach out and allow your energy to connect to another person. This is partly why working with sexual abuse is so difficult.

We have given you the tools. Even if we give you nothing else and tell you nothing else, you can use what we have already given you at each stage when the abuse occurred. Does that take away all the damage? We would like to say it does, but we must tell you that it does not.

What we are going to say seems very unfair: The abuse did not happen because of your choice here on the planet, but in order to heal from the abuse, you have to take the chance to trust some person or some being (as in spirit, the universe). It is not your fault you were abused and damaged in such a way.

We are speaking from the third-dimensional standpoint. From the higher levels, this was a choice your soul made to experience an event that happened in your life. This is not something to say to someone recovering from abuse unless they are already aware of this concept. Remember, you forgot everything about planning your life when you came here. From your point of view in the third-dimensional realm — where reality is, what is happening here on the planet, where this incarnation is not an illusion — the illusion is love. When you have been so wounded and damaged, the illusion becomes love. You close yourself as much as possible to prevent further harm.

When you have an expectation, a hope, that the abuse will end and you will be saved, that somebody will come and love you and pull you out of the horror you are in but no one does, the pain becomes worse. What do you do as the healer in a situation like this? Do you do encodement work? You could, but in this area the person might not allow the encodement work to happen. You know that a person must be open to receiving the healing. You might ask, "Why would people not want to receive healing from this?" It's because they hoped before that they would be protected, that it wouldn't happen again, and that they would be cared for. That hope was shattered by continued abuse.

If you are repeatedly abused, your hope is shattered. Often when your hope is shattered into millions of pieces, you resist hoping again. You resist healing, because if you hope again and there is no release, your hope is shattered forever, and despair sets in. You don't think you could ever come to trust who you are again.

Enact a Healing

If you are a healer, how do you help? We're going to do that now; we're going to help. If you know someone, a personal someone who has been sexually abused, is resistant to being healed, and that resistance is from the fear of being shattered again, bring that person (or those people) to mind. If you do not know of anyone, connect with your soul self and ask your healing team to identify one or more you can send love to. Do not select a large group at this time. Learn how to do this first. It is simple.

Are you ready? Your first step is to double-check that you're in your heart source. Now connect with their healing team, as their healing team is always ready to assist. Each of you sends out a different vibration of love. Love energy, as with any energy, is within a range of vibration. Some of you can send out a higher vibration of love than others. That does not matter. Some people can turn the faucet on higher than others. There is no judgment.

Ask your soul self, who is part of your healing team, "What percentage of love energy are you able to send out today? What percentage can these people, this person, handle?" This is what we mean by "handle": If the love is too intense, it can frighten the people you're trying to help, and they could close themselves down. Very gently send out energy so that you do not frighten them. How can love frighten? It frightens because they do not recognize the energy of love. They have had too many people tell them that they love them and then have been betrayed.

Simply ask for a soul connection with who you have in mind. Ask, "How much of my love energy would be appropriate for the highest good of this individual?" It does not matter how much, as people will only let in so much. Their healing teams will also manage the amount of love energy entering. If you do not receive an answer, ask your healing guides and their healing teams to manage the amount of energy from you to them.

From the connection you have above and below, form your intention to bring in more energy from your chakras that will go out to those you are sending energy to. Your intention is for this person or these people to be loved and healed. Now send energy that comes from your hands and your heart and cover them with love. For many, it is helpful to envision them resting in your hands, receiving love.

Hold that space. Send energy as long as you feel the desire to do so, or until you feel the other person blocking the energy in some way. All you are doing is sending love. As you send the energy, you might feel guided to do encodement work. Remove the artificial encodements ready to be released. If you aren't guided to do encodement work, simply send the love.

The throat chakra is definitely affected when there is such abuse, especially when one in the family, the school, or anywhere knew and could have stopped it. Your throat chakra is involved when living and proclaiming your truth. It also is how you connect and communicate with others in one-on-one relationships — through your truth. When the events of your life have led to an inability to trust because people have proven untrustworthy, your throat chakra is damaged.

That damage to the throat chakra is not only in the fifth chakra; it is also in each of the fifth subchakras of every chakra that is damaged by the abuse. Both the heart (fourth chakra) and the fifth subchakra of the heart can be damaged. When the heart chakra is damaged by abuse, the fourth subchakra in the other chakras, such as the fifth (the throat), can be damaged. Depending on the person, all chakras and subchakras can be damaged.

Be There in Love

When you send love as we have suggested, just be there in love. There is no demand on your part that the people you are sending love to be what and who they are now. Have no expectations of them. Simply send the material of healing, which is love, to them for their use. Even if they do not fully accept that love, that love energy surrounds them when they are ready. The love energy is there for their healing teams to use. Sometimes that love energy does not enter their auras until they are asleep.

Why until they are asleep? You could say it is because their defenses are down and other energies can enter. That is true. Let us give you another reason. It is in your sleep, most learned scholars and most precious ones, that your healing teams are able to work with you because your defenses are down. You are able to connect more with your soul self. You set down the cares of the world. It is one of the reasons that sleep is so important for you. You have read or heard about how the brain and the body renew during sleep. This happens on the physical level and on the spiritual level. It is because those beings who are with you, your guides, your angels, your healing team, are able to gently work with you, to call to you, on that soul level, and ask whether you're ready for healing.

By sending that love energy, you are letting them know that, yes, even if they do not know you, and even if they do not know who you are or what you are doing, unconditional love from the human level is coming to them. It is a process.

If you work with them when they are awake, as your client for instance, or you have done encodement work with them, spend time when they are not with you sending love, surrounding them with love. Any love they do not accept, that their energy and sense of self do not accept, while they are awake is there for when they allow that love energy to seep into their very being. Even if they only accept a minute amount of energy you send them, what a joy when they do so.

Know that some are more resistant to receiving love than others. It is their life path and what they planned. Yes, ones who have been harmed have the responsibility to reach out for healing, to open themselves for healing. It is not any different than if you were in an automobile accident that was not your fault. If you were wounded in such a way and you need physical therapy, it is your responsibility to reach out for it even though the injury was not your fault. You must accept your new situation and move forward.

People's energy fields are damaged differently when sexually abused by a stranger, such as being stolen for the purpose of sex trafficking. The healing processes are similar for both. They do not have to work through being betrayed by someone they loved and trusted, unless of course that happened. When people are victimized by incest by a family member and no one came to their defense, they doubt love in every way. Their trust of those they should be able to count on most shatters the ability to trust in some way. They associate professions of love with the betrayal of not being protected. The ones who have been in sex trafficking close up to protect themselves from strangers. If they see getting caught in sex trafficking as their fault, they need to reestablish trust in themselves.

The prescription, however, is the same. Hold them in love. Whether or not they know you are doing it, send them that love energy. This is what you call the power of prayer. No strings are attached to this love, not even the string that they have to accept it in some way. It is simply there.

Some of you might send love to one who sends that energy back to you faster than you sent it to them. That is okay. Try again another time. We will talk more about the effect sending love energy has on the individual. People who have been sexually abused lose that sense of who they are.

Get Out of the Way of Your Ego

Louise: When we were holding them in our hands, it was like what Amma does for us, holding us in her love. Also, it is what we have done in the past, sending heart-healing energy in the frequency and vibration someone needs.

Margaret: I liked getting out of the way of my ego involvement and just sending love to them in the amount they needed according to their healing team. It seemed like sending love as a reserve for when it's accepted. I liked that we sent love and let it do its course, because they will get it at some level and will use it as they need it. I really, really liked that.

Dr. Cathy: When doing this work, we need to keep in mind that we have no expectations of what the others will do. We simply stay in our hearts and send love.

Margaret: Yes, we have this ego need to be of value and worth, and because they don't get healed, we think they're saying we have no value and worth. A lack of self-worth, self-injury, and self-hatred can happen when we have those expectations.

That's when you do encodement work for yourself. Every time you do encodement work for yourself, you're able to raise the vibrational frequency of the love you send out. It rises automatically, like putting water through a filter and purifying it. If we filter out the ego we don't consciously know is present, we can send a higher frequency of love. From their egos, people might say, "We're not doing any good because they're not accepting it." How do we know they're not accepting it? They might have a hole within them that is so deep it will take more time to see results.

CHAPTER TWENTY-THREE

Heal the Intricate Wounds of Abuse

Amiya and Dr. Cathy

Amiya: This book has surfaced many feelings in you. It has surfaced energies from other lifetimes and from this lifetime. It has also made you more sensitive to those on your planet who have suffered through sexual abuse. If you are having these feelings, know there is nothing wrong with you.

We'll begin where we left off with what happens to the energy field, something we haven't talked about before. Experiencing such a deep wound that incorporates the spiritual results in tears and holes in your energy field. A clouding of structures and implants occurs. You experience artificial encodements and damaged and altered natural encodements.

In the last session, you learned to hold yourself and others in love, within love. That's what we're going to discuss today. Doing encodement work doesn't work well in some situations. You might think, "But it works with the form and the foundation of the structure, such as the structure of your body, a feeling, or an energy part within you."

From your heart source, go into the back of your heart center and into your sacred space. Stay here as we talk. Images, colors, or sounds might come to you; you will all have different experiences. We also want you here to help you determine whether or not this relates to you, whether this is truth for you.

Looking at an image of your energy field, your energy body expands well beyond the seventh layer to where you have no physical form. Your energy moves into being part of the universal energy field. Sexual abuse is also spiritual abuse. Spiritual abuse can tear a hole in your energy body that moves though all layers of the energy body and into universal energy.

We'll use a dramatic representation. Let us say you are shot by a bullet. A small hole might appear where the bullet enters, but a larger hole tears through the body as the bullet exits. Think of your energy body as a bullet moving through the universal energy field. The hole becomes larger going through. This is a result of the combination of the force of the bullet, the energy and intent of who shot it, and what happens to people through their reactions to the event. It could trigger energies from past lives, parallel lives, and future lives, the fears of which can make that hole large. (Again, we're using graphic imagery here.) Your "energy body bullet" can blow through the very fabric of universal energy. Absorb that image for a moment.

Abuse Creates an Energetic Hole

When a hole is made in your energy body and in the universal energy, this opens you to several types of energies. One type, of course, is the absolute love that the universe is made from. Because the reason for the hole is violence, you do not attract universal love but rather the pain and suffering floating around in universal energy. Again, take a moment to absorb this concept. This is an example of how your vibration attracts what is out there in universal energy.

If you have been sexually abused, you have a spiritual wound. The extent of that wound varies according to you as an individual. When the wound blows a hole through the energy field into universal energy, you can attract the pain, sense of betrayal, fear, anger, lack of trust, doubt, and despair that exists in universal energy.

You might be aware of what is known as the collective unconscious as proposed by the master Carl Jung. We are speaking of what he called collective-unconscious energy. Imagine all the energy of time floating around you in some form: anger, fear, betrayal, joy, happiness. Your energy is filled with anger, fear, betrayal, and despair; therefore, you attract the energy of those low-vibration feelings from the collective unconscious.

When you have that hole through your energy field that goes outward into the collective-unconscious energy, you attract the universal energy that holds the energy of this planet for all time. Remember, you are in a place of all time, as there is no time. Paradoxically, there is no space in space. Encodement work has some positive effects, but it does not repair that hole in the same way we're going to teach you.

The wound, the hole, first needs the energy of love. Imagine someone who has a hole of mistrust. Mistrust is one of the most common feelings you have if you have been sexually abused. Sexual expression is a gift from the Creator and one of the most pleasant gifts the Creator has given you. This gift is contained within the passion of physical love when love is involved.

When the beautiful gift of the Creator has been "perverted" by someone's wound of anger, fear, or betrayal followed by betrayal of you, the one who was abused, it opens that wound of the inability to trust. Imagine that that wound, that hole, has borders, and instead of love, pain resides there. You can describe whatever low-vibration emotion is present, but instead of love, there is pain. That wound attracts the other pain in the universal energy field, the collective unconscious. If the person replaces the pain with love, joy, and happiness — not of the event but in general — they attract love, joy, and happiness.

This is a very important concept. If you have any questions about what we have just said, please ask now.

Other Lifetimes Are Affected by Wounds

Margaret: Just to clarify, you're speaking of this lifetime and any other lifetime we've experienced this?

Correct.

Margaret: So it stays with the soul body as opposed to the personality of this lifetime?

That is a wonderful question. Let us clarify. The energy that you, the one with the wound, attract in other lifetimes is outside in the universal energy field. You attract the lifetime energies of other people as well. Having the wound triggers within you other lifetime experiences that are also in the universal energy field. But we are talking about this moment, which is why your wound (what this one calls the "black hole") is so vast that no matter how much love someone gives you, that love is not enough. The borders of the hole are rimmed with pain that can be described as despair, anger, rage, and the urge to kill. These energies that reside along the borders of that hole attract that same low-vibration energy in the universal energy field. As you brought up, it can be your past-life energies, but it is also everyone's energies, because there is no time; there is no space. It just is.

Elaine: Does this wound ever have a specific location, such as the heart?

That is another excellent question. Yes. This is where what you know about the human energy field enhances this information. Your hole can be through your heart. It can be through your solar plexus. It can be through the first chakra. When doing healing, ask your guides to send the healing to the specific location. You don't necessarily need to know where it is.

We'll go through a little process now that will help elaborate that for you. Does anybody else have a question before we do that?

Margaret: A clarification on that last part. If you've had this experience in various lifetimes, can you actually have several wounds, like in a heart and solar plexus, or does it stay with one location?

You bring in another very good question that adds depth to what we are talking about. It brings a complexity we weren't planning on going into at this point, but you bring it up, so that means you're ready for the complexity.

When injuries are triggered from other lifetimes, the wound itself does not expand. Let's go back to the bullet image. (It is easier for people to imagine the bullet, as most reading this book have not been shot but might have been sexually abused.) If the bullet enters a shoulder that has had multiple and various wounds over many lifetimes, the energy of the memory of what happened in other lifetimes surfaces, but that does not make the hole in this lifetime larger. There is an exception: If you focus on the multiple wounds from various lifetimes from the perspective of victim consciousness rather than moving into healing, you bring the past wounds of other lifetimes into this current lifetime.

Remember, the human mind believes everything is happening in the present. That is why it is so important not to repeatedly regurgitate what happened in the past. Every time you do so, you re-injure yourself. Your mind experiences these past memories as happening now. When you keep regurgitating the event, the hole can become larger. But when you recall a wound for the purpose of healing, the hole does not enlarge, as the energy is different from reliving the experience. Consider the image of picking at a scab. A small wound can become infected, making the wound larger. The only time to bring a wound to mind is for the purpose of healing and releasing the pain.

When the bullet goes through you, it triggers the energies of other events and other lifetimes, but it does not make the wound of this lifetime, the actual hole within your energy body, larger. If that seems paradoxical, simply accept the paradox.

You might have noticed that when you do encodements work, you can be distracted by what happens around you and not 100 percent focused on the encodement work. This is an area where your healing team comes in and works with you with great love and affection. What we are going to do with you now (and what we did with you last time) requires at least 98 percent of your focus, because your intent is to send love. If you are not focused, you might send other energies created by whatever distracts you. Their healing team will do what is needed with that love, but your intention needs to be clear so that the only energy you send is the vibration of love.

You can focus your intention more specifically by sending love energy to clear the borders of the wound. Remember, the borders of the wound have the energy vibration of the individual's pain that attracts the energy in the collective unconscious.

When you have 98 percent focus, that energy goes outward to the borders of the wound and dissolves and transmutes the energy around it. You do not have to set another intention other than sending love energy. The love energy is intelligent. Your healing team and healing guides and the individual's healing team know what to do with that energy. Send that energy, that love energy, with your focus, and yes, you can tell them to "clear the borders of the wound of any low-vibration energy" to make your focus clearer. Hold that focus as long as possible.

Here is a fun trick. Some of you have already thought of it. You can call on Archangel Michael and his band of angels to stand in front of that hole. The hole goes out at least into the twelfth layer of the aura, not to the seventh. You can set your intention to have the energy go to the layer of the aura that begins the individuation into the physical body.

Heal Abuse Wounds

Call on Archangel Michael and others, if you wish. And yes, you might call on Metatron and his band to stand in front of the hole and block any incoming energy of pain attracted by the borders of the hole. Be fully anchored in your heart source, and move to the sacred space within the back of your heart center. You will send love energy from there.

To practice this, think of someone you know or know of who has been sexually abused and doesn't seem able to heal. If no one comes to mind, ask your healing guides to bring someone to you who has such a hole and wants to be healed. You don't have to know whether the person was sexually abused or not. Anyone who has difficulty healing might have such a hole.

Create a healing room outside your sacred space that you can enter from your sacred space. Do not invite them into the sacred space itself. You can also create a monitor of some kind to connect with them. Connect with your healing guides. State your intention. Now connect with the soul, the higher self, the soul self, of that individual and ask for permission. (This requires some permission, at least on a soul level, and we'll explain why in a minute.) Ask for permission to send them love energy, no strings attached.

Focus on bringing that love energy from above and below. To bring in more energy, say, "Chakras spin." Bring the energy into your heart, out through your arms, and into your hands. You can also hold the image of the individual within your heart or in your hands. Send the energy to remove or release the pain at the borders of the hole.

Ask Archangel Michael or Metatron and the members of their bands to transmute any energy coming toward the individual attracted by the low-vibration energy of the edges of the hole. We will allow you to do that for about two minutes.

Now gently disconnect. Ask the person's healing team to remove all artificial encodements that were released or jostled free, if you wish, from the individual while you sent that energy. Repair all damaged and altered natural encodements.

Notice that you sent the energy first and then did the encodement work. For someone who has a deep wound that has burst through the energy field into the collective unconscious, encodement work might not work until you send love energy to release the low-vibration energy surrounding the hole.

This exercise requires tremendous focus, because when you're not focused, you can send out vibrations other than love energy, as in your emotions. That is why it is so important for you to focus. If you find you're not able to focus, even for a short time, discontinue as soon as you lose focus. Then ask the person's healing team to please remove any of your artificial encodements that went to that individual. When you send love in this way, you also send yourself. You send them the love energy of another human being connected to the Divine.

Some of you might have noticed how difficult it was to focus, especially if you sent energy to someone you knew. With someone you know, you might have feelings, emotions, and thoughts because of your connection to them outside the healing experience. It is easier to focus if you choose someone you don't really know or a client with whom you have no deep emotional connection.

You can use this tool for anyone at any time, and it is especially good for those who have that hole. The border of the hole contains the low-vibration energy, the pain. As you release that energy forming the border, the hole begins to close. The more that energy releases, the more the individual attracts love, joy, happiness, and contentment from the universal-collective energy field.

The Soul Seeks Experiences in Life

Brenda: Is this pain from the unhealed hole part of the perpetuation and continuation of abusive relationships?

Yes, exactly. And that is another wonderful question. That is what happens in the perpetuation of abuse. People respond from that pain, as they know no other way to respond. That hole brings in energy from the universal energy field that is not of love but of pain. When those energies are triggered, the person responds in ways that others from the universal energy field have responded, such as perpetrating abuse — not just sexual but also physical.

Margaret: Does this also apply to people with PTSD who have killed and maimed other people? I'm assuming they would also have holes, wounds, within them.

Not all of them have holes and wounds. People who have PTSD from their roles in the military or law enforcement perpetrate violence due to their jobs. They knew this could happen. They need their encodement systems and past lives balanced. They might need soul retrieval, which is the Soul Healing Prayer.

With that said, let's look at a situation in which they were injured by friendly fire or an act of betrayal from one of their comrades. The emotional reaction to being betrayed in such a way can produce a hole. This is different from causing pain in another due to what they know is part of their job. Betrayal can result in a hole, even betrayal of themselves. Betrayal is not usually associated with doing a job in which they killed or maimed someone. They were prepared for that. The hole usually comes from something outside themselves. Is that clear?

Margaret: That's clear. I know from a lifetime in the 1500s that I was severely sexually abused by multiple people, including my father at that time. I assume there was a hole at that time. But across lifetimes, I've been the healer. Do I necessarily still have that hole or wound? Or did I even have one to start with? I mean, do we just assume we have one if we know about sexual abuse from some other lifetime?

No. Again, this question demonstrates your development as a healer. You see the complexities. Here is something to know: When you leave your body at death and after your life review, you go to a place of healing where those kinds of holes are repaired. The follow-up questions might be, "Then why do we deal with these energies afterward? Is it because we're not healed?" You come into this lifetime with different things you want to experience. Remember, you make these choices before you incarnate, when you have a very different view of this life.

Let's say you do not want to experience again the sexual abuse of gang rape, but you want the energy of that memory triggered by something else that happens in this lifetime. This all takes place to enhance what you chose to experience in this lifetime. This does not happen because the wound from the past lifetime is unhealed. That other lifetime becomes a metaphor for what you wanted to experience in this lifetime.

You bring in the energy of being gang raped by being raped once or being sexually abused to experience the intensity of those energies without going through what you already went through before. You might ask, "Why would I ever want to do that?" We suggest you have a discussion with your soul self when you leave your body. For now, know that you do not bring holes with you; you bring energy that can contribute to the experience.

For another take on this, let's say an attachment of yours from another lifetime has not returned to the light, meaning they have not gone through their healing process. To put it very succinctly, a ghost is attached to you from the 1500s who might have been physically abused, sexually abused, and betrayed. That being hasn't gone through the healing. He or she might have a hole. As you work to have the being return to the light, you might want to send love to the hole to heal it. This can make the release process easier.

Focus on Love to Avoid Low-Vibration Energy

Dr. Cathy: When doing encodement work, you are centered and grounded. You're in your heart source. You can go in and out of your heart source, depending on what happens. When doing encodement work, you're not necessarily sending them any energy. You're giving instructions to their healing team. You're the facilitator. When you have the intention to send love, you also send energy from yourself and from the universal energy field. Energies that come in from above and below and into your chakras can also collect energy from you. That's part of your healing. Doing this will clear some things for you.

When you are totally focused on sending the purity of love, even at 98 percent (which is a lot), you avoid sending anything of a low vibration that comes from you.

Brenda: If abuse occurs during pregnancy, such as getting hit in the stomach, and the fetus takes the hit, can a hole form in the child's energy field as it does with sexual abuse, or is it only after birth?

I'm connecting to Amiya, so I'll be just a moment.

Amiya: It depends. When there is no intent of damaging the child, the energy field will not be affected by it. Because the injury was not personally directed to the pregnancy, even if the child ends up being miscarried, there wouldn't usually be a hole. Great damage can occur to the energy field if the purpose is to affect the child. Then a hole can definitely form. Let's say the mother is raped while pregnant. If the rapist knows about the pregnancy, there's also an intent from the perpetrator, a wish, to do that to the child. That can produce a hole.

CHAPTER TWENTY-FOUR

Work with the Endocrine System

Amiya and Dr. Cathy

Amiya: In this chapter, we will continue with the brain and work with the endocrine system. This can be done for people in any stage of sexual abuse. When I say "any stage," I mean at any age it happens. When sexual abuse occurs to a young person, and we're speaking especially of penetration and violence, it can retard the development of the brain and endocrine system.

We're going to go step by step through the endocrine system, starting with the pituitary gland. The pituitary gland contains oxytocin and many other hormones, more than we can say. The pituitary gland activates the hormones needed for a woman's eggs to develop. Sexual abuse can affect a woman's pituitary gland and make it difficult for her to conceive. But do not think that any woman who has a problem with conceiving was sexually abused. It is not the same thing.

First, focus on the pituitary gland and ask your healing team to apply the Basic plug-in. We introduced this sequence earlier: the Repair the Energy Field plug-in, the Basic plug-in, the Repair the Energy Field plug-in, the Healing over Lifetimes plug-in, the Repair the Energy Field plug-in, the Remove Victim Consciousness plug-in, and the Repair the Energy Field plug-in. Notice what we're going to do here: the Remove Victim Consciousness plug-in, the Repair the Energy Field plug-in, the Remove Victim Consciousness plug-in, the Repair the Energy Field plug-in, the Implant Removal plug-in, and the Repair the Energy Field plug-in. Let's just bring it all together and call this the Repair the Endocrine System plug-in [see appendix]. How's that sound?

Move to the pineal gland. Ask the healing team, "Please implement the Repair the Endocrine System plug-in." You might notice changes within you, because you can use this whether you've been abused or not. Different things could have caused these problems.

Now use the Repair the Endocrine System plug-in for the thyroid gland. You might need to repeat this plug-in here several times, as the thyroid is greatly affected when you can't proclaim your truth, cry out, or call for help and also when your cries for help go unnoticed or are denied.

Dr. Cathy: This is Cathy. I kind of bled through here. I worked with a client the other day who told her family she had been sexually abused by some kids in the neighborhood, and her parents called her a liar.

Amiya: It is important to know that when someone asks for help (which is proclaiming their truth) and it is denied, damage occurs in the throat chakra, which is connected to the thyroid gland. (We're going to do the chakras in a minute.) You might need to repeat that Repair the Endocrine System plug-in several times.

You could choose to just say, "Please use the Healing over Lifetimes plug-in with the Repair the Endocrine System plug-in," but I suggest you do the entire thing. This is because the people you work with might have had multiple lifetimes in which hanging, beheading, and strangulation occurred that prevented them from being who they were, even thieves. They were beheaded not because they were thieves but because of their choice to be who they were; we make no value judgments. So do that with yourself now. Ask your healing team, "Please use the Repair the Endocrine System plug-in for the thyroid gland. Apply the plug-in again, please." There we go.

Scientists have discovered that the heart is an endocrine gland.

It also produces oxytocin as well as other hormones that help it beat. Say, "Healing team, please apply the Repair the Energy Field plug-in for the heart. Apply the Repair the Energy Field plug-in for the pancreas. Also apply the Repair the Energy Field plug-in for the adrenal glands." You might want to repeat the Repair the Endocrine System plug-in several times for this gland, as it experiences extreme stress. So let's do it two more times: "Healing team, please use the Repair the Endocrine System plug-in two more times for the adrenal glands." Here's a hint: You could also say, "Healing team, implement the Repair the Endocrine System plug-in on the adrenal glands three times."

Now say, "Healing team, please apply the Repair the Endocrine System plug-in for the ovaries." It would be helpful here to specify right ovary and left ovary. (It can be in any order.) Then say, "Healing Team, please apply the Repair the Endocrine System plug-in for the testes, the right testes and then the left testes. Now, healing team, please remove any and all artificial encodements preventing the synchronization and harmonization of the endocrine glands with each other. Please repair any damaged or altered natural encodements preventing the integration and synchronization of the endocrine glands with each other. Link the consciousness of the entire endocrine system with the divine blueprint of the endocrine system. Finally, healing team, use everything we have done for each of the endocrine glands, including harmonizing them with any other endocrine gland we are not aware of." Good.

Repair the Chakras Related to Sexual Abuse

Let us move to the chakras. (This will include the subchakras, so you don't need to mention them by name unless you want to.) We're not going to do as much on the chakras because the book on the chakras [*The Human Energy Field: Chakras*] has much information on what to do. Again, we are focusing on sexual abuse: "Healing team, please apply the Repair the Endocrine System plug-in to the crown chakra, the front of the third eye, and the back of the third eye." Let us interject here that you might get an idea from your healing guides that instruct you to start with a different chakra or go in a different order. Please follow that; it's not a problem.

Continue with the chakras: "Healing team, please repair the front of the throat chakra, back of the throat chakra, front of the heart chakra, back of the heart chakra, front of the solar plexus, back of the solar plexus, front of the second chakra, back of the second chakra, and the first chakra." There will be times you might be guided to use the navel chakra. We'll go ahead and do that: "Apply it to the navel chakra." You might be guided to use what is called the high-heart chakra. "Healing team, please apply the Repair the Endocrine System plug-in to the high heart." Yes, you can use this for all the minor chakras if you wish. Go to the book on the chakras if you need to refresh your memory.

Now make a general request of the healing team: "Please remove all artificial encodements interfering with the full connection of each chakra with the endocrine gland it is associated with. Please repair the damaged and altered natural encodements inhibiting full communication between the endocrine glands and the associated chakra." Do the same thing with the meridians, but you don't need to go through them one at a time: "Healing team, please, repair all artificial encodements inhibiting the connection of the endocrine glands with their associated meridians. Please repair all damaged and altered natural encodements interfering with the direct association of the endocrine glands with their proper meridians."

Repair the Layers of the Aura Related to Sexual Abuse

Now we'll repair the layers of the aura. This is again related to sexual abuse, but you can use it for anything: "Healing team, please use the Repair the Endocrine System plug-in to clear the first layer of the aura, then the second layer, third layer, fourth layer, fifth layer, sixth layer, seventh layer, and a little bit further to the eighth, ninth, tenth, eleventh, and twelfth layers.

"Healing team, please use the Repair the Energy Field plug-in to balance anything with any of those layers of the aura that we just mentioned." Notice what's happening. "Healing team, remove all artificial encodements interfering with the full development of each layer of the aura associated with each chakra — the first chakra associated with the first layer, the second chakra associated with the second, and so on."

One final thing, which is a big one: "Healing team, please apply the same process we just used on the chakras, endocrine system, and levels of the aura to every structure within the book *Hidden Structures*." If you wish, you can go through the book *Hidden Structures* [*The Human Energy Field: Hidden Structures*]. Make a list of those hidden structures, and apply the plug-in to each. Some of you might feel the desire to do that, especially if you are new to this whole thing.

That is all we're going to do today; I think that was plenty. You made some deep changes to the energy field.

If you usually work with clients for an hour, working on their energy field might require less time. One change in the energy field can make significant changes, and too much at once could cause a healing crisis. If you do all this in, say, fifteen or twenty minutes, let them relax with that. If you have a usual hour-long session, you can simply chat about the changes; let them know what they can expect.

Clear the Upper Chakras

Cleo: I realized I don't know what the twelfth chakra is.

Dr. Cathy: I don't really know either. I just know they said, "Go through them." I've seen some diagrams, but they're by different people who get different information. They just go up through the different layers.

Cleo: Why don't we have Amiya tell us what she means by these chakras?

They're telling me it would go into a whole different level of things and take probably about twenty or thirty more minutes to talk about each one of those individually.

Cleo: Well, I'm not asking for that. It's just that we think we know the chakras, and then I realized I never heard of these higher ones.

She's saying to think of it the way you think of the flames, when you first knew about the seven flames.

Cleo: I did, and I kept thinking to myself, "Am I confusing this with the flames?"

No, you're not. They work together. Each of these other chakras works with other parts of the aura, so you actually have all those layers of the aura. I believe I saw something recently that said we actually work with thirty-three layers and thirty-three chakras.

They're telling me you can find that information out there, but different people have different ideas. For example, some put the eighth chakra above the seventh, and others put the eighth chakra within the high heart in the body.

In BodyTalk, we talk about the eighth chakra being an entryway into past lives and genetic information, things like that. When you start with the heart chakra and go up, those are the spiritual layers, the spiritual chakras. They work with your connection to spirit and to the other lifetimes of your soul self. Specific chakras have different information. It would be really fascinating to hear what Amiya has to say about that.

Participant: I also think it's related to the dimension and density we experience. So the higher our awareness, the higher the dimension we experience, and that's related to the chakras. Does that make sense?

It does. Thank you.

Natural and Artificial Encodements Are Different

Participant: With this work, are we removing altered or damaged artificial encodements?

Natural encodements.

Participant: They also mentioned artificial.

We are removing artificial encodements.

Participant: Okay, are all artificial encodements bad, or are they just encodements you pick up as you go through life that might not be good for you in certain ways?

That's a good question. Artificial encodements are encodements that you acquire or create that are not connected with your encodements system or were not created for you by your encodement team. So if somebody sends you love, those are not created for you, and my healing guides are telling me all encodements of love are natural encodements.

Participant: That's nice.

So it doesn't matter if you send them to me, they're created within me, or I create them, all encodements of love are natural encodements. Artificial encodements are usually the ones like anger, fear, jealousy, and emotional pain. We can create those artificial encodements ourselves or somebody can project them on to us. Those are the ones we were predominantly removing, the ones projected on to us. We were also removing any that we develop. For instance, you could have artificial encodements that you developed by believing you caused the sexual abuse. It's a victim-consciousness type of thing. I don't think I've talked about this in any of the books.

Our natural encodements can be damaged just like our chakras, meridians, and things like that. When I first asked about it years ago, Amma told me to imagine dropping a clock on the floor. It is damaged, and maybe the hands on the clock moved. Maybe your encodements are damaged to the point of inactivity. In that case, you can ask that they be activated, and some might be damaged to the point that they need to be replaced, and your healing team will do that

Participant: Replaced or repaired. Okay.

I'm just getting word about how they've talked about structural encodements of light. Some can be damaged and need repair, especially due to things like chemo and radiation (radiation from anywhere, not just treatment of cancer). Electromagnetic pollution can cause that too.

Michelle: I had a curious experience. When I was working with the aura and sending out that energy, the first seven layers of the aura were round and didn't form the shape that we typically think the aura has until it got up to the twelfth layer. It had that egg shape, and in the center was a yolk. Those were the first seven layers. I'd never experienced that before.

That's fascinating. I like that. Thank you for sharing.

Margaret: I did a little bit with Orin and DaBen about the lightbody and lightbody structures. They take you through them, and you work with them and move them. Is that lightbody structure part of the Merkabah? Is it connected to the chakras? Does it have anything to do with what Amiya is teaching to be killed or repaired, or is that just a totally different take on our structures from a different entity?

What I'm getting is that the lightbody you mention is basically another name for the aura. The aura is our lightbody, but light also comes from within us that can stream from the heart chakra and energize every layer of the aura. That can clarify the lightbody. Think of the lightbody as how someone would look if they did not have a physical body. So when we clean the chakras, aura, and all those structures, it gives greater clarity to the lightbody.

Margaret: Okay. Thank you.

CHAPTER TWENTY-FIVE

All Sexual Abuse Is Spiritual Abuse

Amiya

In the first part of the book, we gave many healing tools. We gave you tools for a particular age range, the age range of youth. We took you through what "normal" people (people who have not been abused) have gone through. Most of what happens later in development are normal developmental experiences. Read that material again, and use those tools for yourself or others. We do not need to review every little thing.

Now we proceed to the most difficult parts of the book. This involves actual abuse, such as incest, molestation, and yes, we will deal with what some call ritual abuse or satanic ritual abuse. We will talk about those who identify as transgender people or who identify as gay, lesbian, or bisexual, as well as those who are in a quandary over what to call themselves. (You might notice that younger generations call themselves anything. They might use different pronouns than what you are used to, such as referring to themselves as "they.")

There are different kinds of sexual abuse. One is implied abuse. You might have heard people say, "My stepfather (or father or mother) looked at me in ways that made me feel uncomfortable. He walked in when I was dressing and wouldn't knock on the door. I found peep holes in my closet." There was never anything physical. The person might say she had a feeling of being "slimed." People can experience that even from strangers who walk by. Being slimed often happens in sexual harassment that does not move into physical experience.

Then there are those who were physically molested at home. By "molestation," we mean physical contact occurred but not penetration by a finger, implement, or penis. Molestation is when parts of your body were touched without your permission. Yes, there are times when parts of your body are touched without intention of violation, such as in crowded places. Most women have had the experience of having their breasts hit. Even though unintentional, when people have feelings about abuse, they might be sensitive to inadvertent touches, and those experiences can trigger feelings from the past and activate those encodements, that energy, within their energy field.

Then there is abuse where penetration occurred. The reason penetration is separate, especially when penetration was by a penis, is that penetration almost always injects into the individual, male or female, an entity, a dark being. This being must be removed before someone can fully recover from that experience. More than one being might be present from one experience or many experiences. Group rape, for example, can bring about many different beings attached to the energies of the perpetrators. Not only are beings injected, but the people who molest or abuse might also have feelings they are not even aware of. They might feel rage, guilt, hatred, or shame — their shame or the shame they have toward the one they are abusing and victimizing. We will also work with those.

Abuse Often Involves Betrayal

There is a difference in the abuses of incest and rape. It doesn't make a difference according to how you work with them, but incest incorporates a sense of betrayal and a lack of trust of people the victim knows and loves. When you trust and love someone you believe is there to support who violates you, different energies occur in different chakras.

You also have a different experience with what is called date rape, where the person you have been going out with violates you. You lose trust in others, and you lose trust in yourself for not knowing who is safe. This is different from when the perpetrator is somebody from your family (blood relative or familial relationship of step-parent or step-sibling).

There is also a difference for those who were drugged and don't have a memory of what happened. Other energies, including entities, can enter the individual because the energy field becomes very fragile. Thought forms, elementals, and other beings not related to the perpetrator can invade the one who was raped and drugged.

We will also work with people who have a spirit attachment of perpetrators who have died, especially if the perpetrator was a family member. That perpetrator is often attached to the victim out of guilt or malice.

We do not use the term "victim" as in victim mentality. These people aren't truly victims in the sense that they are less than they were before the events. We use the term to differentiate between the perpetrator and the one violated. Victim consciousness needs to be continually removed from the cellular and DNA levels. Especially in cases of incest, energies go back through the DNA. Victim consciousness also arises from a religious level. Some religious traditions, the Christian tradition being one, say that the father has power over the family. The father will claim that power when violating his children, wife, or partner.

Then there is ritual abuse and satanic ritual abuse. We separate them because ritual abuse can occur that has nothing to do with what you call Satanism. Although we separate them, you work with them in similar ways. We will give you some methods that seem very complex, but we will not give you everything. We don't want you to do further damage because you do not have enough knowledge, insight, or awareness.

Remember that all sexual abuse is spiritual abuse. Your sexuality and spirituality are bound in ways that cannot be separated. This is especially the case in your sexual relationships with others where the intent is more to express the deepness of your love than to conceive children. People who cannot conceive children during their time of lovemaking but exchange the fullness of love energy, experience the oneness that is the primary purpose of lovemaking on a spiritual level. Any children conceived are a symbol of that love. If children are conceived without the love of the partners, they are always loved by the Creator. When you experience oneness with each other, you have a small taste of the memory of the oneness of all.

When you are violated in such a way, the idea of oneness can become abhorrent. You do not want oneness because you associate it with deep pain and betrayal. Healing is needed in these areas.

With satanic abuse, many entities can enter and form an energetic structure. The structure needs to be dismantled and the entities released. As difficult as this might seem, there are female children who, as soon as they begin their menses, are put into satanic ritual abuse by their families to become impregnated, and then the pregnancy is aborted.

This Work Is Reality Based

This is the introduction to the second part of the book. The things we speak about now will be even more difficult than they were in the first part. If you feel triggered, close the book and do whatever healing work you need to do. No matter what your feelings are now or what you feel as you continue reading, know that you are precious beyond measure. You are beloved.

This part of the book will not be about what you planned before you came into this lifetime. We will work in the third-dimensional realm. Nothing you did in this third-dimensional realm caused these experiences that produced such deep wounds, even if you made the choice to be drunk or go somewhere your parents did not want you to go. It has nothing to do with what you wore or even whether you were naked. It has everything to do with the other person. This is the case even if the wound occurred after you said, "No, not now," to someone you knew and whom you've had sex with before. And we will work with rape.

So, precious one, before we end this short message, call on your healing team. Say to them, "Please remove all artificial encodements that have surfaced in me during this time. Repair those damaged and altered natural encodements involved in the feelings, experiences, and thoughts I am having. Activate the precious encodements of me being a sexual being, a loving person, and a beloved person. And please activate the encodements of sexuality in how I relate to the world and how I express myself in the world and in my relationships."

Now connect with your soul-healing angels, and say, "Please find and bring back all the pieces of me that can be returned that have anything to do with my feelings or thoughts of disconnectedness." Some of you might have had an out-of-body experience — "disassociated," as they say in psychology. Then say, "Please find, bring back, clean, repair, and heal all those pieces, and then fully integrate them within me."

That is our short message for today. Our blessings and love are with you unconditionally.

CHAPTER TWENTY-SIX

Recover from Rape

Amiya and Dr. Cathy

Amiya: We will now work on healing some of the more difficult things that happen that pervert your view of sexuality, sex, and making love. We're going to deal with rape first. Some of you might have been raped. In fact, some of you have been, what you call, date raped. It might have been the more violent form of rape of someone you did not know. It could have been incest.

In this section, we are including incest that involved penetration. We will begin with rape that is not incest. However, you will use the following healing strategies in both: the information we gave you earlier and what we provide for incest.

If feelings have already come up with the words we have just used, connect with your healing team. Say, "Healing team, please activate the four foundational plug-ins on any feelings of discord, fear, anxiety, anger, or other feelings coming up." Let them do that work now.

When you are with people who describe their experience of being raped and you're not there as a healer but as a friend, you can connect with them heart to heart as they share with you. They are sharing, at least on a subconscious level, with the desire to heal and release the pain of what happened. Yes, they might have anger, fear, or suicidal thoughts. Your job is to stay in your heart source and connect with them gently, heart to heart. You do not want to forcefully penetrate them, and we use this word purposely. Gently send your energy to them. They might not allow you to enter their hearts.

Try this now: Connect with the energy of someone who was raped. If you are a victim of rape, please do not do this with yourself; choose someone else. Ask your healing team to bring someone to your mind. They will bring someone into your field who wishes to be healed but doesn't have assistance. The person's age doesn't matter.

Heal the Aura and Chakras

Gently send energy from your heart and just touch the seventh layer of the person's aura with your energy. Remember, the seventh layer is like an eggshell; just touch it. You are in your heart source. Ask the person from your heart (this is on a soul level), "May I move in a little deeper with my heart energy?" If the answer is yes, move in to the sixth layer. Ask, "May I move in more deeply to the fifth layer?" Then ask, "May I move in more deeply to the fourth layer?" Notice that you're going from the outer layers to the inner layers. "May I move in more deeply to the third layer?" If you receive a no response at the third, just rest there with this person. If the response is positive, continue to ask: "May I move in more deeply to the second layer?" "May I move into the first layer?" Remember, we're talking about layers of the aura.

Now ask, "May I connect my heart energy with your heart energy?" If you are given permission, enter the heart chakra. If you feel the slightest resistance, stop and rest. At a later time (and that could be seconds, minutes, days, or weeks), you might feel a softening of that energy that allows you to move into the person's heart. Send him or her this belief: "You are precious beyond measure." Reinforce the belief by repeating it: "You are precious beyond measure."

When you first begin to assist someone and you know you will have more than one session together, do this process each time: Connect with your clients gently and send them the belief. Then when you feel they are ready, connect with their healing team. Be sure you are connected with your healing guides. (It is best to connect with your healing guides before you send anyone energy.)

Your clients' healing teams will do what is needed for them at the appropriate rate, speed, and intensity. Simply be gentle and loving. Ask their healing team: "Healing team, please clear all congested energy from this event." If there is more than one event, say, "these events."

Then say, "Healing team, please use the Clear the Gaps in the Aura plug-in to remove the energy of this event from the gaps between the subchakras."

Next say, "Healing team, please implement the Repair the Energy Field plug-in." That is a very long plug-in with many energy structures. You might want to review the steps [see the appendix].

Be gentle and patient. Healing occurs instantly when you ask, but the consciousness has to catch up with the energy. Beliefs and fears can interfere with the healing. You will need to do this each time you work with someone.

Now say, "Healing team, please find within this precious person every low-vibration energy of any person who has in any way violated him or her physically, emotionally, mentally, or spiritually by word, action, or intent." Again, be gentle and allow it to happen.

Before we give the next command, here is a little aside: Even though many of the following instructions are covered by the Repair the Energy Field plug-in, we are going to a deeper level. Amma has spoken of the "general dusting" that occurs with the plug-ins. Now we go into the layers for a deep cleaning.

Heal the Hara Line

Let's clear the hara line. Say, "Healing team, please move to the hara line. Remove every encodement embedded in the hara line of any person who has harmed this precious one."

For this next step in repairing the hara line, you might have the ability to sense the health and well-being of energy structures. If so, begin with the hara line at the point where it connects to the earth star, 12 inches below the feet. Gently move your consciousness up the energy of that person's hara line with the intention of finding breaks, bends, pits (similar to hail denting a car), or other abnormalities. As you move your consciousness up the hara line, simply feel for resistance; you don't need to know where there is a break, bend, or pit.

When you feel resistance, ask the person's healing team: "Please use the four foundational plug-ins to heal this." Notice that you don't have to know exactly what "this" is. Continue moving up the hara line in the same way. When you come to another place, repeat the process. The pitted area in the hara line could be so small that you don't notice it right away, or there could be a tremendous break. Remember, you are focusing on the hara line related to rape. (Rape can happen to men and to women. People know about women and rape, but they might be surprised at how often it can happen to men.)

As you continue moving upward and find resistance of the energy due to an abnormality in the hara line, again say, "Healing team, please use the four foundational plug-ins to heal that area." Keep moving upward.

This one is focusing on an individual who has come to her for healing, and she is stopping at those places where she feels resistance. You might need to stop more or less often. Each time, repeat the request: "Healing team, please use the four foundational plug-ins to heal this place." Continue moving upward until you are about 18 inches above the crown.

Once you are focused on this process, you do not need to repeat the full request (unless it is your desire). You can say, "And in this place," when you find additional areas of resistance, because you are in that intention, that space of working with these plug-ins.

If you have not read the *Hidden Structures* book, you might not be aware of the hara line's structure. It consists of three layers. It carries energy as though it's an empty tube, a pipe. It actually carries the energy of your incarnation. Your entire encodement system unfolded from the energy in the hara line. When the hara line is damaged in any way, it blocks the full energy of your incarnation.

Both the inner and outer layers are very smooth. The middle layer between the two smooth layers is a structured area. Let's call it a matrix. (We are giving you a little more information than what is contained in *Hidden Structures*.)

Say, "Healing team, remove all artificial encodements contained in the matrix, the inner core of the hara line." We are strengthening the hara line by removing the artificial encodements that might have entered through holes or breaks. You don't need to know where they are or where they came from. Although we are focusing on rape, this command will remove all artificial encodements no matter their cause.

When people have artificial encodements in the inner core of their hara lines, they might experience a change in their energy systems as the encodements are removed. Notice we did not use the Basic plug-in, because the Basic plug-in is related to a specific wound. We are asking for all artificial encodements to be removed from the inner core of the hara line.

Now say, "Please repair all damaged and altered natural encodements within that inner core, or that matrix, within the hara line." Then say, "Now activate in that same part of the hara line any inactive natural encodements that need to be activated." Then say, "Healing team, if natural encodements need to be created to make this hara line whole, please do so now."

Here is something fun and a little bit different: Ask to connect the hara line with the divine blueprint. See the connection, feel the connection, and intend the connection. See or form a beam of energy from the divine blueprint to the hara line. You could also take the energy of the divine blueprint and place it over the hara line. This is different from what we have done in the past. There is usually more than one way to approach a situation that needs to be healed.

Use the Spiritual Whirlwind

We are going deeper still. As you might know, the crystalline DNA is unfolding within everyone. For many people, it has already unfolded, but for others, it is in progress or might not have begun.

Say, "Healing team, align the hara line to the divine blueprint as it relates to the crystalline DNA." Remember that the hara line contains the energy of your incarnation. Ask for this person's hara line to be upgraded in accordance with the unfolding of their DNA and even a bit beyond where they are now so that they can stretch into this new reality, this new experience.

For further clearing, use the spiritual whirlwind meditation created by Joshua David Stone while he was on the Earth plane. Now construct the spiritual whirlwind. It looks like a tornado. The point enters the energy field about 18 inches above the crown. Ask the person's healing team and yours: "Please construct the spiritual whirlwind at the exact vibration needed for this precious person to clear any of the energetic debris that was released in the aura as we did our work."

Simply allow the whirlwind to form. If you can see color (and there is sound for those of you who can hear sound), let it come down through your aura. (When you work with others, your healing team will also bring in the spiritual whirlwind for you.) Now ask for another one. The color will change each time as the vibration changes. We suggest that you request three to five whirlwinds, but it can vary depending on the person. Keep asking for them until you feel complete.

Remember, you sent them the belief: "You are precious beyond belief." Now install the second belief using the Belief plug-in: "You are whole."

That is enough for today. We are going to move into much deeper and more focused work to release other energies, including spirits or entities — whatever you wish to call them — from these people. After that, we will move to their emotional experiences, which will vary according to gender similarities and variances. Blessings to you, most learned scholars.

Energy Waits in the Wings

Margaret: The person I was working with wouldn't let me past the seventh layer. That was it. I went through the process Amiya gave. Maybe it's all there for the person.

Dr. Cathy: Even though people only let you in from your heart connection to their heart connection up to the seventh layer, you are still speaking to their healing team. The healing team is doing the work. Not letting love in from you doesn't mean they won't let love in from the healing team. I'm hearing from Amiya now that the amount or strength of their ability to allow you in usually corresponds to how much they allow the healing team to do. Keep repeating the process, and they might let you in more as healing proceeds.

Margaret: It's as if the energy is waiting in the wings for when the person will allow the energy in.

Yes, it is waiting in the wings; I like that. Even if you don't work with them again, your love energy is waiting for them when they are ready. The message I'm receiving is to not ever think that what you have done is wasted.

Margaret: When I used to send general healing to somebody, I'd just say, "If that person doesn't need it, then it goes to the next person who needs it." Whoever's in the most need, gets it.

That will work. You can also just allow it to stay there for when the person is ready, which could be when he or she is asleep and not consciously trying to repel it.

CHAPTER TWENTY-SEVEN

Create a Healing Continuum

Amiya and Dr. Cathy

Amiya: Your healing team is with you making adjustments when something we say applies to you. You might not be aware that some of the things we talk about actually apply to you. Think of a continuum — a continuum of happiness, for instance. You might feel mild contentment and then rapture. A continuum occurs in healing.

We are delighted that your healing team is working with you. As you read, healing occurs. You don't have to consciously ask for healing; however, it is helpful to bring your conscious mind into agreement by requesting it. You do not have to consciously ask for it because you gave us permission by purchasing this book. You are here to assist in the messages that come to heal you as well as help heal others. That choice you made reverberates through the universe.

We are going to present this information in the shortest segments possible. Please listen to your inner knowing, and read only as much as you need at one time. Even though it might not seem like it, much is happening in your energy field.

Last time, we asked you to invite, on a soul level, somebody you know or someone's spirit sent to you who needed healing in this area. Remember, we are working with rape, which is an extreme violation. Remember how you connected with them last time. Begin with a gentle hello, and then very gently send energy from your heart to the outer boundaries of their auras. At each level, ask if you can come closer. Ask for permission to connect directly from your heart chakra to theirs. If they say yes, move closer. If not, gently move in with your energy until they tell you that's enough.

This one is remembering an exercise she used in seminars. She asked participants to stand up, and she said, "Put your hand up like a stop sign when you prefer that I not come any closer." She then stepped forward. Several people allowed her to get closer than she was comfortable with. Others kept her back a foot, two feet, three feet. This also happens on the energetic level.

Begin with a Connection

Let's begin by clearing the energy field. Ask the healing team, "Please use the Clear the Gaps of the Aura plug-in to clear congestion in the gaps in the aura having to do with rape, sexual abuse, and sexual trauma." This is for you as well even if you did not have those challenges. You have congestion in the gaps of your aura just from living your day-to-day life. Then say, "Please use the Clear the Gaps of the Aura plug-in for the gaps within the subchakras of each chakra.

Here's something I don't believe we've mentioned in other books: Ask your healing guides (they work with you as you work with someone else) to align your vibration, your energy, to what is most conducive for that person's healing. Some of you have very strong personalities, such as this one, and that energy can overwhelm some people. If you have a very gentle personality, it might work well for someone who is reticent or shy, but it might need to be raised for someone who likes people with more forceful energy. There's no judgment in any of this. You're simply asking the healing guides to do that.

Good. You are now connected to the one you are working with today.

Rape is when penetration occurs against someone's wishes. (As you know, incest is rape, and everything we do here applies to incest, and we will do more for incest.) There are two general types of rape: One is from a stranger, and the other is from someone you know.

Rape by someone you know includes the euphemism "date rape." The complication with date rape is that the people who were raped, violated, often question whether it was truly rape or whether it was their fault. They might have been on a date and even had intercourse with the perpetrator at some time, but this time they said, "No. No more. Not now." Is that rape? Yes. When people force themselves on others, that is rape.

Remember, rape can occur with any gender. If someone forces sexual attention or activity on you, and you say no and try to get away, that is rape. This is true even if the perpetrator is your best friend (which means that person wasn't really your best friend). All the healings we did in the previous part of the book are applicable in this case. Clear the energy field.

Heal the Energy of Betrayal

Now we are going to work with the sense of betrayal, which also applies to incest. We are speaking of the betrayal rape victims feel when they are violated by people they know. Are you ready, healing teams?

Say, "Please locate that energy of betrayal." This energy can be in you as well as in the person you're working with. "Remove all artificial encodements anchoring that sense of betrayal." Notice we're not yet working with the encodements of the betrayal itself. Continue making requests of the healing team:

- "Repair all damaged and altered natural encodements that anchor the energy of betrayal."
- "Activate all natural encodements that were deactivated by the betrayal."
- "Remove all implants anchoring the energy of betrayal."
- "Activate all inactive encodements needed to remove the energy of betrayal."
- "Soul-healing angels, please find and bring back to this person all parts that are missing and for whom this loss is holding in the energy of betrayal." This means that because someone is missing

a part of the fullness of themselves, the energy of betrayal more easily stays anchored.

- "Soul-healing angels, please clean, repair, heal, and integrate all pieces within this precious individual."

We have removed the energy holding in the energy of betrayal, and now we will remove the betrayal energy itself.

- "Healing team, remove all artificial encodements of the energy of betrayal."
- "Using the Remove Victim Consciousness plug-in, remove all victim consciousness that was produced by this betrayal."
- "Using the Implant Removal plug-in, search for and remove all implants from this betrayal."
- Call on Archangel Michael and, of course, yourself. State, "I am the Sword," and be there in the fullness of your energy. With this next step, form an image of that betrayal still anchored in the person with little strands of energy. Using the Sword of Archangel Michael (or you might ask him to do it), sever the connection of betrayal energy from that person.
- "Healing team, remove all encodements of this energy of betrayal."

A little tip on using the Sword: It is always a good idea to place it directly in the energy of betrayal with the intention of raising the vibration of that energy to the highest level of love possible. This transmutes the betrayal energy. You can use your sword to disassemble the energy, or you can elevate the energy to the highest level of love possible.

Enact Deeper Healing

What you have done so far is what Amma calls "dusting." We will go deeper, but first we want to explain a few things. What is the difference between repairing damaged and altered natural encodements and activating inactive natural encodements? When they're obviously damaged, shouldn't they be repaired in that same request to repair the damaged and altered natural encodements?

Damaged and altered natural encodements have been impaired or thrown off balance. They are still active, but their energy might be skewed due to the damage. This is similar to damage in a chakra. The energy is there, but it might not be working as it should. This is different from total deactivation.

The deactivation of natural encodements occurs when you disassociate or leave your body in any way when the event happens. Inactive natural encodements can also be encodements that were supposed to activate at a specific time and didn't, for some reason. This is similar to a developmental delay. When you deny the part of yourself that is hurt because you do not want to feel that pain, the associated encodements shut off; they deactivate.

As uncomfortable as this is, it is important to confront that pain. When you send a part of yourself away — perhaps you call it the soul, energy, or the psyche — the encodements associated with that part deactivate. They totally shut down, which is different from being damaged. You do that yourself when you send that part away. That is why you want them to reactivate.

Now let's talk about the two different ways of handling the energy of betrayal or any low-vibration energy. You can use the Sword of Michael the archangel to, in a sense, blow up the energy and completely clear it out of the person. Or you can use the Sword to elevate that energy to a higher vibration. You will find that people who have more anger within them about what happened need to see that energy shattered. Then there are those who recognize and understand the concept of being able to raise the energy up to a higher vibration.

What you choose to do depends on the person. If you feel it is in the best interest of the one you are working with to release the energy with greater activity, go ahead and shatter the energy. Don't worry. Because it is touched by the Sword of Archangel Michael, every piece of that energy you shatter rises in vibration. What you do is for the person you are working with. Have absolutely no judgment about their feelings regarding what they need to assist their healing.

Some just want to raise it to the highest vibration. In more violent situations, such as rape and sexual abuse, the person likely feels a greater need to shatter that energy, especially early in the healing process. Those doing self-healing can also raise the vibration. You might find times when you want to shatter the energy, knowing that the vibration of every shattered particle rises to the highest level. Or as you stay in your heart source, you can simply put the Sword within the energy with the intention of raising the vibration of the entire ball of energy. If you have any questions about what we just said, please let us know.

Remove the Shadow Energy of Betrayal

You did a general dusting when you asked for the energy of betrayal to leave; you released the betrayal on the surface. When you use the Shadow Removal plug-in, you remove energy embedded in parts of the body and the energy field. When you work with shadow energy, you work with the leftovers, which are deeply embedded energies.

Now that you have done the general cleansing, we're going to remove the shadow energy for betrayal. Say, "Healing team, please apply the Shadow Removal plug-in to remove the energy of betrayal from the third chakra and every subchakra, front and back." In this case, we start with the third chakra to get rid of the betrayal from the person's sense of self, since that chakra is about inner power. (As in this case, there might be times when you're guided to start with a different chakra.)

Go to the second chakra. Say, "Please use the Shadow Removal plug-in to remove every encodement of betrayal in the second chakra, front and back, and all the subchakras." The second chakra is your sense of power in the outer world, and it is also the sexual chakra.

"Healing team, please do the same for the first chakra, front and back. Now do the fifth chakra (the expression of truth), front and back. Now do the fourth chakra (the heart chakra), front and back. Then do the sixth chakra (the third eye), front and back. And finally do the crown chakra."

Next, we move to something we haven't done much with you, if at all. "Healing team, please construct the energy of the belief, 'I am loved and perfect as I am.'" They are constructing the energies. Now say, "Please place the energy of that belief within every chakra, front and back, as needed." Then say, "Encodement team, please harmonize the encodements within the entire energy field."

When you are raped, you often believe you're imperfect, which battles the sense of victim consciousness. Now, speaking of victim consciousness, say, "Healing team, use the Remove Victim Consciousness plug-in to remove victim consciousness from the cellular level." Then say, "Remove victim consciousness from every chakra, subchakra, meridian, and layer of the aura." We are working with victim consciousness from rape, not all victim consciousness. Every time you use that plug-in, you remove more at a deeper level. We are working specifically with rape and don't want to overwhelm the energy field.

Now, "Healing team, please bring the spiritual whirlwind into this individual to clear any debris in the energy field." You can guide the person through this if you are together, or just see the tip of the whirlwind come into the pranic tube about 18 inches above the person's head. As it comes down, it covers the entire aura. Allow it to go down into the earth. Then bring in another, another, and another.

This is all we will do for this chapter. Remember, we're doing these bite-sized pieces, these little chunks. Next time, we'll remove the energy of the perpetrator from the person you're working with. When the person knows the perpetrator — a friendship or a trusting relationship — the healing is more complex. The same thing happens with incest but not quite on the same level.

Many blessings to you.

Rape Has Different Energetic Consequences

Louise: When teens are sexually exploring, they might suddenly find themselves in the middle of something and unsure what is happening. There is not quite consent, but the energy isn't quite rape. Do both experiences cause damage?

Dr. Cathy: I'm hearing from Amiya that this is rape, under their definition of rape, but the energy is different. It's not as strong because the intent is not the same. Betrayal might not be involved, but shame might be. You can remove both energies using the tools they've given us. That's a very good question.

Celia: When you experience rape, do you get lung illnesses or breathing issues?

Lung issues are usually about grief. If the perpetrator is on top of you and you are terrified, the stress response activates. From both the stress response and the pressure of someone on you, you might have difficulty breathing. The fight-or-flight response might cause you to hold your breath. This energy can embed in you. You can work to release that energy from the person's lungs, and say, "It's okay to breathe now. The event is not happening anymore." Talk to the consciousness of the lungs to help release that embedded energy.

Margaret: I've taught a lot of people who were sexually abused or raped at a young age who later got into sadomasochism. To me, it's like they're attempting to self-heal. They're trying to keep the wound alive until they can get it healed, or they spend a lifetime working through all the ramifications of it. Are they actually healing?

What I'm seeing is that they're actually feeding the wound, which they'll discover through healing. They will need much deep healing and willingness to heal on that level. As they heal, they'll discover they don't have the same need to do that sadomasochistic behavior. They do it to manage the pain. It's on a different level, but it's similar to people who cut themselves to avoid emotional pain. They're trying to avoid sexual pain.

CHAPTER TWENTY-EIGHT

Remove Perpetrator Energy

Amiya and Dr. Cathy

Amiya: Wonderful day to you, learned scholars. I have invited to your sacred healing room today all the many millions of people who have overcome sexual abuse. They are not on the Earth plane but on the inner plane. The purpose of inviting them is to give everyone hope that you can recover from sexual abuse. You can recover from the violation of your dignity, will, and connection to spirit. You can recover from the belief that you are not good enough for others or for the love of spirit. You can recover from the belief that anything you did in the third dimension invited this energy to you.

At the end of the last chapter, we said we would remove the energy of perpetrators still held within. That energy is very simple to remove, but the difficult part is having the willingness to let it go. You must let go of the identity you might have formed that you are a victim as a result of sexual abuse. We are talking about rape in this section, but this applies to all types of abuse. You can use what we tell you here for sexual abuse, incest, rape, torture, and so on. You have to be willing to let go of an identity that is not who you are. (Remember that males and females have been raped. You hear so much about female rape, but there is also male rape.)

In each rape, the perpetrator leaves energy behind. You leave energy within someone when you make love to them, but there is no perpetrator. The one you love leaves the energy of his or her love in you, the encodements of her or his love to you that bind with your encodements of love to him or her. In the case of sexual abuse such as rape and incest, the perpetrator's anger, hatred, and shame can bind with that same energy in you. An infant who is raped does not carry much energy of self-hatred, but it binds with the development of the little one's self-esteem.

Insert New Beliefs

We worked with some beliefs earlier, and we will work here with more beliefs using the Belief plug-in. Before we use that plug-in — which removes the energy of the old beliefs that the new beliefs will replace — first ask, "Please remove the matrix of energy that says, 'I am impure and undeserving of being pure.'" This is where Archangel Michael and his band do their work with you as the Sword. If you, the person reading this, have been abused in this way, call forth that energy. Even if you have not been abused in this way, go ahead and call forth that energy that could be within you for some other reason.

Say to that energy, "You are not of me. I am created from the love and light of the Creator. The Creator is only love, and I am only love. I am pure, holy, and deserving of all love and everything that comes from love."

With the Sword of Archangel Michael, sever that attachment, or as we've taught before, place the Sword's tip in the matrix of energy, and let it shatter the matrix in such a way that all is transmuted into sparkles of love. When that is complete, use the Belief plug-in. Say, "I am pure, holy, and entirely the manifestation of God's love." Repeat: "I am pure, whole, and entirely the manifestation of God's love."

When you work with others, find out what name they use for the Creator/Source/All That Is/God. It does not matter what it is; it is what they connect to, so use that name. If they have no sense of this connection, come up with some ideas, and ask them, "May I use this word? May I use 'Creator' or 'Source' or 'Great Spirit' or 'All That Is'?" Ask about their spiritual tradition. Of course, if you are working with people at a distance, you can use whatever name you wish.

Call to their soul energy to activate the encodements of the name they find most comfortable. In some cases, that name will go back to another lifetime. When they have no sense of self in this lifetime, call for their soul selves. If they prefer to say higher self, call for that energy. Use the names and terms comfortable for them. Whoever or whatever they are, it is all love.

Now insert another belief: "I believe I am deserving of being whole and loved with the purity of love." Once those beliefs are within them, they will no longer need to hang on to identifications such as "sexual abuse victim." Those are labels imposed by others. They no longer need to hold on to these labels that are not who they are.

Sever Attachments

Ask the healing team to surround the people you work with, and ask your healing team to surround you. Command, "I call forth the energy of any perpetrator who has left the energy of anger, hatred, power over, shame, or rage. I call forth that energy from myself. I call forth that energy from this person now." Then say, "With this sword, I sever the attachment to that energy and transmute it into the highest level of love possible at this time."

Look for the golden structure within their physical hearts. It might seem clouded. The golden center itself is not clouded, but clouds can form in front of the golden center. Just as the sun shines brightly even when there are clouds, the golden center is always there in its perfection. Call to the person's healing team: "Healing team, remove all artificial and natural encodements from this person that have caused a cloud to form in front of the golden heart structure." If you wish, you may gently use your sword to brush that cloud away. As the sword touches that energy, it transmutes.

Now speak to the one you are working with. (If it is you, speak to you). Aim your energy at the third chakra, the sense of self-esteem and knowing who you are in your internal world. Say, "You are precious. Nothing that happens to you and nothing you do can change that. I call forth from deep within you the memory of springing from the love of the Creator, from love itself." You may use any words similar to this, if you wish. This is just a model.

Next, focus on the second chakra. Say to this person, "I call forth now, in the name of the love from which you were created, all energy that has perverted for you the act of sharing your body with love." Gently place within your client the energy or the belief: "You can, by your choice, share your love physically with another with only the memory of sharing love."

Call forth the consciousness of the cells. If you have the ability, notice what that energy is like. Is it clear or cloudy? Does it contain pain? Say, "Consciousness of the cells, I call forth from you any low-vibration energy that is clouding your joy and your ability to reproduce in absolute love and joy. Cells, I call forth any memory within you that has nothing to do with joy, happiness, contentment, and love."

When that energy comes out, you can do one of several things: You can tell it to be gone. You can call on Archangel Michael and his band to transmute it. (That's actually what happens when you tell it to be gone. It depends on who you are working with and what they need.) You can take your sword and place it within that energy, or you can sever the energy and release it. No matter what method you choose, this energy transforms into love. Once you sever the energy and its message and say, "No, this cannot be," you change the message and release it to love.

Heal the DNA, Aura, and Chakras

Continue healing, starting with the DNA.

- "I call forth the consciousness of this person's genetic code. DNA, any changes made in you through this act of violence, I command you to return to the fullness of how you were to be."
- "Healing team, I call on you to use the Repair the Genetic Code plug-in to return the DNA to its fullness, to how it was created in love."
- "Healing team, please follow that genetic code. If energies have come from past generations of rape, sexual abuse, torture, or anything passed down from generation to generation, call that forth. Release it and use the Repair the Genetic Code plug-in."
- "Healing team, find the genetic code and all hidden areas in the

genetic code (what your scientists call junk DNA) that contain love and can unfold and blossom." It is like a bud gently opening into a flower. "Begin that opening so that love infuses this person's cells in every way. May the knowledge and memory of the love from which they were created unfold."

- "Crystalline DNA, I call on you to pour out your awareness, your knowledge of love into this blessed person" (or into you, if you wish).
- "Healing team, remove all congestion between the layers and gaps in the aura."
- "Healing team, remove all congestion in the gaps of the subchakras of each chakra."
- "Healing team, go to each energetic structure in this person to this person's soul star, soul seat, dantien and hara line, earth star, and the personal individuation point, and clear the energy of trauma and abuse from around these areas. Clear any perversion of who this person truly is."

There. That is the process we give you today. Be at peace and be filled with love.

Dr. Cathy: Questions?

Margaret: Will there be something specifically for healing perpetrators, or will that be too much for people reading this book?

It might be too much for people reading this book if the perpetrators are still alive. We'll see what Amiya says. But when we work with releasing attached spirits, healing is definitely involved in that.

CHAPTER TWENTY-NINE

Release the Pain of Rape

Amiya and Dr. Cathy

Amiya: Working with people who have gone through the horrors of the third-dimensional world is a treasured opportunity and a gift for you as well as them. The only choice they made at the fifth-dimensional level was for spiritual expansion, but when working with people on the third-dimensional level, you don't talk about fifth-dimensional choices when they are crying in your office or home.

We will tell you who is also crying. When people rape, they hold other energies. Phrasing it metaphorically, those energies also cry about what happened. They cry for their lack of self-control and their inability to stop what they did. Most people who choose to rape (we're speaking on the third-dimensional level) actually try not to rape. They try not to have that drive to hurt another.

Yes, some rape from choice, and they do it serially. They do it with anger and hatred and from a sense of power. It has nothing to do with sex, which is supposed to be sacred and represent the oneness of God. It is a way to break the sacredness of a gender (whether the rape is of a male or a female) and take out the perpetrator's anger on someone else. That energy becomes lodged in the one who was raped.

Most of you know that when you become angry, that energy goes out to the one you are angry with and can implant in that person. Everyone has done this; you have sent energy out to someone in anger. Those of you who know about energy attempt to call that energy back. As you have learned to elevate yourself, you have learned to manage those emotions that escape you.

In the situation of rape, those who rape cannot manage those emotions. They cannot manage or bring what they have done back to themselves. They hurt someone with the deepest violation. You have probably heard people say that some things are worse than death. As you know, once death of the body occurs, you move into another realm. Pain and suffering are over, if you allow them to be, and you move into the light. However, some do not move on and are trapped with their feelings. Some of these attach to others, which you will learn about later.

Specialists Work at Your Vibration

Rape is trauma. People hold on to trauma to protect themselves. They are afraid of letting that violent energy loose, whether it came from another person or from watching something happen. The energy of violence can enter people when they are traumatized. People can hold on to that violence to protect themselves from other violence.

The problem is that the energy you hold to protect your heart hides your heart. It hides that golden structure within your heart and the glory and joy that come from it. This makes life difficult. You might believe that you need to hold on to the violence and anger of another because you do not know it is not your anger. If this is the case, we ask you now: Are you willing to take the risk and let go of the anger that comes from another? Are you willing to let go of that self-loathing and despair that come from another?

If you are not willing to do this now, are you willing to become willing, or are you willing to become willing to become willing? Your healing team supports any step you take in the direction of release. Amma, the Divine Mother, and Abba, the Divine Father (or whatever words you use to describe that energy) are here to assist you.

If our, Amiya's, vibration is too high for your pain or it hurts you on an emotional level, we call in others whose vibrations match yours. This is not a judgment that you are lacking; it is a judgment on our part that this is what you need. Think of it this way: When you take a bath or a shower, you might prefer the water to be much hotter than the temperature others prefer. You select the water temperature on a subconscious level, but it matches what your body needs. We, Amiya (actually your healing team, Amma, and Abba), call specialists who work at your level of vibration.

There are specialists who release anger, despair, or shame. You didn't know that, did you? Specialists work with people caught in first-chakra issues, heart-chakra issues, crown-chakra issues. All are of the vibration that matches your needs. When your healing team calls us or others to work with you, they are calling in specialists of the vibration just for you. That is how important you are to us. That is how special you are and how much we desire to work with you to free you from pain.

Release What Holds on to Pain

When you say, "Heart source," declare your heart source, or go through the seven steps, you place a protective energy around you. When you set your intention for your heart source to expand around the people you are working with because they are unable to form their own protection, you accept a sacred responsibility to protect them from outside influences. When you say "heart source" and expand your heart source around the people you are working with, you fulfill that protective responsibility. You do not bring them into your sacred space; you simply protect them with the energy that springs from the depths of you and your knowledge and understanding.

It is helpful to then call on the Sword of Michael the Archangel. Those of you who have already received the Sword, say "I am the Sword." If you have not received the Sword, call on Archangel Michael, the purveyor of truth who uses that Sword, to transmute energy to the highest level possible for where you are at this time. That archangel is with you. Or you can request, "May I have your Sword to work with you?"

Hold out your hand to wield the Sword. Archangel Michael will place it in your hand, and you will place it in your heart center. Say, "I am the Sword," any time you need it. That Sword can be your finger, or you can call forth the Sword that you wield as a protective energy. In no way is that Sword meant to kill or destroy anyone or anything. It is a tool that severs attachments and transmutes energy to its highest level. When you work to heal another, you work with a form of spiritual lovefare — the journey of love to transmute negativity. That is who you are as you come to work with others.

We have placed within the energy of this book the activation that your healing team is with you and you are surrounded by love. The heart source of those who have made this book possible surround you if you do not know how to create the heart source. You affirm that with your understanding, desire, and agreement.

Call now, "Healing team, be with me. Surround me with my heart source and the heart sources of those who have participated in making this book. Surround me with those who stand with Michael's Sword to protect me and raise my vibration of energy that now manifests as pain and not love, and transmute it to the highest level possible for me. That transmutation will continue."

Connect again to your healing team, and say, "I am willing, on whatever level of willingness I need for myself, to release the pain of that event (or those events) that I still hold within my cellular memory. Healing team, find every artificial encodement within me, whether from this lifetime or another or whether from within me or from the one who violated me. Find that artificial encodement and release it from me now. Find that artificial encodement that holds on to the pain and release it now. Repair all damaged and altered natural encodements whose lack of wholeness contributes to me holding on to all pain, by whatever name I use for that pain.

"Healing team, activate any encodements that became inactive." Those encodements usually become inactive due to fear. "Activate every encodement I need so that I might release this pain in whatever form it takes, whatever name I use for it. Activate or create within me the encodements to remind me of the love from which I am created and that I am love, because I don't feel love for myself right now because of what happened to me. I want the lie that I am not beloved to leave me now. Please activate those encodements."

Let that energy relax in you. Let it occur.

Release the Pain and Perpetrator Energy

Now that you have released what was holding on to this pain, call forth the pain. Use whatever word you need to envelop the pain from the event, the betrayal: pain, anger, rage, hatred, self-abhorrence, shame. Say, "I call forth all the pain from this event that is within my body, cells, and aura." If you are Christian, you might want to say, "I call you forth in the name of Jesus." If you are not Christian, you could call it forth in the name of whatever being you wish. This one would say, "I call you forth in the name of the love of All That Is, the Creator, the Source."

As you listen to yourself say this, feel the energy of that command even if you were not raped. Say to it, "I have learned much from you even though I might not recognize it now. Your job is finished. You have protected me, and now I choose to be who I truly am."

Take out your Sword or call on Michael the Archangel, and say, "I now sever every strand of attachment that you have to me. As I do so, if more artificial encodements need to be released, damaged and altered natural encodements need to be repaired, activations need to occur, or something needs to be created and activated within me, please do so now. I call on the power of love to do so."

Take your Sword and sever that attachment or attachments. If you wish, you can place the Sword in the middle of the energy of pain, and say, "I transmute you now to the highest level of love possible."

As you transmute the pain that was lodged in you, you transmute yourself and accept all you have learned: the wisdom and compassion you have gained and the knowledge that you can overcome such pain.

The pain you released held in other things. It held in the energy of the one who raped, abused, and violated you. Command this energy to come out of you: "I command that all energy within me that is not from me to come forth now." Let it come.

When you feel that rustling of energy has moved out of your body, say, "You are not mine. I will not carry you anymore. You must leave now." You have several options how to have it leave: You can blow it out of your body with your breath, you can place Michael's Sword within the energy with the intention of raising its vibration, or you can send it back to the one it belongs to with the intention that the person learns from the energy and that you will not carry that person's pain.

Repair, Cleanse, and Integrate

The next step is to heal the energy involved. Say, "Healing team, please use the Heal the DNA plug-in and repair my DNA from any changes that resulted from not-love that caused me to hold on to pain and that could pass down generationally. I call on you to change that now." (When you're commanding, you don't necessarily need to use the word "please." They know you are in appreciation as you ask them.)

- "Healing team, use the Healing over Lifetimes plug-in to release any and all energy that I had of a similar nature from souls involved in this lifetime."
- "Soul-healing angels, I am ready to bring back those parts of me that I tossed away because it hurt so much. Clean, repair, and heal them of all anger, fear, and emotions of not-love. Integrate them into me so that I am whole and good as new."
- "Healing team, remove the shadows surrounding the golden center in my physical heart so that the essence of my being can show forth."
- "I call forth the wonderful clearing energy of the violet flame, which is in my third eye, to go down through my body and clear and cleanse."

You might need to repeat this process a few times. Healing takes place in layers. For some of you, it will occur all at once. Use this process as often as you need. You can use it for any type of pain or wound you hold on to.

Louise: I did not feel the energy physically, but I felt as if I experienced it through the eyes of those reading the book with the need to heal. I could feel, in a way, what they were letting go of and how they allowed healing to occur, knowing they were beginning to release and feel a different way. It was very interesting. It was like going in through their eyes but not being a part of them. It was good.

Dr. Cathy: Wow. Thank you, Louise. Anybody else?

Mimi: That was very, very powerful.

Thank you, Mimi.

CHAPTER THIRTY

Remove Perpetrator Beliefs

Amiya

In this chapter, we will do something in which the processes are similar but the intentions are different. We haven't shared this information before. This can be used with anyone who has been sexually abused or has had any kind of trauma perpetrated on them by another person. We're doing this with rape, incest, and other sexual abuse. We will remove the energy of the perpetrator's beliefs placed within the one who was abused.

We have talked about removing the energy of a person and about removing the abuser's feelings of hatred, anger, and shame placed in the energy of the one abused. We have not talked about removing and changing the beliefs of the perpetrator placed within the one that was abused.

Rape, especially stranger rape, is an act of hatred toward the woman or the man. It is not personal. That might seem strange, but it is not specific to the abused person; it is specific to the gender. For example, a man could be responding to issues with his mother, sister, or some other female that caused him problems. When he rapes, it is an act of hatred toward that gender and not toward that person.

What you call date rape is more personal because the person knows the perpetrator. In addition to hatred of gender, this kind of rape focuses on the belief that the perpetrator is better than the one who is raped. The perpetrator has the need to exert control over someone.

With pedophilia, there is lust (not love) and sometimes hatred. The driving force is power over the person abused.

When perpetrators penetrate people, they inject their energy of hatred through their action of abuse. At the same time, they inject the energy of their belief that women, men, teenagers, or whomever are not worth anything. You have probably noticed how many more derogatory terms there are for women than for men. Many of the derogatory terms for men are based on women — their mothers, for example. This is a symbol of patriarchy in which the other gender is denigrated to display derision and power.

Become Familiar with Common Installed Beliefs

We'll first do the removal in the more detailed way; then we'll do it the very easy way. It's important for those of you learning to know how to work with the details. Sometimes the "general cleansing," as Amma calls it, occurs with the general use of what we do. When we go into detail, it can get into the deep crevices where the "dust" is hidden and compacted.

The underlying reason for the assault can be fear, hatred, or self-loathing. Let's take hatred. You can fill in the blank as to the hatred of what. It could be self-hatred projected on to another. With hatred, a belief is projected on to and injected into the person who is abused. Examples of beliefs include:

- "All women are worth nothing."
- "All women deserve to die."
- "All women deserve to be subjugated."
- "Men are no good."
- "Men deserve to die."
- "Men deserve to be punished."
- "Men deserve to be subjugated."

These are a few of the beliefs that might be placed into another by the assault. You can identify a belief when working with others through your intuition or through muscle testing. You can even ask them: "Do you have a belief that needs to be removed?" Refer to a resource of beliefs you might have, and muscle test to learn which is appropriate.

We will start with the specific. Remember the Belief plug-in? With this plug-in, your encodement technicians first remove the energy of the old belief or any belief contrary to the new belief. When you know the old or non-supportive belief is about hatred, such as women are no good, women are shameful, or women deserve to be punished, then place within the person a belief similar to women are precious and valued, men are precious and valued, children are precious and valued, or whatever belief needs to replace the old.

There are two parts to this. The first part removes the energy of the person who brought in that belief. Request, "Healing team, remove all encodements — be they artificial, natural, damaged, or altered — that belong to the perpetrator and are holding in the perpetrator's belief (you can add the belief here, if you wish) about this person. Remove and balance those now."

Some people move through the aftermath of rape more easily than others. When rape occurs to people with good self-image and self-esteem, the trauma of the rape (as difficult and as horrific as it was on the third-dimensional level) is not as severe as it is for people who already believe themselves to be less than, no good, or shameful.

People who have good self-esteem before the rape might need fewer sessions and less work than those who had poor self-esteem before the rape. People who experienced trauma before the trauma of the rape will generally need more assistance than those who had no trauma before the rape. The greater the traumatic effect, the more you will need to do. Have no judgment about how long the process takes.

Some people might need only one session to remove the perpetrator's energy if they had good self-esteem before the trauma. With those whose trauma added to the poor self-esteem, you might need to carefully go through each chakra to remove the energy of the perpetrator. Here is an example:

- "Healing team, remove all encodements of the perpetrator holding this belief" (you might have the belief in mind) "in the first chakra."
- "Remove all encodements of the perpetrator holding the belief in the second chakra."
- Go through the rest of the chakras.

You might need to request: "Remove all encodements of the perpetrator causing problems with the soul star and the core star interfering with the movement of energy down the prana tube." This happens especially in a person who already had a poor self-image and poor self-esteem. That isn't to say you wouldn't do this with someone who had good self-esteem before the trauma. You can always make the request, as the healing team will only do what is necessary.

Be aware of the differences in people who had self-esteem issues before the trauma and those who did not have those issues pre-trauma. The more people have already been affected by trauma in their lives and believe they are less than, the greater the effect rape will have on their systems; it will travel throughout their energy systems in a deeper way.

To repeat the process:

- Go through and remove all encodements of the person who is holding in that energy of the non-supportive belief.
- Use the Belief plug-in. Go through the plug-in step by step or simply ask the healing team to implement it.

Use the Belief Plug-In to Install Positive Beliefs

Set your intention on the issue you would like to heal. Move into your heart source, and connect with your healing team. They will:

1. remove all artificial encodements preventing the full activation of the new belief
2. repair damaged and altered natural encodements preventing the full activation of the new belief
3. activate any inactive encodements for the new belief
4. ask for the creation and activation of all encodements for the new belief if they are not present
5. remove all artificial encodements holding in any conflicting belief

6. repair all damaged and altered natural encodements holding in any conflicting belief
7. deactivate or remove all natural encodements of the old belief
8. use the soul-healing process to bring back pieces of the person whose absence is either holding in the limiting belief or preventing the full integration of the new belief
    a. find and bring back all pieces of the energy lost during the wounding event
    b. clean, repair, and heal all pieces
    c. integrate all pieces within the person
9. harmonize the encodement system

Begin by stating the belief you wish to integrate within the person. Here are some examples of positive beliefs:

- "This person is precious and loved."
- "Women are wonderful."
- "Men are wonderful."
- "Women are sacred."
- "Men are sacred."

Use whatever beliefs the people you are working with need. If you don't know, you can ask them what they need. Then use the Belief plug-in.

You can repeat this process as often as necessary using as many beliefs as are needed. Usually more than one non-supportive belief is installed in people when a rape or sexual abuse occurs. Remember, the beliefs and energy of the perpetrator can settle into their energy fields.

If you are able to work with people immediately after the rape, that energy will not take root or spread through their energy field. If you are working with people you don't know — on a crisis hotline, for example — you can provide immediate assistance. Remember, you can do all this within yourself without others knowing. They have come to you for assistance and have given you permission to work with them. You can do this energy work while speaking with them. Their encodement technicians work in any healing situation, whether the people involved understand encodements or not.

If people come to you or call the crisis hotline after they have been raped and they are ministered to with love, affection, support, and total acceptance, it prevents that energy injected in them from spreading. In other words, the thought form injected into them is stopped from taking root. In some cases, it is an elemental that has more energy, definition, and personality than a thought form.

When the thought form is present, any time the person has a similar thought or feeling, the thought form of the perpetrator becomes stronger. That thought form then moves into other chakras, spreading from the first chakra to the second chakra and to the third. It spreads throughout the energy field in many different ways. Think of it as a spore that is planted and then spreads outward. We are speaking of energy. Your loving intervention stops the propagation of that spore. As soon as possible, address the issue, remove the non-supportive beliefs, and add the new supportive beliefs.

Become Familiar with Common Positive Beliefs

The following might confuse you if you're not familiar with planning your life before incarnation. If that's the case, ignore it for now. When you incarnated, you forgot all, or almost all, that happened before. In this life — what we call the third-dimensional life — any abuse people experience was not their fault. Release from your confusion anything else we have said about the fifth dimension. What is important right now is to release the energy of the abuse from the people who were violated now. This is true for those who are aware of the concepts of creating their lives before incarnation. These releases or the pain cannot be bypassed. Release the pain. Release the energy of the perpetrator. You can do this.

There is no time. Read that again: There is no time. Whether you are in meditation or deep in your heart source, you can move back in time. You can say, "Take me back to the first instance this happened." Address that energy at that time. When you are able to be in the space of no-time, you can stop further propagation of the injected thought form. But because the person is in the third dimension, you still need to do some of the other work.

Let's examine common beliefs that need to be placed back in the person. We will start with two basic ones we have mentioned many times.

- "I am love incarnate."
- "I am the power and presence of God."

Someone might say, "If I'm the power and presence of God, why did this happen to me?" The answer you give, of course, is not one you would give the person while in third-dimensional pain. This is a supportive response: "Whatever happened is not your fault." In the third dimension, it was not anyone's plan. In the third dimension, the experience of rape, incest, molestation, or any type of sexual abuse was in no way the person's fault. It's not within the third-dimensional plan. Only when working with people on the higher spiritual levels — when they are ready to work on higher spiritual levels — do you bring in the idea that they agreed to a plan before they incarnated.

Here is another belief to install with the Belief plug-in: "What happened to me is not my fault. My recovery is my responsibility, but what happened to me is not my fault." If you feel the person needs to use different words, adjust the wording of the belief. For example, you could use these words: "What happened to me is not my responsibility. My recovery is my responsibility." Change the words as needed for each person. You might need to be more specific in the belief about responsibility, such as, "(Perpetrator's name) was responsible for the rape."

You can install this belief: "I am the perfect, sacred, and beloved child of God." If you believe a thought form of hatred of the person's gender was injected, you can install this belief: "I am whole and entire. As a woman, I am sacred." For a man, use the words: "As a man, I am whole and entire. As a man, I am sacred."

Heal Guilt and Shame

The same beliefs are installed for people who blame themselves because they were drunk, used drugs, or were in a place "they should not have been." The truth is that no one ever deserves to be raped, molested, or violated by incest. No one ever deserves that. Just because people are drunk, high, poor, or dress in a particular way does not give anyone the right to violate them.

It is important to release the energy of guilt and shame that they had anything to do with the abuse. This is an example belief you can install: "It was not my fault when someone chose to rape, molest, or incest me." Adapt the belief to what happened to the person. Again, we are speaking of the third dimension.

Even when talking about the plan for the current incarnation, it is never someone's fault. For people who are aware of the process of making their pre-incarnation plan, you could install the belief: "I grow in wisdom and knowledge of my soul's path from what happened to me."

Remember these things for healing when a person assaults another:

- Placed within the one abused is the energy of the perpetrator and the perpetrator's feelings.
- Perpetrators can place within their victims the energy of their beliefs (such as women are evil), which can take root in the person who was assaulted.
- The energy placed within the abused can grow and spread throughout their energy field.
- When the abused people add their feelings, the energy placed within them by the perpetrator can strengthen.
- Remove the energy of the perpetrator's belief.
- Use the Belief plug-in to install a new belief that counters what the perpetrator inserted. Have that belief ready. Write down a series of beliefs you think are important for you or for the person you are working with, and install them one after another using the Belief plug-in. Remember that the Belief plug-in also contains steps the encodement technicians go through to remove any contrary beliefs.
- Even though you are aware of the higher spiritual realm of why these things happen, many, if not most, of the people you will work with are not aware. Work on the third-dimensional understanding that they are not at fault and did not make that choice.

Alleviate Past Damage

Margaret: Say this happened to someone we know or to a celebrity. Can we go back to the beginning of the event and work with the person to alleviate some of the damage?

Yes. Let's return to the first part of this book. Remember how you connect with people very gently, moving in with your energy? You might only go to the seventh layer. Go as deep as they allow even when connecting to their hearts. They might be willing to accept your energy on a deeper level if you do these steps:

First, announce who you are. We're speaking on a soul level, correct? Announce who you are and that you wish to send them love and healing. Then tell them how precious they are. You will know within you, or you will feel from them, whether or not it is acceptable to move further into their energy.

This is the same as in any other kind of healing. You can send the energy of healing; if they do not accept it, they do not accept it. You are not taking over their will. You cannot force healing on anyone. Someone can force energy on someone, and that can do damage. But you cannot force healing on anyone. They can resist any energy propelled into them.

That is the long answer. Anything else?

Mimi: Yes, I have a question. I assume that anyone in their pre-incarnational plan who accepts the idea of being violated also has a plan to heal from the event.

You can assume no one has a plan that cannot be healed. Remember the difference between healing and curing? Healing incorporates the mental, emotional, and spiritual. Curing involves the physical only. You can have a physical healing without mental, emotional, or spiritual healing. Let us elaborate a bit more: Anybody living in this time frame in which divine energy is flooding the planet as it moves toward ascension has a plan to heal and raise the vibration of the planet even if not consciously aware of it.

Cleo: Listening to this gave me the idea that perhaps I will focus some of my intended healing on people who have no one to pray for them or to help them when they have been violated.

That would be a wonderful thing to do.

Cleo: Of course, I wouldn't know the details, but I can set the intention.

You can set the intention in several ways. You can do it very simply by stating, "I would like to work with people who are in need of healing and have no one else to work with them." You can do this mentally. Be in your heart source, go to the back of your sacred space, and connect with your healing guides. If you have the desire, that makes you a healer. Connect with your healing guides, and ask specifically for a person who fills those qualities you ask for and is within the vibration you can work with. This is a form of protection for you.

Cleo: That's very helpful. I would not have known to do those things.

If you have a sense that darker energies might be involved, always call in Archangel Michael and declare you are the Sword. Always call in protection.

CHAPTER THIRTY-ONE

Clear Beliefs That Form from Abuse

Amiya and Dr. Cathy

Amiya: We know you read our books for the experience of learning and for your healing. You sometimes wonder, "How did that healing happen? I didn't know I had anything related to what I just read that needed healing." Yet, you feel the difference. Some of you are fascinated with the various ways in which healing can occur, and you have used many healing modalities.

This excites and delights us. We don't experience excitement in the same way you do, but in the human term of "excitement," it is a sense of delight in watching you and the vibration on your planet grow as you work with others. You cannot heal without it affecting someone near you, and they cannot heal without it affecting someone near them. These concentric circles of healing move outward in waves from you and from one to another. Every person who accepts healing, even on a subconscious level, also accepts the delight of sending that healing outward.

It is true that someone who refuses to accept healing limits the flow of energy somewhat, but it goes around them and outward.

Energy is intelligent. Even though you might think, "Oh, I'm asking for healing for myself or for one person in particular," on that deep soul level you are aware that your healing energy flows outward to someone.

How does this happen? Changes occur in your encodements system. Changes take place in your aura and chakras. All the little parts of you experience change, as you learned in the *Hidden Structures* book [*The Human Energy Field: Hidden Structures*]. Changes are everywhere, and they do not stop with that seventh layer of your aura; they reverberate outward.

You are a system. The planet is a system. The universe is a system. What affects you affects every other energy that comes in contact with you. All energy flows outward, even the energy of discord. That is why Amma gave you the heart source and taught you how to use your body (including your energy body) to keep you centered and grounded and to transmute energy. Your heart source reflects your energy, and if the energy is not the vibration you need — if it comes to you because you have a similar vibration within you — your heart source can transmute that energy. How about that? If you make it a practice every day (even several times a day) to declare, "I am the Sword," the energy is transmuted.

Staying Centered Transmutes Energy to the Highest Vibration

When you work with someone for healing (it can be for yourself, but we're specifically talking about others), being in your heart source, being centered and grounded, and being the Sword of Archangel Michael, assists in transmuting all energy to the highest vibration possible. Your energy, or the energy coming into your energy, transmutes to the highest level of vibration of you. Think about what Amma has taught you. Using a numbered line, if you have an energy vibration of +5, you can easily work with the energy vibration of -5 or lower. Working with -6 would be more difficult, and -7 would be a stretch.

The more you stay centered and grounded using your heart source, the more your vibration rises. When you watch television, for example, if a scene triggers something in you and you ask for healing of what was triggered, your vibration rises. As you have probably learned about the one bringing in this information, she loves what she calls the whodunits, the mysteries and the suspense. These programs can do a lot of triggering. She often says, "Healing team, find the wound that was triggered, and use the four foundational plug-ins."

You have so many easy ways to heal yourself. You have heard, "Ask and you shall receive." This is especially true in the area of healing. It is not especially true when you ask something that is contrary to your life purpose or your life plan. We know it is frustrating when you ask for something and it doesn't happen or a vibration within you disallows it, but that is a whole other topic and another book.

Get In Touch with Buried Energy

In this chapter, we will work with how to counteract what the individual who was abused learned from the experience. The purpose is to not just counteract what was learned of a lower vibration. In the last chapter, we counteracted beliefs from the abuse by inserting beliefs everyone needs: "I am love incarnate. I am the power and presence of God. What happened was not my fault; it was the fault of the person who was the perpetrator."

We reminded you to work on a third-dimensional level. You do not tell someone, "Oh, you planned this before you came here to learn more about love." That discounts their individual experience in this third dimension. This is where you, as a healer who knows about the fifth dimension, keeps one foot in the third dimension and the other in the fifth dimension.

We believe most of you have heard the term "spiritual bypassing." If not, let us explain: Spiritual bypassing is where you take a pain — let's say the sexual abuse we are working with, such as rape, incest, or molestation — and say, "I need to forgive that person, so I'm going to work on forgiveness. I do not need to go into my pain and release it." That bypasses the energy that needs to be released.

Every person needs to get in touch with the energy buried within, in some cases to acknowledge the energy so that it can be released. This is part of the plan in learning about love and the effects of not-love. When you can acknowledge your pain and what you lost and grieve for what you lost, you can release the low-vibration energy and move into the higher levels of spirituality.

Do not allow anyone to tell you that you are not spiritual because you hang on to these things. This simply means you have energy within that hangs on. When you did the exercise to release certain beliefs, we had you release the energy within that causes you to hang on to those beliefs and to the energy of the perpetrator. It could have come from another lifetime, but there was something within you that caused you to hang on.

When you work as a facilitator of healing, it is crucial that you not judge others if they desperately hold on to their pain for some reason. When you are in your heart source, you lack judgment even of the perpetrator. You have compassion for people in great pain. You do not know the complexities of their life paths. When you judge, you discount their glory and that they are love incarnate. You discount their pain. In essence, you are saying, "If only they wanted to get over it."

"Wanting to get over it" has to do with the ability to release what they most fear. If they believe pain protects them in some way, they do everything they can to hold on to the pain. Your job as a healing facilitator is to gently release, step by step, the fear they hold on to. This applies to everything, but of course we speak here of sexual abuse.

Learn What the Abuse Taught

Let's go into this different area. What did the one who was abused learn in this situation? There are several ways you can look at this. First, you can look at the positives. For example, they can learn resilience. They learn to say, "I am stronger than I thought I was. I am more resilient than I thought I was." That is positive, is it not? "I have discovered courage I didn't know I had." That is also positive.

If what they learned was to isolate, then it is important to work with them. What would they rather have than isolation? Would they rather connect with another? Begin with where they are. Maybe they have a friend or someone they would like to connect with, but they are afraid. Help them get in touch with their inner knowing, which they might very well discount. As in the case of rape, the people who were raped might think, "Why was my inner knowing not available when I turned down that street? Why did it not come to me when I accepted that date with a stranger? Why didn't it tell me I was in danger even in my own bed?" They doubt their inner knowing and themselves.

Place within them beliefs that support their inner knowing, strength, and courage. Sometimes you have to work in a coaching way or send them to a therapist. Help them examine:

- signs that the situation could have been dangerous
- things they could have done in the third dimension that might have prevented, say, date rape, such as avoiding being given a drug by never leaving a glass unattended or never taking a glass from someone else

The person might get in touch with certain things and wonder, "My friend (or mother, sister, brother) told me not to do this, and I did it anyway. Why didn't my intuition kick in? Why didn't I listen?" Listen to what this says; they are victimizing themselves. That is victim consciousness. Pull them out of that as thoroughly and as quickly as you can.

You might ask them, "Why do you think you didn't listen?" They might come up with a number of ideas. Then ask, "What did you learn? Can you take this event and pull something positive that you learned from it?"

They could say, "I learned not to trust anyone."

You could respond, "Yes, that is something you might have learned. But did everyone do that to you? Is it possible you can trust at least one other person on this planet?"

You gently open their hearts to trust again by gently opening their awareness of who they are. You can request that they sit down with pen and paper and write out what they learned from the experience. Suggest that they be honest and let what they have learned to flow. If they learned that they cannot trust anyone, point out that that belief does not support the fun and joy of life.

Have them move away from the general term "everyone" to the specific term "someone." If they know the name of the one who abused them, they can say, "I cannot trust John," or "I cannot trust Susan." If they move to gender, race, or religion, help them realize that what happened did not happen because of everyone in that category; it was one person. If it was a gang rape, then it was those people; it was not everyone. Help them come to see this by asking, "Can you trust your best friend? Can you trust that person?" Help them discover who they can trust: siblings, parents, friends, authority figures. Discover who has supported them in the past, and ask whether they can still be trusted.

Use the Basic plug-in to heal the wound that caused the lack of trust. When you work with people who are unfamiliar with the plug-ins, go through each step of the Basic plug-in. Read the steps or recite them from memory. Be gentle. Know that if you trigger them, it is not your fault. Gently back away, not to leave them but to release the pressure. Allow them to go through their emotional process. If the emotion is fear, have them breathe deeply. If you are in fear, breathe deeply.

What to Do When You Are Triggered

If you get triggered, go back into your heart. Place your hand on your heart chakra or physical heart. Breathe. Look around, and see that the person who abused you is not there; you are safe. If you are reading this alone, have someone you know who you can call to help pull you out of the emotion. As silly as it might seem, you can go into your heart and start doing the multiplication tables. If you never learned the multiplication tables, count on your fingers. Do something left brained to pull yourself out of those feelings.

When you are able, say, "Healing team, please take that part of that wound, whatever it was within me that got triggered, and please use the Basic plug-in." You might want to go through each step of the plug-in. Many people enjoy the soul-healing prayer included in the Basic plug-in (and all the plug-ins).

List what you learned. You might want to draw a line down the paper and list two headings: "What have I learned that supported me and my healing?" and "What have I learned that isolated me from others?" That doesn't mean isolated from everyone but from a particular group, such as, "I avoid poor people" (or another socioeconomic class), "I avoid Caucasians" (or another race), "I avoid Catholics" (or another religion), "I avoid men" (or women), or "I avoid gay people" (or another sexual orientation).

If you were abused, it was by a person or people — a limited number and not hundreds or thousands. If you were abused within a religion, you were not abused by all the people of that religion.

When you have your list, focus on the supportive things you've learned. It could be "strength" or "resilience." It could be as simple as, "I will purchase my own drinks. I will never leave my drink by itself, whether it's alcohol or water." There are strategies you can use. The key, however, is to use them from curiosity and not from fear. Think of it as buying or renting a house. You know what you want, and you look for places with those things. When you don't see what you want, you either eliminate it or decide whether it is important to you. You ask yourself, "Will this be according to my needs?"

Deal with Limiting Beliefs

Have the people you help look at what they have learned that limits them, the beliefs that keep them inside and avoiding a particular race, gender, or sexual orientation. This is where you can begin to unfold what needs healing. Sometimes it is as simple as using processes to insert beliefs. You can use the Belief plug-in, but some people will not resonate with that. You might need to refer them to another modality that inserts beliefs in a different way, such as BodyTalk or PSYCH-K, which this one uses. When nonsupportive beliefs are limiting you or those you are working with, work gently. Beliefs that are nonsupportive in one way are protective in another. You might not see how that is, but they need them. Be gentle and nonjudgmental.

Beliefs you might need to install include: "I am safe." "I listen to my inner knowing." If you do this work often, you will find some who say, "There was something in the back of my mind that said, 'Take your drink with you when you go into the bathroom,' but I didn't want to insult him" (or her). Install a belief such as, "I always do what I need to do to protect myself." If the person did not want to insult someone, you can install the belief: "It is right and healthy to follow my inner knowing."

Beliefs form when people are assaulted. Before, we dealt with beliefs injected into people by their perpetrators. Release those beliefs, and work with the others.

Healing Comes Just from Reading these Books

Cleo: I'm grateful I don't have clients because it's such a responsibility. This just reminds me of how much I do not want responsibility for anybody else. I've had this feeling for a long time, independent of healing.

Dr. Cathy: Isn't that a wonderful thing to know about yourself?

Cleo: I guess I need to heal the wound that caused this. Maybe I was betrayed or something.

I suggest that if you think there is a wound, then ask for healing of the fear of responsibility.

Cleo: Okay. Sure.

You do spiritual work with others on the inner plane.

Cleo: I presume so.

There's a difference in responsibility toward people still in their bodies and those who have left their bodies. You might request, "Healing team, bring me the energy of people open to working with me." Do that work for a little while, and then they're released at the end of the session. That's a different type of responsibility.

Louise: I've had people come to me for counseling in a casual way, but it's not casual, and a part of me understands what to do and how to do it. It has struck me several times that I am, in this lifetime, absorbing what Amiya is presenting and that information is being applied to a different lifetime as a different personality. So what we're learning could be for our benefit in other lifetimes. Does that make sense?

It makes perfect sense that you're learning on the third-dimensional human level. There is no time, so you're learning for all your lifetimes. When I channeled the back-cover blurb for the PTSD book [*Trauma and PTSD: Resolve the Pain to Recover Your Life*], it came to me that you can read the book with an open heart to healing and receive healing even if you know nothing about encodements. This Encyclopedia of Healing will teach people who are working in the area of healing or those who want a new modality. It is also for people who are called to the book who will just read it and allow the healing to occur.

Cleo: That's me.

That's one of the strongest qualities of these books: You can just sit there and read. Cleo, you've mentioned how much you're getting from reading the *Hidden Structures* book even though you were present during all the channeled messages. I haven't had time to go back and read all the books, but I know it would be wonderful and beneficial for me to do that.

CHAPTER THIRTY-TWO

Release Energetic Attachments

Dr. Cathy

I'm going to teach you a process I have used for years that I've gathered from people I've worked with as well as from the beings I've channeled. These are the bare bones of how I do a spirit release.

When you work with a client who was sexually abused, especially when there was penile penetration, a dark being is probably attached to the second chakra. There could be more than one being in various places, but the second chakra usually has at least one. (Instead of "dark entity," I often use the term "those who have forgotten who they are." These are what some people call demonic beings.)

I went to Catholic school for ten years. We were taught (and this is true in all Christian religions I know of) that once an angel made a decision against God after having seen the face of God, that angel was never allowed back into God's presence. This was because the angel had seen the magnificence and glory of God and turned against God.

I was delighted to discover that God, who is totally love, never denies a part of God's self or any of God's creation no matter what we do in life, and this includes angels. We are always welcomed back to the glory of our Creator. This is what I do when I work with the dark entities, the ones who have forgotten who they are.

I also have a process for people who have died and lost their way who attach themselves to those still living, such as to loved ones. You might find a stranger, a spirit you didn't know in life, who likes your energy and thinks, "Oh, I'm going over here. Maybe this person will help me go somewhere else."

We'll begin with how to release those who have lost their way. In sexual abuse, this includes rape and incest. Incest is rape by someone who is a family member or one considered a family member. Everything we've discussed about rape applies to incest. Incest has additional overlays due to the family nature of the perpetrator. When people are incested by someone who was supposed to love them, someone who says they're important, an additional layer of pain and abuse occurs.

Those of you who have read and worked through the book on healing trauma and PTSD [*Trauma and PTSD: Resolve the Pain to Recover Your Life*] have healed a great deal of what is involved with any type of sexual abuse. The work in this chapter includes the method we used to release entities in that book.

Sometimes Spirits Lose Their Way

Let's begin with releasing the attachments of people who lived on this Earth. I will give you an example. I worked with a college friend I hadn't seen in about thirty years. I came back into her life after she was in an automobile accident in which she was paralyzed from the waist down. I reconnected with her to help in any way that I could.

As I worked with her one day doing BodyTalk, I sensed a spirit, a man who I believed was her father. When I helped her connect with him, she verified that it was her father. I couldn't say for sure that she had been sexually abused, but I asked her, "Is there something your father could have done that he wants to ask forgiveness for?" She said, "Yes." My perception was that sexual abuse was involved.

I began working with him. He was typical of family members who become attached to the ones they abused, physically or sexually. Once people leave their bodies and they're aware they have done so, they realize, "Hey, I'm going to get in trouble for what I did." They feel great fear, grief, and regret, and they believe, if they grew up Christian, that they're going to be sent to hell.

When people leave their bodies and do not return Home to the light, they don't go through the process of life review and to their place of healing. They receive healing after a being of love guides them and helps them put everything in their lives into context. When they haven't passed over, they still have all the feelings, all the pain, they had when they lived on Earth. They just don't have a body. When they know they no longer have a body, they have the additional knowledge that they're supposed to go for their life review. From their experiences on Earth, they expect to be punished and separated from God forever. Even though this occurs after death, they have the sense of finally being caught.

Some people know what they did was wrong, and they have shame about it. They're willing to take their punishment even if they believe that means going to hell and total separation from God forever. They hope to burn away their shame, and they want to apologize.

I've worked with those who were abused and have family members attached, and they want little to do with the perpetrators. They might say, "Okay, I'll go ahead and talk to them, but I want them out of my life. I don't want them to come back in any way." They just want to get rid of them. That shows you how much healing the abused need, which is perfectly understandable.

This healing is a process. When I worked as a therapist, I used to say my client load increased when I became aware of an attachment. When I do this work, I prefer that my clients be involved as much as possible. I help them connect with the beings attached to them. I want the clients to experience their power of being in control.

Go Through the Spirit-Release Process

I don't often do spirit-release work during the first session unless that is the primary reason for the client's problem. First, we call in wonderful protective beings such as Archangel Michael, Jesus, or whoever the client brings into the session. These beings are present and protecting.

When I sense an attachment, I start by asking the client several questions: "Do you ever have thoughts and feelings and wonder where they come from? You might be having a great day and suddenly you have horrendous thoughts or feelings of rage, shame, or depression." If they say, "Yes," which they often do, I talk to them about how we can have energies attached to us.

This is important: You need to find your own way of doing this. Only do this if this work calls you deeply from your heart. You can have some disastrous results if you do this out of ego. For example, the attachment — the being who's lost its way or forgotten who it is — can attach to you. This is not something to do out of ego.

I talk to my clients about people in their lives who have passed on. If I suspect a parent, I will usually ask, "Do you have a parent who has died?" If I get a sense the attachment is male or female, I'll ask about that gender. When they verify that a father or mother has passed on, I say, "I think your father" (or whoever) "is with you." I then explain the process. I tell them we'll do this together, and I assure them there is nothing to worry about or fear.

The attachment (the parent or other perpetrator) is usually behind the person on one side or the other, and I sense where it is. If you focus behind the client, you can often feel the difference. One side seems heavier or denser than the other. I have the client locate this density. (You might not be able to sense this energy, and that's okay. It's about being in your heart and being focused.)

I say, "I want you to bring your attention to the space over your left shoulder." I always start with the side where there is no attachment so that they can feel the empty space first. Once they do that, I say, "Okay, now do the same over the other shoulder, and tell me the difference."

They usually say, "It's heavier over here."

I respond, "That is where I sense your father," or mother, brother, grandparent, aunt, uncle, whoever.

Be sure that people are in their hearts. This can be scary and cause them to go back into their heads. Have them go back into their hearts and breathe deeply. I then instruct them to bring their attention to the area where they experienced the density or to where I felt the density. For this example, we're going to say that the attachment is the client's father.

I ask, "What did you call your father?"

The client says she called him "Dad."

I then give her the words to say and tell her I need to know his answers to the questions I give.

I say, "Ask him, 'Dad, is that you?'"

A look will often cross the person's face.

I ask, "What do you get?"

People might respond with, "I got a yes." Sometimes they don't sense a word, but they feel movement or see a color.

After they respond, I tell them what I sensed. I ask the client, "Does that feel right to you?" (I make sure I use the word "feel.")

If the client didn't experience anything (that happens occasionally), I ask whether I can proceed as if the being I sense is there. I've never had anyone not give me permission. I tell clients everything I say and what I hear back. I still have the clients connect with the energy of the one attached so that they can, hopefully, get a sense of what's happening.

Act as a Spirit Therapist/Coach

As I proceed with the healing session, I become the therapist to the spirit. If you're not a therapist, you won't do the therapy part, but you can coach the spirit. I identify who I am and tell the entity, "I know you did things to _____" (client's name). I often feel energy from the spirt: sadness, anger, rage, shame.

I ask my incarnate client, "What would you like to say to this person? You can do it out loud or to yourself." Most prefer to say it out loud. Remember, these beings did terrible things to the ones they were supposed to love and protect. Now the clients have me (or the one leading the release work) as a witness.

Clients say whatever they want. The perpetrators might try to downplay what happened or make excuses. I stop that immediately by saying, "That's not true, and you know that's not true. You did this because you didn't have self-control." Sometimes I have to speak firmly, but I do so from my heart.

I do everything I can to not allow the discarnate beings to say anything that will hurt the people I'm working with. I do not relay any information from the discarnate beings that I believe would hurt my incarnated clients. I reword it in some way, such as, "He's making excuses. He's just trying to get out of responsibility for his actions."

Usually, that doesn't happen. The being accepts responsibility and feels terrible and scared. After connecting with the spirit, I have the clients ask, "Why are you still here?"

Many times, beings answer: "I'm scared."

I then have the clients ask, "Are you afraid of going to hell?"

If the answer is yes, and it usually is, I tell the spirits, "I have to tell you something. There isn't a hell. There is only God who loves, and God wants you to be fully with God. God wants to heal you of everything that has happened in your life." This part often takes some back-and-forth conversation. I attempt to help them realize they don't have to fear God. If they do not release their fear, they will resist leaving.

When the spirits are ready to go, I ask whether they would like to say something to the ones they are attached to. It's not unusual for them to cry. I tell the clients what's happening. Once it gets to that point, the spirits often say, "I'm sorry." They can't take back what happened, but they can apologize.

My clients then have the choice whether to forgive or not. They might say, "I forgive you," but they might not mean it sincerely; they only say it so that the perpetrator will leave. Accept that. That's where the people are in their healing. Sometimes the clients will say, "No, I don't forgive you. I want you away from me. I don't want you near me. I don't want you to come back. I don't want you to do anything with me. Get out of my energy. Stay away from me."

When that happens, I talk to the spirits. I tell them the one they abused has to work through this. I might say, "You hurt her terribly, but I want you to know that God loves you, and you can be forgiven. Are you willing to let her go now?"

Sometimes more conversation is needed to help them sort things out. Usually they get to the point of being ready to leave. I sense the light opening behind them along with a family member or a spiritual figure. When I believe the spirits are ready to leave, I tell them to look to where I see the light. I ask whether they see anyone they know. When they recognize someone, they often move toward that person. I ask whether they have anything else to say to the ones they're attached to. Their last words often are "I'm sorry" and "I love you."

After the spirits go into the light, I check in with my clients and ask how they feel. The usual answer is, "Lighter."

That completes releasing the one who was attached, but there is more to do with my clients. For example, their energy fields might be damaged by the attachment. You can use the Repair the Energy Field plug-in, or you can use my favorite modality: Call in the Healing Band of Mercy, a group of angels who repair the energy field after attachments are released. That's how easy it is. You might think, "I don't know about it being that easy, because you have to be able to sense energies." Remember that I've been doing this for close to thirty years.

This is an amazing experience. There is a joy that comes when someone has gone Home. Imagine escorting a terrified child home to safety and how wonderful it is to see that child safe in his parent's arms. This is the same. I talk to my clients about the sacredness of what they just helped accomplish, such as, "You helped your dad go back to God and be totally healed."

Angels Provide Assistance

Brenda: If we can't sense the energy of an attachment, should we not get involved in this?

That's an excellent question. I have learned over the years that attachments are usually revealed to me when I'm ready to work with them and when the client is ready. If you believe this is the case, refer the client to someone who can do this.

Michelle: Do you ever have to call in angels or other spiritual beings to help?

Yes, although that usually occurs with dark beings.

When Archangel Michael comes to take that being away, does it happen gently or is there a struggle?

It depends on how willing the person is to go. Archangel Michael uses as little force as possible. Sometimes a group of angels comes, which usually happens when an attachment is being stubborn but not malicious. Michael can sometimes intimidate the spirits, and they will leave. I had a case with an angry, mean, and violent being who was attached to two girls. He came in through a Ouija board. The guy was a rapist and unrepentant. I told him he had to get away from those two, but he refused to go to the light. I called in Archangel

Michael, who came in with a group of angels. A bit more force was involved than usual: They literally picked him up and took him. I was told he was going to a place of learning.

CHAPTER THIRTY-THREE

Remove Dark Beings

Archangel Michael

What a wonderful day it is, fellow members of spiritual lovefare, for those of you who hold the Sword within your very cells. Know that the Sword has nothing to do with killing. It has to do with transmuting low-vibration energy to the highest level of energy you call God, All That Is, Love Itself. You can apply the Sword to any aspect of your life to raise its vibration.

I want to tell you a story. All That Is wanted to learn about what All That Is, is. In other words, All That Is wanted to explore different aspects of love. Just as you volunteered to be on the Earth plane and forget who you are, others volunteered from the angelic realm and agreed to act to forget who they are. Notice we said "act," as if they were against God. These others had to forget they had seen the face of God — pretend — and take on a role of denying their Creator.

I'll let that sink in.

Those you might call demons are no different in their roles than you, but their memories of who they truly are were wiped cleaner and more forcefully than yours. As this world evolves and raises its vibration, the children coming in are forgetting less of the love that they are. Their memories are not wiped as thoroughly as they were before the vibration of your planet began to elevate.

These demons had their memories wiped only once. They are not continually born as you humans are, as you souls are. They continually reinforce within themselves that they can never return to God, that they can never return to the light, and that they are not of the light. Their indoctrination is continual, whereas your indoctrination changes over time as you come to realize the love that you are.

Dark Beings Have Different Vibrations

Demons have different vibrations. This one we speak through [Dr. Cathy] likes to call them those who have forgotten who they are, which is true. They volunteered to forget, and then forgetting was impressed on them more and more.

There are various vibrations of forgetting. Some demons attach to people, resulting in minor inconveniences. Do you consider a mosquito flying around you a minor inconvenience? A mosquito is different from knives coming at you. A mosquito is frustrating. It distracts you, sometimes biting you and causing a little pain. Then you go on a hunt to find the mosquito and kill it.

Some demons are like mosquitoes. These dark entities support humans to forget love. They can attach to those who act in ways that are contrary to love. Other demons are similar to Godzilla. You feel helpless when faced with such power. Some will take over your body, if you agree, in what you call possession. That does not happen as often as people think. The main way dark beings interfere is through oppression. Wouldn't you say that a mosquito oppresses you? If they're darker, more evil, they oppress you even more.

I am giving you the basics so that you know what can happen when you work with someone who has a dark being attached. When this one becomes aware of a dark being, her focus changes. She is aware that the person with whom she is working is afflicted by a being who has accepted the lie of who it is not. This being has accepted the lie that when it is discovered, it will have failed its oppression and be returned to what you call hell. It knows that, from various religions, it will be returned to the pain of hell, and it fears that pain.

Those who use rituals to return these beings to hell do not help them remember who they truly are. When you use spiritual lovefare, you work with the truth: the belief that all is love. Your job as a human being who practices spiritual lovefare is to reveal love. You can take certain steps when a dark being enters people and attaches to them through rape, through penile penetration as a fluid or energy injected into them.

Begin the Release Process

You are the Sword. Declare, "I am the Sword," and feel the strength of your energy. Here's something you might not know: When you declare "I am the Sword," you do not need to use any other words to call us. We come to you faster than instantly. When you say, "I am the Sword," the energy of that declaration goes out with the information that you need us. As many as are needed for your specific situation come. Yes, you can still call me and members of my band. The dark energy is our brother who has forgotten who he is. (There really is no gender.) We recognize that energy and our hearts yearn to have him remember who he is.

Be in your heart source. If you become fearful, return to your heart source. If you receive ideas of vengeance, return to your heart source.

The release process is easier and goes faster when the one who has the being attached works with you. It might seem strange, but people can be so scared that they are afraid to release the darkness. When the person helps release the darkness, nothing holds on to that dark being.

Earlier in this book, you received instruction on how to release discarnate beings. You released the artificial encodements holding on to the attachment. Do the same here. Proceed as we have instructed you, as Amiya have instructed you. You have done the preparatory work. Your preparatory work is to be in your heart source and be the Sword. Do all the following steps from your heart source and with the intention that this dark being, who has forgotten who it is, comes to know itself as an aspect of light and that it returns to the light.

Once the dark one is discovered, do the preparatory work discussed earlier. Tell the one to whom the being is attached how you will proceed. Give her words to say to the being, and let her know she is not alone. You will be there to handle the situation if anything comes up. The people should help as much as possible so that they feel and experience their power in being able to work in this way. People who have been sexually abused, such as through incest or rape, struggle with feeling powerless because of being overcome. The truth is, they are more powerful than they know. When you help them participate in this process, they can experience power.

Connect with that being. Your connection lets the dark one know you are in control. You will give the one who has the attachment certain words. There will be a time when you take control, and you will need to identify when that time comes. This takes experience.

Have the one who has the attachment tell the one who has totally forgotten who it is, "You have been discovered. When you are discovered, you have failed." The being knows the truth of those words. Everything the being does is meant to be done in secret; it is easy to fool the human. But when this dark being is discovered in, say, the second chakra, that is when its failure begins. When you speak those words to the dark one, you are announcing that you know the truth. The dark being then moves into fear.

Help the Dark Being Move to the Light

Now you begin the work of getting the being to move on. Next, say, "I know that when you have been discovered, you have failed. When you have failed, you will be punished."

If you do not act to remove that darkness immediately, it can stay and cause havoc, such as projecting fear and sending messages of how this person deserved everything he received. It tells lies. But stay there with that dark being, staying in your heart source, and speak firmly from the heart, from the power that you are: "I know that you will be punished. I can prevent you from being punished. I can help you go to a place where you will never experience that punishment again." Depending on how sensitive you are, you might, as you speak these words, feel the vibration of that dark being move from fear to hope.

That dark being must make its own decision to move into the light, but you can provide a little help. Say, "I can prove it to you. Look deep within yourself." You need to encourage dark beings, as they are usually reluctant to look deep within. Repeat, "Look deep within yourself." If they refuse, this one says, "You must be afraid to look within." These beings are taught from the beginning to never show fear. They cannot be afraid because that is part of being a failure. To avoid the appearance of fear, the beings almost always begin to look within. Encourage them to look deeper, deeper, and deeper.

Suddenly, both the being and the person it is attached to feel a shift. Often, the dark being feels confused. Ask it, "What do you see?" Often, it communicates, "I see light." This light can be the brightness of white light or a red light, like fire. Whatever light the being sees, this one quickly reinforces it: "Yes, this proves that you are of the light and you can return to the light. You are of the light and you can return to the light." The vibration of that formerly darkest of dark beings begins to change.

This one knows there is not much more she can do, and she calls for help. She tells the being, "I would like to call those you knew in darkness but are now in the light to come talk with you. Are you willing?"

The being then replies yes or mutely nods its head.

She then says, "I call for those who are now in the light but knew this one in darkness to come and talk to this one and share the truth and their experiences." Hundreds come. She describes it as being able to hear chattering but not knowing what is being said. She can feel a change and usually so can the person the being has been within.

This one asks the being, "Do you wish to go with them?" When they say, "Yes," she stops them. "Before you go, do you have anything you wish to say to this one you have been within?" Usually it wants to say, "I am sorry."

She gives them other instructions: "Before you go, take with you anything you placed within this person. Take out structures. Dismantle them. Take any debris you have left. Gather it all together, and take it with you. Then leave with those you have been speaking with." And they go.

Repair the Energy Field

The person's energy field needs some repair work. Call the Healing Band of Mercy, a group of angels that works specifically in this area, to repair the energy field after the person has released any kind of attachments. You can also work with the healing team to repair the energy field using the Repair the Energy Field plug-in.

Sometimes other dark beings come to "rescue" the dark being. You can call in reinforcements, as it were. Tell the dark being and the person you are working with that they are protected. Because you are the Sword, we form a barrier between that dark being and any force coming to rescue it.

You can do this release work repeatedly. It is not something to do from ego. If you are in your heart source, it is never out of ego. If doing this work feels beyond you, refer the person to someone who can do it.

After you have released the dark being, say to the person who once had that dark being, "Do you realize what you have just done? You have taken this being who fully believed it was evil and there was no way it could be saved and returned it to love, to God. That entity now goes to a place of learning." Some dark beings do not want to go, but they are still taken to a place of learning. If the being asks whether it will hurt, be honest. "Yes, there can be pain, but it is the pain of coming to know who you truly are. Once you have discovered who you are, there will be no more pain."

That is what I wished to tell you. Thank you.

CHAPTER THIRTY-FOUR

Release the Energy from Incest

Amiya

Incest is an unwelcomed sexual event by a person considered family. This person does not need to be biological family. For example, the person could be a stepparent or a parent's best friend and be considered part of the family.

The primary work you do to release the energies of incest are the same as we have already described. Incest goes energetically to the very fabric of your concept of God, of who Spirit is. You learn that parents are all-powerful. They manage your life and are supposed to be your protectors. Parents, even grandparents, give you love, nurturing, and support. When a person who is supposed to protect you and care for you sexually violates you — especially from the time you were born — your whole sense of who you are as an individual and who protects you is thrown off balance.

Think about the intimate act of changing an infant's diapers. The person changing the diapers cleans the genitals, a necessary act to prevent infection or irritation. The infant goes to a medical professional who examines the genitals. The infant might feel discomfort, but it is a clinical experience with no sexual overtones. Those who have had the unfortunate experience of it being not clinical but abusive know how that feels on energetic, physical, and emotional levels.

Infants having their diapers changed in a matter-of-fact manner many times a day, with all the touching and cleaning needed, have no emotional side effects from those events. If that activity moves into an experience of the adult manipulating the genitals in some way or having the child manipulate the adult's genitals by using the baby's sucking reflex, the energy transmitted to the baby contains fear and shame. On one level, the infant acquires the energy that something is not right. That energy can surface years later if abuse energy is triggered, such as during a sexual relationship. This comes from the cellular memory containing the energy of the perpetrator.

Young children who learned that doing sexual acts to an adult is love have a difficult time with sexual boundaries. This can cause problems in their relationships with older people. For example, these children might offer to do something sexual as a way to show affection or to get what they want. Instead, the older people are horrified and rebuff them considering them to be evil or perverted. This begins confusion about what is right regarding sex. Suddenly these children are considered wrong and bad, and they don't understand why.

People tend to forget that if children who engage in such behavior as youngsters want to continue giving pleasure, as it were, to people they like, this has nothing to do with who they are. They are only doing what they were taught by their perpetrators. These children were formed and fashioned to have the belief that to give pleasure was to manipulate or suck on a person's genitals. They transfer that belief to other people they love or feel affection for because this is how they were trained. What children learn does not tell you who or what they are; it says something about what happened to them.

These beliefs need to be changed. This process is complex, as beliefs regarding sex, sexuality, self-worth, who you can trust, and more are tied in a knot. You can, of course, use the Belief plug-in. The complexity is that when beliefs are changed, the person needs to act according to those beliefs, which can be difficult for a child. It is difficult enough for an adult. The energy of the new belief is present when it is placed within the person. The signature of the act needs to be rewritten in the brain, and that is done by action.

Using a non-sexual example, if you believe it is unsafe to express anger and you change that belief to it being safe and appropriate to express anger, you reinforce that belief by acting on it. When you act on that new belief, you receive feedback that it is safe and appropriate to express anger.

If children are not in a safe place in which they can use their new belief, it is difficult to reinforce the belief. When you place within a child the common belief that it is not appropriate for a person, other than a doctor, to touch their private parts, the child must be able to act on that belief. Parents train their children by saying, "It is not okay for anyone to touch you, and if you ever feel uncomfortable, you can say no." The problem comes, of course, when the person who inappropriately touches the child is the parent who is supposed to assist the child.

Do you see the complexities of what happens? Mistrust and confusion develop. The child wonders, "Who can I trust?" The younger the age when sexual abuse begins, the more difficult it is for the children to sort through their beliefs when they are older. Who can they trust? What is safe? What is right? Those who are incested or sexually abused as young children have a more difficult time working through sexual issues as adults. They need mutual love, trust, and great patience as they work through sexual issues with their partners.

Healing from incest is about unraveling and untangling what is the truth about love, sex, and sexuality and what is distortion. Always remember that these people love. It doesn't matter what happened to them or what they think of themselves. They were created in love. Part of the creation in love was to be the physical expression of love between two consenting adults.

The age of adulthood has changed over the years. Two-thousand years ago, people died in their thirties, and an old person was in their forties. The consenting age as an adult was younger. Marriages were arranged soon after women began their menses. In your society today, since you live much longer, women at that age are still considered children.

In today's society, you are trained that you have the right to say no to what a person wants to do to you. There should not be the need to say no. It should all be based on yes. It should be based on love. Passion can happen with deep love or infatuation. Passion is to be enjoyed when there is consent. Do passion and consent occur with children? Children cannot give full consent because they do not know what is actually happening. Children are learning how to please people. They are learning how to be who they are. The adult's role is to teach them in a safe environment in which the adult is also the protector.

Add New Beliefs

How do you work with healing incest? First, apply the information from this book. All the strategies we have given in past books about repairing the energy field are important. If penile penetration occurred without full consent, remember to look for entities.

Here, we will focus on working with beliefs. We will work with adults, as working with children can be difficult because their brains have not yet developed to the point where they have abstract thought. That is one reason why it is important to get children out of situations in which they are being abused and moved into a family of love. If a child is transferred to another home, it's important that the adults do not respond with horror or revulsion to what they might think are sexual advances by the child. If the child was trained to get what he or she wanted by giving pleasure to the man, the family needs to refrain from horror if the child reaches for the man's penis to get what he or she wants.

You simply say with great love as you gently take the child's hands and look him or her in the eyes, "We don't do that here. You do not have to do that. There are other ways to ask for things and to love. How about a big hug?" If the adult knows how to pray to heal the wound that caused the child to act in such a way, please use that prayer. Retrain with love, not with horror. Adding horror or revulsion adds another trauma and creates more confusion for the child.

We've told you about the children. You have to firmly, gently, and lovingly retrain them to change their behavior. Guide the child to give pleasure and show affection to adults by being nice and giving hugs. When working with adults, use the healing strategies given in this book. If you have been reading through this book and are following each healing experience, you have been doing exactly what is needed.

Balance Beliefs

Let's talk about teenagers who have developed abstract thought. Even with abstract thought, you will not find many teen who can immediately see the future consequences of their actions. Think about your physical passion. You might have learned about sex from your family, friends, or another source, but did any of them impress on you the power of physical passion? The experience is stronger than what you have heard. You have to be able to think through things before you feel passion. Very often, teens get caught up in the passion and cannot think through it.

How to respond during physical passion is complicated by energies from sexual abuse. The abused person often has softer boundaries and doesn't know how to say no. Teens rarely want to look at the effects of sexual abuse. They often don't want to admit they were abused. The shame can be overwhelming.

People who were abused as children, especially women, often have a more difficult time saying no. This can result in date rape. (If date rape has occurred, apply the healing processes we've given you for rape and date rape.) When abused people become adults, often in their thirties, they become aware that their lives have been significantly damaged by sexual abuse.

What remains is balancing beliefs. This works best with teenagers and adults. The following are some crucial beliefs:

- "It is safe and appropriate for me to have sexual relations with consenting adults." This belief can be adapted as needed.
- "It is safe and appropriate for me to have sexual relations with my partner." This applies to a person with a loving spouse or partner.
- You can add, "I deserve a loving and passionate relationship."

Does balancing beliefs instantly change things? No, but it gives a foundation to sexual relationships. Changes occur more deeply when people have loving, kind, and patient partners with whom they can gently and slowly explore and learn what is safe. For some, safety begins simply with being able to hold hands and have their arms around another person without the expectation of engaging in sex.

Some therapeutic techniques blend with our message. We are speaking through a person who was a therapist, and she knows the importance of being able to touch without the demand for sexual relations — holding hands, cuddling, rubbing each other's backs. The goal is to rewrite the past. The one who was wounded needs to develop a sense of safety, and perhaps both partners were wounded.

Teach both partners to work with their healing teams. Every time a fear surfaces, have them request: "Healing team, please use the Basic plug-in to heal the wound that was triggered when my partner touched my shoulder" (or my back, etc.). Touch can surface cellular memory of what happened in the past even if there was no sexual intention in the touch. How many times have you held hands, even briefly, with a person and had no sexual intent? Holding hands was a sign of support. Walking down the street holding your child's hand and enjoying that connection is nonsexual.

When engaging in sexual relations, people can have the continual need for healing any time they are triggered. Difficulties can arise if those who are triggered are going through the healing process by themselves without their partners' full involvement and support in the healing. It is difficult to find people who can be patient, loving, and caring while in the throes of passion. Without a loving partner to carry some of the responsibility, the abused person can feel alone and burdened with having to carry all the responsibility for healing. The truth is that it is ultimately the abused who is responsible for his or her healing.

We have deviated. If you, or the person you are working with, has been triggered, you can immediately ask your healing team to use the four foundational plug-ins: the Basic plug-in, the Healing over Lifetimes plug-in, the Remove Victim Consciousness plug-in, and the Implant Removal plug-in.

Move to the Belief plug-in. People can find great solace when led through all steps of the plug-in. It gives them space and time to experience their healing team working with them. Say to their healing team, "Please locate the wound that was triggered." If doing all the steps, you would say, "Healing team, please use the Basic plug-in. Encodement technicians, remove all artificial encodements, repair damaged and altered natural encodements, activate the natural encodements that went inactive, and create any natural encodements needed for the full experience of joy in this person's sexual relationship with her (his) partner."

Then you would move to the soul-healing part of the Basic plug-in. Say, "Healing team, please find and bring back all the pieces lost when this wound occurred. Clean, repair, and heal all the pieces, and fully integrate them within this person." Offer thanks to the healing team. If the one triggered feels safe being hugged or having her or his hand held, ask, "Spirit (or whatever name you use for God), please fill this precious one with all the love that was needed at that time but was not received. May this person come to know what love truly is and how love is truly expressed."

Work with Triggers

If you were abused or your partner was abused, you might stop many times when making love or just hold hands to do these healing prayers. Many things are triggered, such as cellular memory. If you're working in a therapeutic situation with a client, it helps to talk about what occurred. For abused people, loving another physically was perverted in a way that deeply damaged them.

You or your client can use commands, such as: "I command all energies that tell me that making love to my partner is inappropriate (or wrong, painful, etc.) to come out of me now." You can also say, "Thank you for protecting me. I do not need you any longer. Leave now." You can also get in touch with the energies and breathe them out. It might seem strange to think the energies were protecting you, but they set up a defensive layer around you to prevent you from more emotional pain. They are no longer needed.

If those energies are difficult to release, call in your healing team: "Healing team, please remove any artificial encodements holding in those energies. Please repair any damaged and altered natural encodements holding in those energies." In a commanding voice, say, "I call forth all energies within me that tell me that a sexual relationship with my partner is wrong or painful. Leave me now."

If another wound surfaces, go through the foundational plug-ins again and repeat the process. This can be a slow process. Be patient with all concerned. Be in your heart, and hold yourself in love. When working with an adult, the process of working with encodements, releasing energies, changing beliefs, and removing entities is similar to untangling a fine gold chain. It takes patience and care. You are untangling the finest gold threads of the person's sexuality. Move back and forth between the healing prayer, calling forth the energies caught within the person's cells, and releasing all in healing prayer.

Through it all, you retrain and revitalize the psyche of the person who was abused. You also assist the one abused to learn the safety and power in the words "yes" and "no." If you are in a relationship with a person who was abused, go no further than what the person says yes to. Ask whether you can hold his or her hand, rub your finger or thumb on his or her hand, and so forth. Only when the response is yes do you continue. If the person says no, then stop. Your actions should only progress with a definite yes.

CHAPTER THIRTY-FIVE

Install Self-Value

Amiya and Dr. Cathy

Amma: You have been bringing in information to help resolve great pain across the planet. Part of that pain is due to adult women not being valued as people; they are not valued in the same way as adult males. That means children, girls, and women are not valued for all their gifts.

If you studied the history of sex and sexuality over the past thousands of years, you would find an ebb and flow of respect for human beings on all levels. As you read this book and do this work to bring healing to others, you also trigger things within you: your views from this lifetime about sex, sexuality, and relationships between men and women, men and men, and women and women. You trigger what it is to be of value or not to be of value.

Think back to a time when you did not feel valued. It could have been in your family, as in many families, males are valued over females. In many families, children are not valued until they become useful. Years ago, usefulness came at an early age when children could work in the fields to support their families. Now, in the Western world, the developed world, people have money and the sustenance needed to support life, but respect and love for one to another is often not there.

Think of a time in this lifetime when you did not feel valued. See yourself at that age. Go into the back of your heart center, into your sacred space. Call to that aspect of you at that age when you did not feel valued (and that lack of value might have had nothing to do with gender). Introduce yourself to this aspect that did not feel valued. Connect with that aspect heart to heart.

Reach out with both hands and ask that aspect to reach out and take them. Look at that wonderful, beautiful aspect of yourself who did not feel valued. Look at that aspect of you in the eyes. This aspect of you wants to speak with you. Include these things in your words: Thank this aspect of you for what it has learned and experienced, even the sense of not being valued. Tell this aspect of you how wonderful, how beautiful, and how delightful and valuable it is to you, and tell it how much you respect and love it.

Say a prayer of healing for this aspect of you, whichever prayer you wish. Talk to this aspect of you about your gifts, your talents. Anytime you feel this aspect of you resist listening about your gifts or talents or you resist sharing that or have difficulty coming up with your gifts and talents, go to your healing team. Ask for healing in whatever way you're guided.

Place your hand on this aspect's physical heart. Say to this aspect of you: "Within your heart is a golden structure. Within that structure is your strength, courage, and who you are as love incarnate. Within that golden structure are you and the Creator, the love that created you." Bring energy into your body with your breath, and send it gently out from your hand into the heart of that aspect of you. Say to your healing team, "Please activate all encodements within the golden structure so that this aspect of me (which means you as you are now) knows the truth about the radiance of who we are."

Embrace that aspect of you lovingly, gently, and completely. Bring it into you, merging into oneness. That aspect is no longer separate from you. Ask your healing team: "Please align all encodements that have been healed within me, and do the same within that aspect."

You can use this wonderful healing experience at any time with any aspect of you, any wound within. You can also do this healing with others, if you wish.

Self-Value Is Part of Sexuality

My healing friends have mentioned to you before, and I will mention it again, that when you do this work, much surfaces within you. Everyone has wounds regarding sexuality. What is it you say? It is "the nature of the beast," the loving beast, the beast you tame within. When you do this work with a person and you feel those energies come up in you — the untamed beast, so to speak — as soon as you finish with the one you were working with and have said your good-byes, it is time to work with you. Ask to heal the part that surfaced, that wound. It might not have anything to do with sexual abuse; it could be a feeling of not being valued for who you are.

Not feeling valued is part of your sexuality, because your sexuality cannot be separated from who you are. Your sexuality is how you experience the world, joy, and the sensual parts of yourself — taste, touch, scent, sound, and sight. Your sexuality is connected to Source, the love of creation, and the love of Source's creation. It is connected to you and your creations. A big lack of awareness among people is realizing that sexuality is not just about sex; it is about your experience in the world.

When you work with another, you might feel something within that you identify as sexual or having to do with your sexuality. A wound might have surfaced that you need to heal. Your healing team is there and will do what they can without your conscious permission, but there are times when they need your willing cooperation to release the pain of the past and the old beliefs that hold you down. They need your willing cooperation to bring in and activate your beliefs of who you truly are.

A Gentle Healing

Margaret: I would do anything to help my mother when I was a kid, and it wasn't always appreciated. That also happened with my husband, his siblings, and their mom, but I'd never equated it with my mom. My mom's parents didn't value themselves, and I'm sure it's a chain that goes back in time. I found the healing very gentle.

Mimi: In this lifetime, I've never felt that I didn't have value. I'm sure there are many people who feel the same way. So I left that open for healing over other lifetimes. The

exercise made me wonder how people can think they're not valued because we all have value. I've always known I had value, period.

Dr. Cathy: That's wonderful. Some people who took care of their families when they were children might not have felt appreciated for the work they did. This isn't sexual, but it can be healed with the process Amma used. Not everybody came from abusive homes.

Elaine: I grew up in a home where the males were valued more than the females. It's almost impossible for me to understand where Mimi's coming from, that she was always valued. I felt I was never valued. In this exercise, I went to a teenage incident. There was a gentleness and a kindness that I suddenly felt that I didn't realize was there.

That's a gift in itself, isn't it?

Elaine: Yes.

CHAPTER THIRTY-SIX

Support Witnesses of Abuse

Amiya

We begin this chapter with what happens to those who witness incest or rape but who are not the victims. We will later discuss the people who, in a sense, give themselves as sacrifices to perpetrators as their sexual objects to protect their sibling(s).

When a child witnesses abuse but can do nothing to intervene, parents or family members are often the perpetrators. It is not unusual, when brought to the non-abusive parent's attention, for that parent to refuse to believe that abuse is taking place or to act on it. Besides simply refusing to believe it, the parent might fear changes in the family that could result in violence or homelessness. If they throw out the perpetrator, for example, the single parent and family could end up on the streets with no money, home, or way to feed, clothe, and care for the children. The non-abusive parents are caught in a conundrum, and their fear and stress keep them from seeking further options or possibilities.

Work with the witnesses in all the areas previously discussed as if they had been abused. The big difference is that an observer rarely has an entity attached to them. Witnesses usually seek help when they are adults. They are probably suffering from trauma and might have PTSD. You would use the information contained in the book on trauma [*Trauma and PTSD*] and repair the energy field. Balance their energy and look for congestion that is muddying and covering their soul star, pranic tube, and hara line, and then remove the energy of the perpetrator from them.

Those who witness abuse often take on the energy of the abused person because they are trying to relieve some of their pain and heaviness. To facilitate healing, you will need to use the plug-ins to heal the wounds and remove the energy of the pain. Begin with the four foundational plug-ins.

Find the First Wound

Go into your heart and connect with their healing team. Request: "Please find the wound that needs to be healed first." You or your client might not know which wound is being triggered and needs to be healed first. That is why you say, "Find the wound that is being triggered," or "Find the wound responsible for this feeling." Then say, "Please apply the four foundational plug-ins to the wound."

Witnesses of abuse who share their experience with you might not want you to do anything. They might just want you to listen. As you connect to them heart to heart, which is important as they share, ask your healing guides to ask their healing team, as much as is allowed by the soul self, to please apply the four foundational plug-ins to whatever they are saying.

Your healing team might apply the plug-ins to the wound being discussed, and then five seconds later, as they are telling you something else, their healing team will apply the plug-ins to the new wound. So even while listening, you can ask for healing to occur.

If you are reading an article about a person who was wounded, or if you are listening to a newscast or a podcast of a person talking about a wound, you can connect with that person heart to heart (remember to connect gently) and ask for healing. Go in gently from your heart to the other's heart, because you don't want to be invasive in any way. You might only be able to touch the outer limits of the person's aura because of defense mechanisms that are in place preventing the person from being hurt again.

You can ask for healing as much as the soul self allows. You're not doing anything to violate the person's freedom of will, as everyone always has the choice to receive or not to receive. You can use everything suggested earlier in this book and in others, especially the trauma book [*Trauma and PTSD*] and heal the energy field.

Alter Beliefs

People wounded by what they witnessed have different beliefs they need to integrate. Beliefs form and fashion the person. They can hold in shame and powerlessness. This one has a memory of a client who felt powerless, guilty, and ashamed because he was unable to protect a younger sibling. Although he was only seven when the abuse occurred, he saw himself as the adult he'd become and believed he should have been able to help.

People see how they are now and apply that to their child selves. How can a seven-year-old protect a five-year-old sibling from an adult? This is where beliefs need to be changed and balanced. You might use the Belief plug-in or any other process you are aware of.

People who were young when they witnessed abuse need the belief that they were powerless at that time to intervene and stop it. They must realize that they did not, even as a twelve- or thirteen-year-old, have the power to change what the adult was doing. You can use the Belief plug-in or another technique. This one also uses PSYCH-K or BodyTalk, depending on which she believes will resonate most with the client.

If using affirmations, be aware that simply repeating an affirmation does not move the belief into the subconscious mind. Use all five senses to form an image of the new belief in action. You do not embed the belief that the person is entirely powerless; you embed that they were powerless at that time. You can balance that with another belief that they can help now, but back then they did not have the knowledge or strength to do anything; it was not their fault. You might want to install the belief: "When I was a child, I could not change what happened to my sister." You might follow that with, "Today, I can listen, support, and be her advocate."

Have them see themselves helping now by giving support and being an advocate. Have them bring an image to mind of what that would look like. Have them use all five senses so that the subconscious mind fully knows what that belief means. As an example, that man could imagine: "I'm listening to my sister. We are at the lake. I hear the gentle lapping of the water as it hits the dock. Sunlight sparkles off the water, and I smell fresh-mowed grass. I see the tears on my sister's face. We are connected heart to heart, and I listen to her." The power of just listening validates her and shows that he believes her and is there for her.

In the conversation, the one abused might say she wants to confront the perpetrator. That's where the one who felt powerless as a child can now say, "I am willing to go with you. I will stand there, and I will protect you. I couldn't protect you when you were five, but I can protect you now." That is another way to form the belief "I couldn't protect you when you were five, but I can do everything I can to protect you now." You could also form the belief by saying, "I stand in support of my sister (brother, whomever) because I have the power now." Support can be protection, listening, or holding hands. It can be whatever is needed.

Install New Beliefs in the Subconscious

It is important to establish the subconscious belief that the witness was not at fault for the abuse. You can adjust the belief as needed. You might also need to address survivor's guilt. Some options include:

- "What happened to _____ was not my fault."
- "It was not my choice who was abused."
- "It was not my responsibility who Dad (Grandpa, etc.) chose to abuse."

Sometimes you must develop what seem to be obvious beliefs:

- "I was only seven years old and weighed 60 pounds. I did not have the ability or strength to stop the abuse."
- "It was beyond my capabilities to stop the abuse."

You can add beliefs for their present state:

- "I now have the power and ability to support _____."

There are times the observer buried what happened or wasn't aware that what was happening was bad. Depending on the situation, you can install beliefs such as:

- "I didn't know it then but I know now that what happened to _____ was terrible (or choose the appropriate descriptive word)."
- "I didn't know it then but I know now that what _____ said was true."
- "I was only _____ years old and believed what Dad (Mom, Grandpa) said was right. I know different now."

Balance the Witnesses' Energy Field

When working with people who witnessed abuse, you need to balance their energy fields. You need to remove the perpetrator's energy from them and the energy they carry of the one who was abused. You also need to remove the guilt, shame, and other feelings the observer developed at that time. Just as you can find fear within the one who was abused, you can find fear in the one who witnessed the abuse. You can find shame in the one who did the abuse, and you can find shame in the one who witnessed the abuse. The witnesses' feelings might be those of the perpetrator, the one abused, or their own feelings.

This is a fairly simple process that you can use if you are comfortable doing it. Know your limits. Ask your clients where they are feeling tense or tight, such as their shoulders, and ask them to focus on that area. Have them connect to that energy, and ask them, "What do you feel?" Then ask, "What is the first thing that comes to your mind?" The answer might be shame, anger, fear, and so on. Then ask, "Who's shame (or anger or fear)?" In other words, whose energy are they carrying? Sometimes they will name one person; other times, they will name two people or a group of people.

Have them command all the energy of the shame (that is not theirs, for example) to come forth. They could command: "I call for the anger of other people I am carrying to come out of me." When that energy comes up, have them say, "You are not mine. I will not carry you any longer. Leave now."

After that energy is gone, have them focus on the area of their bodies that had hurt. Ask, "Does it feel better? Do you notice any differences?" They will usually say that they feel lighter or that they have more mobility. If they still feel discomfort, have them call forth their own feeling energy: "I call forth my energy of shame (or anger, fear, powerlessness, etc.)."

When their energy comes forth, remember that one purpose of that energy is to protect them. To release that energy, have them thank the energy and then release it: "Thank you for protecting me. I don't need you anymore. I have learned what you can teach me." Depending on the person, you could have them say, "Thank you for teaching me. Thank you for letting me know how terrible I felt about what happened. I don't need you anymore. Leave now." Have them take a deep breath and breathe the energy out and away from them.

You might need to do further encodement work. Ask their healing team: "Please remove the artificial encodements holding in the energy of the emotion and repair the damaged and altered encodements holding in that energy." You might ask the soul-healing team to find and bring back all the pieces the person lost when it happened. Go through the steps to clean, repair, and heal all the pieces, and then ask the soul-healing team to fully integrate them so that your clients have the wholeness of their energy within them. This assists them to stand firmly in their truth. Repeat the process to send away the energies of guilt, shame, regret, or whatever feelings they are working with.

Replace Destructive Beliefs

The one who witnessed the trauma might have developed destructive beliefs reinforced by the perpetrator, such as: "You can't do anything. You're just standing there. You can't protect anyone." You can assist the witness to develop beliefs that counteract the non-supportive ones:

- "I am strong and powerful."
- "I am self-confident."
- "I am an advocate for and support those who have been abused and hurt."

Beliefs that don't directly relate to the abuse can have powerful effects. They can be countered by other beliefs, such as:

- "I passionately and clearly express my truth."
- "I passionately and clearly do what is necessary to live my truth."

You can install a belief that addresses two areas:

- "No matter what happened in the past, I now speak my truth."
- "I now stand up for my sibling."

Some people feel powerless because they couldn't assist when they were young, and now, in the present, they think they're powerless everywhere. That can be countered with the belief:

- "I am now powerful and in control of my thoughts, actions, and words."

You can find more examples of positive beliefs on the internet. Search for affirmations in the topic you are working with:

- affirmations, abuse
- affirmations, personal power
- affirmations, inner truth

Other keywords include:

- trauma
- sexual abuse
- losing weight
- success
- good relationships
- communication

Read through them with the intention of finding ones for yourself or for another person. You can then modify them to better fit your or their needs.

For those who have witnessed abuse and feel guilt and shame because they couldn't stop it, the goal is to relieve the shame and guilt. They can breathe out the feelings, or you can use encodement work and then install beliefs that support your clients now in how they want to be. Sometimes you need to have them imagine their child selves, and then, as they are now, kneel in front of that young version of themselves and talk to them: "I'm so sorry you went through this. I'm so sorry you feel responsible because you could not do anything. I will take care of you now."

Call on your healing team to use the plug-ins to bring healing to that child. Once the child feels healed, have the person as an adult invite the child to move into their hearts and come together as one. Then ask the healing team to integrate the encodements of both people.

When witnessing abuse, the person can dissociate — send away the part of them that hurts. That might be the part that feels powerless. Anger, fear, and shame can be attached to those pieces. It's important for that to be healed. The soul-healing process found in the plug-ins helps tremendously.

Again, know your limitations. There are certain things you can do without doing therapy. If you get to a point where it feels like therapy is needed, it is time to refer your clients to someone else, unless that is your background.

Unsupportive Witnesses

Margaret: Perhaps the witnesses were too young to know what was happening, they were in alignment with the perpetrator, or they believed what they were witnessing was loving action. They didn't learn until they were older that what they witnessed was wrong, and they might still not believe that what they saw was wrong.

A witness who believes there was no problem will not likely come to you for healing. Instead, the one who was abused will say to you, "My brother still refuses to admit what happened."

Sometimes people are in alignment with the perpetrators because, as children, they trusted their fathers (or mothers, grandparents, family friends, etc.) but now they realize what happened was wrong. These people might need a belief such as, "I did not know then, but I know now. I now give my support." That person might need to just apologize to the one who was abused: "I am so sorry. I didn't know. I understand now. I couldn't be there for you." They can make amends.

Margaret: There was a situation in which people didn't tell the truth and continued to lie about what they saw. Do I, as the healer, do long-distance healing if they're amenable to it, or do I just let it be?

Send them all the love they need so that they have the support and the ability to resolve things now.

CHAPTER THIRTY-SEVEN

Incest: Bargains and Betrayal

Amiya

As you read this book, you are discovering that you are not only a learned scholar but also a person with an open heart; you have compassion and empathy. What a gift you are being as you do the processes we have given you. Many of you have held a person in mind during these processes.

Yes, we're almost finished. You can breathe a sigh of relief, right? You have done wonderful witnessing and work. In this chapter, we bring our work with incest to a close. Yes, there is so much to heal. Use the processes we have given you. Your healing guides and healing teams are ready to work with you. Adapt what you have received for your needs.

As you know, incest is a tremendous betrayal in every way. It is a betrayal of what an adult is called to do with a child, which is to love, nurture, and protect — not to abuse. We want to address an additional betrayal: One who is incested often attempts to make a bargain with the abuser. They say they will do what the abuser wants if the abuser will leave their sibling(s) alone. The abuser says, "Okay, as long as you keep that promise, I will not do that." Then, years later, perhaps as an adult, the person learns that their abuser incested their sibling(s) as well, meaning they were doubly betrayed. They were betrayed in the sexual realm and in the deal they made.

Think about that a moment. They had a semblance of trust, maybe a residual trust, that the one abusing them would not abuse anyone else in the family, but their sense of good that could come from that was destroyed.

Everything we have said in healing betrayal applies here. Use the foundational plug-ins on this betrayal as you have used them on other wounds. This is a deep wound. Ask that God fill them with all the love they need but didn't receive. There is an ocean of betrayal energy in these cases. People who have been incested see the whole of the events, no matter how long the incest lasted, as one event. Of course, it was many events, but they bring that awareness into one energy. Then there is the next betrayal of when they discover the deal with the abuser has been violated. They are betrayed again. They close themselves down even more to trusting people. It brings an additional layer of pain, betrayal, and mistrust into their hearts.

Remove the Energy of Betrayal

In the *Hidden Structures* book, we discuss the golden center within the physical heart. I'd like you to connect with that golden center now. Go deep within the physicality of your heart, the energetic substance of your physical heart.

Everyone has this golden structure. It doesn't matter whether they appear to have love energy in them or not. As they grow up, even before they are born, the golden structure can be enveloped with pain. Very few people know about the golden structure, but it is there. When people have been repeatedly betrayed, including the biggest betrayal that they were not able to protect their siblings, something similar to concrete or steel forms around their golden structure. Within the golden structure is also the energy of trust. Yes, trust is in other places, but it is also in the golden structure. The more that golden structure is hidden, the less trust they are able to have for anyone, including themselves.

This betrayal is deeply felt because they offered their abuse as a sacrifice to protect another. When they find out that it didn't, they become hopeless and despaired, feeling everything they went through had no value.

We're not going to repeat all we've done before, but use those strategies. We're going to work with beliefs, including trust. There are various beliefs and layers of pain to work through. Work with the four foundational plug-ins over and over again. Use them as you work with cellular memory. Look for areas of mistrust in the DNA, both as miasmas and similar patterns of wounding that go back generations. When you work with extreme pain, such as with incest and trauma, look for changes in the DNA. Use the information in each of the books about the energy field.

When you work with women, remove the energy of incest and betrayal from their eggs. Women form all the eggs they will ever have while in the womb. Request of their healing team: "Please clear the encodements of incest from every egg." This clearing is especially helpful before a woman has children. Work separately with the DNA. Use the Heal the DNA plug-in throughout the layers of healing.

Abused people will mistrust God. Your first higher power, your first god, is the first person in control of your life — a parent or parental figure. When a parent betrays you and you come to know there is a higher power beyond your parent, the mistrust of your parent transfers to a mistrust of God, whether it be of Amma or Abba. (Many people prefer to use a non-personal term for God. Amma and Abba are personal terms. In another language, they mean Mama and Daddy.) If that parent, the representation of God, betrays you, you feel betrayed by God. You always wonder: "If God loves me, why did God allow this to happen? God could have stopped this."

Unless a person has dealt with these issues personally, we suggest that he or she is best addressed by a person who is knowledgeable, wise, and deeply spiritually connected. When people talk about having anger toward Spirit, God, or their parents, you become a listener and send love. Listen, affirm, and have no doubt whatsoever in what your clients are saying. Be present as you surround your clients with as much love as you can. As you listen to this person's pain, you might ask their healing team to please do encodement work as needed. You might also need to ask your healing team to do encodement work on you.

Install New Beliefs and Work with Encodements

Sometimes it's difficult to come up with beliefs. As we said earlier, one way to find beliefs is to go to your internet search engine and type "affirmations, trust," "affirmations, sexual abuse," "affirmations, anger," or other keywords. You will find affirmations other people have developed for specific purposes. You can then adjust the affirmations for you or for the person you are working with.

If you want to stay with encodements, use the Belief plug-in. You have several methods of working with beliefs, so choose the method you believe will work best for your clients. Ask their healing team which is the best method. You can dowse or muscle test your clients (or yourself) to determine the best method for them. If they ask specifically for a particular method, use that one.

The key is to install the new belief so that the old, nonsupportive belief is removed. If the pain is not deep, what you might call "ordinary mistrust," then you might only need one or two sessions to fully install the new belief. But when you are dealing with mistrust on the deepest level, such as the betrayal of incest and not being able to save a sibling, you might need several sessions. These sessions could be interspersed with other encodement and healing work. Determine the layers that need to be addressed. One is people's beliefs surrounding their failure to protect their sibling(s). In many cases, their deal with the abuser delayed their sibling(s) from being abused, so their sacrifice had some value.

As you work with your clients, take what they say at face value. This is their truth. There could be other interpretations, but you are working with their truth. Do not further betray them by expressing doubt. With encodement work, you do not need to be a therapist, but you need to know when to refer your clients to a therapist. Your job is to listen with acceptance. Any type of abuse, including sexual abuse, triggers past-life abuses. People can have dreams and memories that are not necessarily of this lifetime, but they're still valid memories. As they go through healing, they will learn to separate what happened into specific categories, such as whether an incident was from this lifetime or another lifetime. It could take years for them to be able to do that.

Showing doubt, not listening, checking your phone, or doing something else distracting will be interpreted as betrayal. It will confirm for them that nobody is willing to witness with them, be with them, or stand firmly with them. Another betrayal, of course, is sharing what you have learned, unless you are a therapist sharing information with permission. Only work on a deep level if you are trained to do so. Professionals have learned many nuances. Always be in a place of love within your heart source as you listen, affirm, and do interior healing work.

Encodement plug-ins are valuable forms of the work we teach. Each contains encodement work as well as the soul-healing process. Many people respond well when you take them through the soul-healing process. Incest victims and other sexual-abuse victims describe feeling as if parts of their souls were ripped out of them, sullied and dirtied. With the soul-healing process, you call those pieces back and cleanse them, which your clients can sense, feel, and imagine. It's more difficult to imagine encodements, as they are abstract. Those who are sensitive can feel a difference with encodement work even if it is not easily imagined.

Use Prayer

If your clients are not familiar with encodements but they are familiar with prayer, make a commitment to pray for them. If you work with a person for whom the tradition of prayer is important, asking to pray for them is meaningful. The healing work you do, including encodements, is prayer. Even if you do not do encodement work, their healing team works with them when you pray for them. Your healing team automatically does encodement work. They did it before Amma brought in the information about encodements.

A powerful prayer is to ask for your clients to be filled with all the love they needed but didn't receive. You can do this daily. Do this daily for yourself. That love, as powerful as it is, must go through the energies of mistrust, betrayal, and pain. People, including you, can put up blocks to receiving love. Send love over small amounts of time, unless it's for you; send yourself love for as long as you feel comfortable receiving it.

Remember that when you connect with clients who have been abused and you go heart to heart with them with a beam of energy, gently send that beam to where it touches their energy fields. Then gently move through the layers of their energy field. You might feel a resistance before you get to the heart center. Never violate them by sending your heart energy forcefully and deeply, especially when there is resistance.

Process Guilt from the Body's Natural Response

We have one other issue to discuss as we close the topic of incest. Many people who experienced incest feel guilty because they felt some pleasure or enjoyment during the act. The pleasure can range from feeling special due to the abuser's attention or to the body's response. You are aware that your body responds, correct? When you watch a sensual movie, hear an erotic story, or read a book containing sex, your body might automatically respond. Men might get erections. Women might experience vaginal secretions and tingling in the genitalia. Those are natural responses you do not intend to happen.

When a person's genitals are touched, in many cases the body will respond. A woman can orgasm. A man can ejaculate. That does not mean they enjoyed the situation. You have the paradox of hating what is happening but enjoying the attention. The earlier the incest begins, the more children feel they are receiving positive attention, unless it is physically painful. The older the people, the more they realize what is happening is not true love.

When people feel shame due to their bodies responding and any pleasure they experienced, there are several things that you can do. The first is to give facts about how the body responds. The body doesn't always respond, but it often does without you wanting it to. This one worked with a woman who felt shame and guilt over this issue. She asked the woman to imagine holding a kitten. She said, "Is the fur of that kitten soft? Do you intend for it to feel soft?" She then explained how, just as the woman's body responded to the softness of the kitten's fur, her body can respond to other kinds of physical stimulation. Find examples you can use about how the body sensually responds.

Healing involves many complexities; you can see how it is tangled. Not everyone will respond the same. Know your limitations. Do self-healing, and know you are doing the work of love.

***Louise:** This reminds me of years ago when my husband and I were in the process of renewing our foster license with the state. We attended a class about children who were sexually abused. Because of their natural response when they were touched, there could be sexual arousal, and we had to be very careful in personal interactions with them. For instance, giving hugs and kisses before bed was fine for some children, but others needed certain rituals to feel love and acceptance and not be triggered in any way.*

CHAPTER THIRTY-EIGHT

Remove the Patterns of Ritual Abuse

Amiya and Dr. Cathy

Amiya: We are going to discuss another difficult topic in a short period of time. We do not want a great deal of information in the book on this, as we do not want people in their egos trying to do things they have no training for. When we say "training," we are not talking about "step one, step two, step three." We mean the spiritual realm, where you are deep within your heart and stay in your heart source.

In this chapter, we will discuss ritual and satanic ritual abuse. It's a very heavy topic, is it not? All of you reading this, spin your chakras. Ask your heart source to extend to the farthest reaches of your aura, which is beyond the room you are in. As you grow spiritually, your aura extends.

This next process is something this one we speak through does when using BodyTalk. We will do this with your healing team, and we will call it the Wei Chi plug-in [see the appendix].

Focus on the issue you need help with, and ask your healing team to implement the Wei Chi plug-in. The wei chi is the protective energy of the body. Your encodement technicians will perform the following steps:

- remove all artificial encodements that interfere with the strength of your wei chi (or wei qi)
- balance and repair any damaged or altered natural encodements interfering with the strength of your general wei chi
- activate all inactive natural encodements that need to be activated for a strong wei chi
- examine yourself (the soul, the spirit) and create any natural encodements you need to make your wei chi strong
- find and bring back any pieces of you that were disassociated or sent away from being wounded
- clean, repair, and heal those pieces brought back and fully integrate them on all levels of your being — physical, mental, emotional, spiritual, and energetic
- harmonize your entire encodements system to what has been done
- use the entire Wei Chi plug-in again and apply it to the emotional wei chi
- use the entire Wei Chi plug-in again and apply it the wei chi affected by the weather — be it damp, cold, windy, or hot — on all levels
- repeat the Wei Chi plug-in on your wei chi that has been damaged by electromagnetic frequencies
- strengthen the wei chi against electromagnetic frequencies

Now your wei chi is strengthened on all levels as we continue with this chapter.

Ritual Sexual Abuse

There are differences between ritual sexual abuse and satanic ritual sexual abuse. Ritual sexual abuse and almost any repetitive sexual abuse by one person to another usually involves some type of ceremony. The perpetrators decide what they will do, and they usually approach people in the same way. There is not — and this is different from satanic ritual sexual abuse — a connection to darkness, as in worshiping an aspect of darkness. They do this not for darkness but because of their woundedness.

Ritual sexual abuse without the satanic element involves the darkness of woundedness within the abuser, but it is not related to any spiritual entity except those entities injected into the victim when there is penetration and especially ejaculation. For healing simple ritual abuse (meaning not connected with worshipping darkness), use the same techniques you have been using throughout this book. Repair the energy field in depth using the processes described in the *Human Energy Field* books: *Auras*, *Chakras*, and *Hidden Structures*.

Use the soul-healing prayer repeatedly, and teach it to your clients so that it can be used any time something comes up. First, connect with your soul-healing team. Say, "Please find and bring back all the pieces I lost when this wound took place." Then, "Please clean, repair, and heal all these pieces, and fully integrate them within me. Thank you."

Why do we suggest the soul-healing prayer instead of the Basic plug-in? You can certainly use the Basic plug-in. Your entire healing team is part of the soul-healing prayer. Many people seem to resonate more to the soul-healing prayer, as it feels more personal than standard encodement work. No matter which healing you do, your encodements team is always working to remove artificial encodements, repair damaged and altered natural encodements, activate those that were inactivated, and create new ones.

You do not have to do each step of the Basic plug-in with our clients, but we recommend that you do. It is very helpful to do encodement work, the Remove Victim Consciousness plug-in, and the Healing over Lifetimes plug-in. If you are aware that implants are present (energetic implants or physical implants), use the Implant Removal plug-in.

We're going to add some new information. Something happens in the brain of the person who is ritually abused. Think about neurology. When you form a habit, electrical impulses move through your brain. Some people call it "forming a pattern" in the neural network. The more this happens in the same way each time — perhaps the ritual is eating, violence, shopping, gambling, or turning on the television — a pathway forms in the brain. You need to remove those patterns as much as you can.

We will give you this process in the form of a plug-in, but your clients need to assist by not recalling memories of the abuse in their minds. Recalling the abuse retraumatizes them and their brains. Because recalling abuse is typical, you might need to repeat the process many times.

You need to allow healing to occur. A scab of sorts forms, and your clients should not "scratch at the scab." The more they focus on their memories without using prayer and healing, the more they anchor the pain, which keeps the pathway in the neural network active.

Remove the Energetic Pattern from Ritual Abuse

The following process releases the ritual part of the abuse:

Call for the consciousness of the abuse within the person. You can use the word "ritual" or "habitual." You will work with the consciousness formed during the pattern of abuse and relate to it as if it is an individual. It is a consciousness just as you are a consciousness; it is a manufactured consciousness. At first it was a thought form, and as the abuse repeated, it took form as an elemental. In long-term abuse, it can, in a sense, form a personality. That personality might take the shape or form of the chronic abuser.

As you call forth that consciousness, be sure that both you and your client are in your hearts. Remember what we did with the wei chi earlier. This is a form of protection that can protect you from your feelings about and responses to what happens. Declare to that consciousness: "You are not part of this person. You might think you are, but you are not part of this person." You can use the person's name.

You can call on Michael the Archangel, or state, "I am the Sword." If your clients are strong and able to do this, have them declare that they are the Sword. Be sure they connect with Michael the Archangel to receive the Sword. If that is not within their belief system, then you are the one with the Sword. Call on Archangel Michael to be there. Call on their favorite spiritual beings, which might include Yeshua, Buddha, All That Is, or Universal Energy. The term they use does not matter.

Sever the connection of the consciousness from the person with Michael's Sword. Place the Sword within the consciousness of the abuse, and after you sever it, transmute that energy. This is not a real being, so it is not as if you are trying to kill a human being or a spirit.

You are removing something created of pure energy. You can transmute that energy.

Proceed with your usual encodements work. Request the healing team to

- "Remove all artificial encodements that have been holding in this consciousness."
- "Remove all artificial encodements of the consciousness that have been left in the brain."
- "Remove all artificial encodements of the consciousnesses that have been left in the chakras."

Remember that you've already severed the consciousness; you're now removing everything that might attract that consciousness back. Request the healing team to

- "Remove all artificial encodements that have left any of the consciousness in the meridians."
- "Remove all artificial encodements that have left any of the consciousness in the DNA."
- "Remove all artificial encodements that have left any of the consciousness in the aura."

Here's a shortcut: "Remove all artificial encodements from any structure mentioned in the *Hidden Structures* book that are left over from the consciousness of this abuse."

Now we're going to do the same thing but substitute natural encodements for everything we just did with artificial encodements. Again, here's a shortcut: "Healing team, we ask you to use the same format we just used to remove artificial encodements to now repair damaged and altered natural encodements holding in the consciousness."

Here's something we have not spoken of much: "Healing team, if any structure we mentioned has encodements that are severely damaged and cannot be repaired, we ask you to replace them with new, healthy, and vibrant natural encodements." (You don't need to add the "new, healthy, and vibrant," but it assists the person you're working with if you say it aloud.)

Now we go to beliefs. Ask the healing team: "Using the Belief plug-in, install the belief 'No matter how often I was abused, I am still in my perfection.'" You can add this next belief to that one, or it can be separate: "Abuse does not change the essence of who I am." Or it can be worded another way: "No matter what happens to me, my essence as love incarnate remains."

You might come up with other beliefs appropriate for the person you are working with. We have mentioned several in this book. As you work more with your clients (or with yourself), you might become aware of other beliefs that need to be placed within them. It is good and helpful to always reiterate the beliefs, "I am Love Incarnate," and "I am the power and presence of God."

Here are some beliefs we do not mention often, but they are just as crucial:

- "I deserve true love." (This is not the fabricated love the abuser gave them but true love.)
- "I deserve to love someone with all my heart."
- "I deserve to be loved with all of someone's heart."
- "I deserve to love others."
- "I am the perfect, dearly beloved child of God."

If you find this is needed, ask the healing team:

- "Remove all artificial encodements and repair all damaged natural encodements holding this person in the shock of fight, flight, or freeze. Activate all needed natural encodements that will release this person from being frozen in the fight, flight, or freeze response."
- "If any new encodements need to be created, please create them, and activate natural encodements that release this person from the fight, flight, or freeze response."

Sometimes the fight, flight, or freeze response activates the hypothalamus-pituitary-adrenal axis. Ask the healing team:

- "Remove all artificial encodements holding the person in the hypothalamic-pituitary-adrenal axis."
- "Repair all damaged natural encodements holding the person in the hypothalamic-pituitary-adrenal axis."
- "Activate any natural encodements that need to be activated to release the hypothalamic-pituitary-adrenal axis."

- "Create any natural encodements needed so that the person can be released from the stuck-ness of the hypothalamic-pituitary-adrenal axis." This axis is important for the body's stress process, but it does not need to be stuck.

Lastly, activate the spiritual whirlwind process given to the world by Joshua David Stone (or popularized by him). Image a tornado above the person's head. Ask that this spiritual whirlwind, or this spiritual tornado, be of the exact vibration needed to clear the person's aura and energy field. The whirlwind is a little larger than the width of the person's aura. The bottom tip starts about 18 inches above the crown in the pranic tube and passes through the body and aura. The frequency/colors vary according to the frequencies needed to release the congestion in the aura.

You can call the whirlwind down three, five, ten, or more times, however many the person needs. Videos on YouTube explain the process, but be sure to search for "spiritual whirlwind" and "Joshua David Stone," as there is another spiritual whirlwind associated with a religion. This is a wonderful process to use for any kind of pain or trauma.

Satanic Ritual Sexual Abuse

Satanic ritual abuse is a complex problem. The people who were abused in this way need someone who is trained in either the psychological and spiritual realms, or they need to be trained by someone who has done this work.

The patterns that form in the neural network during ritual abuse also happens with satanic ritual abuse. There are additional complexities with this abuse due to the ritual worshipping or adoration of darkness. Keep in mind that someone who perpetuates this type of abuse has been deeply wounded. Everything we have said so far for ritual abuse — in any abuse — needs to be noted in satanic ritual abuse with some additions:

With satanic ritual abuse, the ritual includes the attempt to block out the person's light. It is of great importance and integral to healing that you stay in your heart source as you work with clients who have experienced this type of abuse. The steps we gave you to remove the consciousness of the ritual can be used to remove the sense or consciousness of darkness from your clients. You can use the same steps to remove any dark energy that has invaded them or any sense that they are evil.

Energetic structures were constructed in the people who experienced satanic ritual abuse. If you do not know how to release these structures or are unable to follow your healing guides' directions, you can cause a collapse of the structures within your clients' energy. This can cause great emotional and energetic damage.

Healing in this area is not something to undertake lightly. If you feel a deep calling to work with such people, then you need to get training. This one we speak through has worked in this area. She listened carefully to her healing guides even though she didn't call them at the time. During that time, she was told by her guides the reason she could not see the energies was because she believed what she was seeing rather than what she was being told. Remember that. This is why it is crucial to remain in your heart source.

When you work with someone who has been satanically ritually abused, be aware that the structures are connected to each layer of the aura and to the structures described in the *Hidden Structures* book.

As much as those who perpetrate this type of abuse attempt to invade the sacred space in the back of the heart chakra, one or more angels hold the Sword of Michael the Archangel and produce a great flame that prevents it. Structures are often created in front of the back of the heart chakra to prevent the people from entering that area themselves.

Something else can be involved with female victims of satanic ritual abuse. This might be difficult to hear or read, but in many cases, a goal of satanic ritual abuse is to impregnate the female and then abort the fetus to capture the soul of the child within the structures they made. They use a process to release that soul. This one is starting to have tears in her eyes remembering working with someone in this area.

You also need to look for entities. You have been shown how to find entities in the second chakra. Also look in each chakra. They are hidden in the layers. Sometimes they are hidden in the structures. If you do not have the training and that connection with your healing guides, do not do this work. Do not work through your little ego. If you are able to do this work, you will work with layers and go back and forth between them, removing structures and releasing the trapped souls of embryos or fetuses. It is a long and difficult process.

Another layer in healing is removing the energies that block the person's connection with spirit in the deepest way. The issue is trust. Someone might say, "How can we trust a God who allows such things to happen?" No matter what happens, that person is never without light surrounding them.

Stay within the Light

We have no more to say about satanic ritual abuse even though there is much more. This type of abuse is real. Yes, some people make up these experiences, but many times these are not pure fabrications; their memories can come from other lifetimes. When you become aware of people who have been abused in this way and you know you're not able to work with them that deeply, give them support by holding them in love.

When working with clients who have experienced such abuse, remember to very gently connect heart to heart if they allow it. Very gently send that beam of energy to their aura, and gently enter the aura until you feel a resistance from their energy. Do not invade. In many cases, you might not be able to penetrate too far, or you might not be able to tell where that resistance is. Then imagine your hands are filled with love, and hold them within that love. Send that love to them. They might reject it, but that is not your concern. The love is there if they need it.

Now call on your healing team. Begin with: "Please use the Basic plug-in to heal any wounds that surfaced in me as I read these words." Some of you might have experienced new wounds.

Next, request: "Please use the Healing over Lifetimes plug-in to heal any memories that surfaced from other lifetimes. Use the Remove Victim Consciousness plug-in, even if I don't feel like a victim, to remove any powerlessness I feel." Or you can say, "Implement all the steps to remove victim consciousness to address the powerlessness I feel in the face of those who have experienced such horrors."

People would prefer to deny that such darkness exists, but it does exist. These events are part of the dark side, which is the difficult thing about this book. Stay in your heart source, stay within the light, and support those in pain during their recovery.

Amma wants us to tell you that she is now enfolding you in her love. Our blessings and love to you.

You Can't Always Believe Your Eyes

Dr. Cathy: This is the story Amiya wanted me to share with you: I worked with a precious woman for about eighteen months, and it was through that experience that I learned about structures. People think I'm clairvoyant because I can describe things in detail. Some of that has developed, but I am clairsentient and claircognizant. I've always wanted to "see," and I have a very few times.

I was chatting with spirit about my not being able to see and how I wanted to. The answer I received was simple, powerful, and true: "If you could see, you would believe what you see and not what we tell you."

I had an experience in which I thought Mother Mary was reaching into the energy field of this precious woman I spoke of. Mother Mary was going to help me dismantle a structure. Her hand was ready to enter the aura, and suddenly I heard a strong, "No!" I stopped immediately. It was not Mother Mary, but a disguised being who was going to disrupt what I was doing.

People say they won't believe it unless they see it. Sometimes you can't believe your eyes. That experience was a huge lesson for me.

CHAPTER THIRTY-NINE

Perpetrators Also Need to Heal

Amiya

You have carried much pain over the course of this book: the pain of those you know who have experienced sexual abuse, your pain, and the pain of those you don't know. You have imagined what this is like for them and tapped into their pain. Carrying that pain in the way you have has released this energy and brought healing to the planet. You have been very generous, and we thank you for your service.

Before we begin this last chapter about sexual abuse, connect with your healing team, and make this request: "Please apply the Healing over Lifetimes plug-in to every unhealed wound that has anything to do with sexuality or sexual abuse in any realm that surfaced for me as I read these messages."

Those who many call perpetrators, we call precious souls. That might seem to be a difficult idea for people who have been abused. This is where you come to a separation between what you know deep within you. All the people on this planet, no matter what they have done or not done, are precious souls. They are love incarnate. Some people seem soulless to you. Their expressions are blank. They seem to have no feelings about anything they have done — no empathy, sympathy, or contrition.

How does a person come to be that way? Some people are born with neurological deficits in their brains. These deficits need to be resolved for them to have empathy and to understand the impacts of what they have done. If you read some of the recent literature, you will see that some people have less blood flow to certain parts of their brains. The blood activates nerves and energy centers related to empathy and compassion. When you read some of these stories, as this one has, you realize that much happens neurologically. Sometimes those neurological changes occur in utero or during the birth process.

Feeling anger for what happened to a person who was abused is natural. You and the abused person must work through that anger and pain. We have given you ways to do that in this and previous books. Some people need different strategies than what we have given you. If you are a therapist reading this book, you can use your standard way of working with people and do encodement work internally.

Most Perpetrators Were Abused

Almost all perpetrators were sexually abused as infants, young children, or as older children. You have compassion for those who have been sexually abused. We challenge you to open your compassion to those who were sexually abused and then became perpetrators. Some therapists, including this one we speak through, find it difficult to work with perpetrators. It has been difficult for her to find compassion for those who cause such pain, such as in others she has worked with who were abused. We challenge her to open her heart to compassion for those whose brains were affected by their abuse.

The methods you use to bring a perpetrator peace and healing are the same you use for any person who was sexually abused. In addition, you must deal with the patterns that formed in their brain's neural network that cause them to release the energy of their abuse and subsequent impulses in a sexual manner. You might not be aware that some men (and women) with the impulses or desires to abuse others did so once or twice and were so horrified by their actions that they killed themselves. Some people go to great lengths to keep away from children. They choose not to have children. You do not see the struggles and pain many who have these impulses go through when they wall off the pain and shame of what was done to them and what they have done to others. In other words, they push their souls away. They push their love incarnate-ness away.

Why do people perform what you call "horrific" acts? The reasons depend on the person. You, as love incarnate, as the power and presence of God, have one response: to be with them in a place of love. You do not have to work with them individually, but we challenge you to be love incarnate and recognize them as love incarnate. Send them love. Use the same processes we have given you in this book.

You might not want to work with people who have done such things or if you're not a therapist. This is a special calling. You must be totally yourself as love incarnate. You must go deep within your heart source and stay there. Now, go deep within your sacred space in the back of your heart center. Call for those spiritual beings who can assist you to be only love for those who are so desperately wounded. You might see those who need help on the news. They have been arrested for what they have done. Immediately go into your heart source. If you feel revulsion toward them as people and not just toward their actions, those feelings are signs that you are not in your heart source.

Go into your heart source. Send them love energy. If you have difficulty sending love energy, know it is just as difficult for them to accept love energy. The harder they are — the less light in their eyes, the windows of the soul — the more layers of hardness they have built around them to keep away any energy of love, caring, and compassion.

Yes, people might come to you feeling horror about who they think they are. They are willing, on some level, to do something to overcome their impulses. Usually, they will not come unless ordered by the court system. The primary reason traditional therapy rarely works for those who have such impulses is that healing needs to take place in the spiritual realm. Traditional treatment ignores accessing people's spirits, and prayer is not fully accepted.

You can help if you wish. You can help by surrounding abusers with love. You do not need to know them, and they do not need to know you. Every time you come in touch with your anger, revulsion, or abhorrence toward abusers, first accept your response. If you deny your feelings, you push them within. Return to your heart source. Connect with your healing team, and ask them to find the wound within you that causes you to respond in such a way.

Take Additional Steps for Healing

You might notice we're not giving you step-by-step instructions on how to help those who might come to you or those you have learned about. Since you are reading this book, you have the steps for working with encodements to help people who have been sexually abused. Use those same steps.

There are some additions. For example, look for generational abuse. Request their healing team to please use the Heal the DNA plug-in. You will need to call forth their energy of being perpetrators, which might contain the energy of a parent, a grandparent, or another. Go back to where you have been instructed to call forth those energies when working with abuse victims. Call forth these same energies, and help the abusers release them. You will be working with the pain of their past when they were abused as well as the pain that wells up when they address their past pain.

When working with these broken people, it is crucial that you do not send them anger, revulsion, or abhorrence. If you cannot be in that deep place within your heart source, in your sacred space in the back of your heart chakra so that you connect with them with love, then do not do anything. Do not add anything else to them that is not love. You do not do this work from vengeance; you do this work from a place of deep healing and compassion.

As people heal, they need to come to a place where they can recognize their pain and the pain of those they harmed. They need to forgive themselves so that they can truly heal. If you think they don't deserve forgiveness, this shows your woundedness. Even for the worst things you have done or not done, you deserve to forgive yourself. Forgiving yourself does not mean what you did or didn't do was right or that consequences are resolved. It means you release your shame and guilt, acknowledge what you learned, and accept that you are love incarnate.

As with healing from any trauma, when feelings or symptoms

surface for your clients, connect with your healing team, and ask them to use the four foundational plug-ins. Symptoms can include inappropriate arousal, the desire to be in a place they should not be, and thoughts or desires that are precursors to abuse.

Working with those who are so broken requires special people. Those facilitating healing need to be trained in the psychological dynamics involved. Facilitators must be able to remain in their hearts no matter what they hear. They must be fully cognizant that they are working with people who are as they are, love incarnate.

Remember, this book is about working with energies in the third-dimensional realm. It does not focus on deeper spiritual explanations of why these things happen. If you go into the spiritual dynamics of love, people can use what you call "spiritual bypassing" to avoid working with their pain. You want them to realize that they are love incarnate, and they must continue to work with healing. Help them get in touch with the gifts and talents they have denied. Continue doing the spiritual healing over and over. Use the Basic plug-in or do soul healing if they cannot understand encodements. For them to heal, they will need to connect spiritually. Spirit is always there, ready to connect with them.

Very simply, use all the tools we've given you in any of these books to work with these people. Help them connect with themselves spiritually. Help them believe that they are love incarnate. When they talk about a time when they hurt someone, they wounded themselves as well as the other. They need healing using the same tools you use when you do something you regret. You can then help them learn to cut the energetic cords between them and their victims. In addition, you can teach them how to send healing energy to their victims — if they can do so without being triggered to repeat abuse.

For abusers to heal, their childhood wounds that trigger abusive actions need to be healed. This includes impulse control. Once they give in to the first impulse, it's much more difficult to overcome the second impulse and then the third until any impulse control is gone. They lose themselves and push their souls away. This is why perpetrators are so difficult to move into healing.

There will be a time when researchers learn to activate the human brain to engender empathy, compassion, and impulse control. When this occurs, many people will be helped. There is a dark side to learning to activate the brain, as those who want to control people would also learn how to work with the brain. Everything seems to have the dark and the light, does it not?

This Is a Deep Calling

You have heard it said that there must be a special place in hell for those who do these things to others. There is a special place of healing for everyone in all situations. Society needs to believe each person is sacred. Society needs to heal in this area. Your prison systems have no real sense of rehabilitation, because the emphasis is on retribution. If you instead had treatment centers devoted to healing in all areas, you would have true rehabilitation. When we speak of rehabilitation, we are speaking of people coming to know who they truly are as love incarnate and the power and presence of God.

You can use many other strategies to bring healing to the perpetrator. Integrate your spiritual, energetic, and cognitive methods of healing. Your job is to be in your heart source. You can use the methods given in these books, including releasing the genetic lineage. How far back does the genetic lineage of abuse go? Ask your healing guides to help you determine how far back you need to work with a person to identify the beginning of generational sexual abuse. [**Note from Dr. Cathy:** As to the number of ancestors, ten generations of ancestors is 1,022 people. Physical abuse was not outlawed in the U.S. until the 1870s. The true prevalence of sexual abuse was still being argued when I was a new therapist in the 1970s.]

If you feel called to work with perpetrators, it is a deep calling. It requires you to step into the darkness and hold their light. You must battle the consciousness of darkness within those wounded on a level that requires you to be an immovable force in your heart source. You cannot deviate from being an instrument of love and the power and presence of God. You cannot help another release shame if you feel shame for them.

For success, they must be willing to do the work, but few are. Society has deemed them unable to be helped. They can be, but they need to be surrounded by love and care. In working with them, you help them release shame. You help them come in touch with the knowledge and wisdom they can gain. They can do this if they are willing. They will never be willing if a person is not there to hold space for them as love incarnate. The tools in this book apply to what happened to them as children and what they have done as adults.

The perpetrators need to call forth the consciousness of the abuse done to them and the consciousness of themselves as abusers. Then they need to release that consciousness as we have shown you. You must be there firmly with Michael's Sword to transmute the energy that reveals itself. This takes great work and great spiritual knowledge of who and what love is. It takes the willingness to believe that even those who you might consider the worst of humanity — your Hitlers and Idi Amins — were also created from love. Something happened to deny the love.

Healing does not absolve their guilt of doing things that deeply harmed another. The event is still there and will always be there. But they can let go of their internal guilt. They can let their shame go even though it never takes away the fact that they brought harm to a person and possibly ruined a life.

Some things within this topic are difficult to realize and understand. The truth is that the deepest healing only comes after the perpetrators have left their bodies and they are welcomed with love. They are brought to a special place of healing.

All Life Is Precious

You might have many questions, but we're not going to answer them all in this book or any book in this series. Your society needs to grow in acceptance and love. It needs to respect life in all forms and recognize that all human life is sacred, be it what you judge guilty or innocent. (This includes your planet and the animals, for life in all forms is sacred.) Only when this world recognizes that human life is sacred — not money, corporations, profit, or greed — and you discover how to save that human life, can peace and healing come.

How can everyone come to know who they are as love incarnate and live that way? Is that a utopia? Is it the Garden of Eden before the fall? There are ways to bring this about. It takes much evolvement and spiritual connection. It takes the willingness of those who know that they are love incarnate to stand as love incarnate and send that love to any person, no matter what they have done or what has happened to them.

We challenge you to see all people as precious and as sacred as newborn babes, no matter their race, color, or socioeconomic status, even if they have grown well out of the precious newborn-baby stage. Begin that process with yourself and your family. If you can accomplish this with your family, with those you say you're supposed to love even if they have hurt you, then you can move to working with those who are the most damaged. That is a challenge, is it not?

Our blessings to you.

CHAPTER FORTY

Live Love

Amiya

This has been a difficult series of channelings, especially for the last half of this book. You have come in touch with many things that mean much to you regarding your sexuality and the things that have happened to you or to people you know.

This last chapter is of blessed love and peace to all beings, all sexual beings, on this planet. We had told this one that we would save the work regarding the transgender experience for this last chapter, but there really isn't anything separate for transgender people than there is for homosexual people, questioning people, or bisexual people. It doesn't matter what you call people regarding their sexual orientation. Members of the younger generation see no difference. Why does it matter who you love?

That is the true question: Why does it matter who people truly love? The Judeo-Christian scriptures say that God created people as male and female. Is that true? God created you as a human being exploring life in every way that you explore life, and that includes your sexuality. God created you to love. Maybe you identify as male, female, neither, or both; it does not matter in the least to the Creator. Those who say that people should not go against what the Creator created them to be have a very narrow focus and understanding of creation.

You can find love and affection between genders in the animal kingdom, including similar genders and same genders. Notice we said "similar" genders. You might think, "It either is or it isn't." No, there are similar genders, similar ways of expressing yourself. People you call "trans," the terminology in your world today, are assigned female or male at birth. You are probably aware that some babies are born with the genitalia of both genders. Parents decide how the child will be raised, whether as male or female, and the genitalia that the parents do not want the child to have are surgically removed. A person makes that decision for the child. They might make the wrong decision.

There are more biological differences than you will ever know, more than X and Y chromosomes. Hormones and neurotransmitters combine. How much estrogen flooded that growing being in the womb? What is the balance of serotonin and dopamine? Scientists have discovered more about this, but most of you are stuck in the knowledge you gained when you were children — what your parents or biology teachers said.

In biology class, some of you learned that brain cells could not be replicated. Scientists now know this is not true. An area in the brain produces stem cells that become neurons. You might have learned that your genetic code does not change. Now scientists know that 95 percent of your genetic code is changeable by your emotions and what happens to you from the chemicals you breathe, eat, and place on your body. Your DNA changes by the drugs you take. LSD produces chemicals that can change the DNA. Ayahuasca, which is used in healing and meditation in certain places, changes the DNA. People think of DNA changes as negative, but they are not necessarily bad. Some changes in the DNA release serotonin, which balances the dopamine-serotonin level and can lift depression and anxiety.

People Fear Differences

Many people are frightened by what can change in the body. Your personality can change, but the essence of who you are — love — does not. You were created by the Creator who knows all. If you were assigned female at birth (we will use that terminology), but you feel that you are literally male according to the way maleness is defined in your society, the Creator did not make a mistake. Your biology is different, but biology did not make a mistake.

Let us talk about transgender people. Before they have hormones placed in their bodies by injections or pills, they believe their inner selves do not match their outer selves. Like everyone, they have hormones of both genders within them, but their inner selves, the parts that cannot be quantified, determine whether they experience themselves as male or female. Those with hormones balanced between male and female can be what you call androgynous, if society does not push them to match their genitalia.

Many in your younger generation see no reason to differentiate or label who a person loves. They do not use the terms "gay," "straight," "trans," "pan," or "omni." They use the name "love." They express their love physically (and we're speaking of love physically shared by mutual consent) with those whom they love. Whoever they fall in love with is who they love.

You love some people in a romantic way and not others. They might be of one gender or the other, male or female. (We are using divisions again according to most in your society.) You can't always control who you fall in love with. Some people feel great fear and confusion when they fall in love with those of their gender. They never knew they could love a woman sexually or love a man sexually.

There is no negativity in who you fall in love with. Difficulties can arise if you fall in love with a person outside your committed relationship. You would have to sort those problems out and make some decisions. You can experience great pain in these situations.

Accepting who people are — how they identify themselves and who they love — is part of the first ray, the blue ray of accepting the will of God. It is not your business or our business who a person loves or how they identify themselves. It is not our business unless we are asked to assist in healing areas that interfere with coming to know who a person truly is.

Think about that for a moment. You know, in the depths of yourself, that another person's path is not your business unless your paths intersect. You have been growing and developing spiritually and expanding. You are aware that life is not as you were taught; it is much more expansive than you knew. You might have grown up with a God "he," a Creator "he." Now you realize that creation has a feminine aspect. Yet that feminine aspect of creation has told you there really is no feminine and masculine God; there is simply the Creator. But humanity needs to relate to God in an anthropomorphic way, which is why you have the division of a male and female God.

The primary question in your society is, "Why do differences in others produce such fear?" What people do in the privacy of their homes, even if they live in the apartment next door to you, has nothing to do with you. Why are people afraid of that? Why are people afraid of a person who is different than they are or who uses a different name for God? You're aware that the name Allah is not a different God. It is not any different from the name of God in Spanish — *Dios*. It is simply a language.

The only people affected by who they love are the people who love them and the people they love. The problem comes if those people they love do not return that same love.

Healing Brings Clarity

How do you bring healing to people who have been abused, who have been vilified, because they feel alien in their bodies? You use the same tools we have used every other way. You use the same tools you used in the trauma book and at the beginning of this book. All healing is healing.

People might come to you feeling alien in their bodies. They cannot express themselves as they believe they truly are because their bodies, when they look at them, betray them. What can you do to assist this person? You can do encodement work. Ask your healing team: "Please go into the wound that has the greatest effect in keeping this person from coming to clarity." That wound could be what parents have said, what neighbors have said, or what they read in the newspaper or in a book.

The first step is for them to gain full clarity. Use the Healing over Lifetimes plug-in to be sure that no wounds from other lifetimes have transferred that had to do with gender assignment. This could be an unresolved issue of being born male or female. Once that has been changed and healed, your clients will gain greater clarity. This does not mean they will change their minds about feeling alien in their bodies, but they will come to greater clarity within themselves, and that is the key.

The key to living the life a person was born to live, that they planned before they came into this life, is gaining clarity. To gain that clarity, it is important to heal the wounds that cause cloudiness: of the father not accepting, the mother not accepting, or the demeaning words or physical abuse from schoolmates, other people, or the church. Those wounds need to be healed for people to gain clarity about who they are. It does not matter whether that clarity is what gender they might identify as.

You might be familiar with people now wanting to be referred to as the pronouns "they" or "their." Other than you being confused about which pronoun to use, what business is it of yours what a person wants to be called? Doing that is called love and acceptance. There is no cure for homosexuality or transgenderism, because there is no illness; there is nothing wrong with it. The people having this experience were created that way. They are not violating the Creator's will. Their experiences are more complex than those of most people. People who have not had to struggle with whether they are gay or straight or whether they are male or female have no idea what that is like for those who do.

People are born the way they are because they cocreated themselves in that way with the Creator and their council, who they spoke with before they incarnated, before they even chose a body. You might think, "Why would anyone choose to be something so difficult that people would beat them up or kill them for being different?"

That is where healing needs to be done on this planet, the idea that everyone must be the same and exist according to the way it has been in perpetuity. It has never been one way in perpetuity. History is written by the victors. Scriptures are written by those in power. The one thing that needs to go through every scripture of every religion is love. You live love. You live that beautiful thing. When you cannot accept others as they are — we're speaking here of sexuality or gender identification — then you do not know about love.

Celebrate Differences

Imagine walking in a field of wildflowers or having a garden of 100 rose bushes. The flowers are not all the same, but do you pluck the ones that are different and throw them out? Do you scream at, denigrate, or destroy the flowers that are a different shade of color than the rest? Or do you enjoy the differences?

Enjoy the differences in human beings who express themselves differently. What would your world be like if everyone was an engineer? What would you do without your artists and healers? What would you do without those who enjoy cultivating the land and growing food? All people, whether they identify with a particular sexual preference or gender, even if it is not how their bodies looked when they were born, bring a difference and love and excitement to this world.

Let us end this book in this way: Love is what you were created from, and love is who you are. When you do anything that does not accept that love from which others were created, you have something to look at within yourself. When you judge others as being wrong because they love differently than you do or they see themselves differently than you see them, the issue is with you, in your relationship with yourself.

If you cannot accept others as they are, you are the problem; you are the one who is wounded. That does not mean that you accept toxic people in your life. It means that you accept them as they are, and then you make your decisions.

If you allow people to love who they love, as long as the others want to be loved in that way, and you listen to how they express themselves and how they look at the world, your life is richer. Diversity — whether in wildflowers, trees, or the same species — is meant for enjoyment. It is meant to stimulate your creativity of thought in how infinite the Creator is. The Creator who created a very tiny seed and turned it into a redwood, a Sequoia, or a baobab tree, is the same Creator who made that lumbering, emotional animal called the elephant. The same Creator who made the avocado made the zebra and the hippopotamus. Does that not demonstrate creativity to you, the infinite power and ability to create anything?

Humanity has such a fear of differences because it is not in touch with its heart. Love and accept everyone, because the Creator is the one who made all as they are. And here is a secret: The Creator makes no mistakes. The Creator did not make a mistake with you or with any being, tree, mineral, bird, or ocean. It is as it is.

Humanity interjected itself with its biases: This dam needs to be built, these trees should not be there, or that person should not live. When humans come to accept the sacredness of all life — *the sacredness of all life* — they will move from denigrating people because of who they love to accepting them. They will move from killing, torturing, and imprisoning people to discovering how they can help those people come to know who they truly are. There is a difference between rehabilitation and punishment. People vilify others for their sexual orientation or gender identification because humanity does not love as a whole.

What can you do as a lightworker? Spend time daily sending love to this planet, to the people who find it difficult to love because they were not loved in the way they needed. Some were born with different things that happened in their brains. Does that make the Creator wrong? No, that means there is a different life path. There's so much more that we could talk about in this area that is difficult to understand from your human perspective.

Nothing changes the love of God for anyone. There is nothing wrong with loving anyone. There is nothing wrong with expressing that love to those who wish to have that love expressed to them. This entire book has been about bringing healing to the areas in which people were not accepted as who they were, not loved in the way they wished to be loved, or forced to physically act for another in a way they did not want, whether that was rape or incest.

Come to know who you truly are: You are love. All people are love, even those you can't stand to be with. Go within and ask for healing and how you can be love for those people and for yourself. Sexuality is about showing love. It is not always physical, but it is always about love.

Thank you, learned scholar, for being with us. If you need healing from things that have surfaced, connect with your healing team and ask. You may call on us. We are with you. Our blessings to you.

APPENDIX

Encodements

Encodements are your smallest energy structures. They are introduced in Amma's first book *Change Your Encodements, Your Life, Your DNA*. I've prepared a video series that will give you an excellent introduction to encodements. You can access the videos at https://drcathyphd.info/chakras2.

Your Healing Team

You have a group of beings available to work with you on your healing. When working with the information brought through from Amma or Amiya, your healing team can consist of a number of members:

- Your soul self, which is what Amma prefers to call the higher self.
- Your body-soul, which is the soul of your body that keeps everything running. (This is close to what some call the body elemental. You, by the way, are the soul who has borrowed the body you inhabit, but you are not the soul of your body. You are not your body, right?)

- Your encodement technicians — beings trained to work with your encodements.
- Your soul-healing angels — angels who work specifically in what some call soul retrieval.
- Members of Amma's Healing Friends.
- Anyone else you invite.

You can connect with your healing team and get to know them. You can even ask for a name to call them.

The Heart Source

Before we begin each session, I invite people to join me in hearing what Amiya has to share. We have a ritual: First, we establish the heart source, which is one of Amma's favorite teachings. Second, we gather in the healing-lecture room.

I suggest you enter your heart source each time you open this book. Your heart source will keep you centered and grounded. When in your heart source, you can evaluate whether what you're reading or hearing is the truth. Your heart source is a wonderful place to be when evaluating information.

The most important thing about being in your heart source is that fear is not present. If you are in fear, you aren't in your heart source. There is much you can do from your heart source. Amma says she has told us very little about what all we can do from our heart source. For now, be in your heart source to stay centered, grounded, protected, and in a place of love.

To form your heart source, do the following:

- Focus on the front of your heart chakra and move deep within.
- Focus on the back of your heart chakra and move deep within.
- Focus on the front of your brow chakra and move deep within.
- Focus on the back of your brow chakra and move deep within.
- Connect your heart chakra and brow chakra with a beam of light. (Just imagine this.)
- Send that beam of light up to the center of the universe. (Don't worry about where that is.)
- Send the beam of light down to the center of Earth.

It takes some practice to construct and stay within your heart source. Practice it. Being in your heart source is a powerful tool when chaos surrounds you, no matter what the chaos is. Please go into your heart source before reading any of the messages in this book.

The Healing-Lecture Room

The healing-lecture room is a room of light where anyone who reads or listens to this material is gathered. When you're in the healing-lecture room, you are with all who avail themselves of this material. Remember, there is no time.

Whenever I establish the room, the perimeter is surrounded by angels. The angels are often from the bands of Archangel Michael, Raphael, or Gabriel. For these messages, Amma's Healing Friends surrounded the perimeter. They also infuse the room as well as your heart source with an electric violet light.

Consciously join us in this room. We are all here with you.

Plug-Ins

When I began working with encodements, I found that I was repeating the same requests. I asked the encodement technicians whether there was an easier way to do this, and they responded yes! They said I could assemble a collection of steps for them to complete and give that collection a name. I call each collection of steps a plug-in.

When you ask your healing team to please use a specific plug-in, they know what to do. Using plug-ins simplifies the process and saves time. You don't even need to know the steps of the plug-in although it helps to be familiar with them. Following are the plug-ins Amiya refers to in this book.

Basic Plug-In

Focus on the issue you need help with, and ask your healing team to implement the Basic plug-in.

Your encodement technicians will perform the following steps:

- remove all artificial encodements related to, interfering with, or preventing what you are focusing on
- repair any damaged or altered natural encodements related to,

interfering with, or preventing the balancing of whatever you are focusing on

- deactivate or remove any natural encodements related to the issue that are no longer needed

Your soul-healing angels will perform the following steps:

- find and bring back all pieces of your energy lost during the wounding event
- clean, repair, and heal all pieces
- integrate all pieces within you

Your encodement technicians will perform the following steps:

- activate any inactive natural encodements related to the issue that need to be activated
- create and activate any new natural encodements needed that you do not have but need
- harmonize the encodement system

Healing over Lifetimes Plug-In

Focus on the issue you need help with, and ask your healing team to implement the Healing over Lifetimes plug-in.

Your encodement technicians will perform the following steps:

- remove all the artificial encodements resulting from the core wound from this lifetime for the issue you are working on
- repair the damaged and altered natural encodements resulting from the core wound of this lifetime for this issue

Your soul-healing angels will perform the following steps:

- find and bring back all pieces lost at the core wound
- clean, repair, and heal all pieces
- integrate all pieces within you

Your encodement technicians will perform the following steps:

- activate all inactive natural encodements needed to assist in healing this wound from this lifetime for this issue
- create any natural encodements needed to assist in the healing of this wound from this lifetime for this issue

The wound from this lifetime may have triggered a wound that occurred in a **past lifetime**.

Your encodement technicians will perform the following steps:

- remove all the artificial encodements resulting from the core wound from the past lifetime
- repair the damaged and altered natural encodements resulting from the core wound of the past lifetime

Your soul-healing angels will perform the following steps:

- find and bring back all pieces you lost at the core wound
- clean, repair, and heal all pieces
- integrate all pieces within you

Your encodement technicians will perform the following steps:

- activate all inactive natural encodements that are needed to assist in healing this wound from the past lifetime
- create any natural encodements needed to assist in the healing of this wound from the past lifetime

Similar wounds in **parallel lifetimes** may have been triggered from the wound in the current lifetime you are aware of. Your encodement technicians will perform the same steps as above, substituting "parallel lifetimes" for "past lifetime."

The wound from this lifetime may have triggered similar wounds in **future lifetimes**. Your encodement technicians will perform the same steps as above, substituting "future timelines" for "past lifetime."

Implant Removal Plug-In

Focus on the issue you need help with, and ask your encodement technicians to implement the Implant Removal plug-in.

Your encodement technicians will perform the following steps:

- remove the artificial encodements holding on to the implant
- remove the natural encodements holding on to the implant
- remove the encodements of the belief that you need the implant
- remove all the encodements from any lifetime, past, present, future, or parallel

- remove all the encodements from any connections to your soul family
- remove all the encodements from any connection to your monadic family
- remove all the encodements from any galactic influences
- remove the encodements of the implant itself

Your soul-healing angels will perform the following steps to bring back the pieces of you whose absence is either holding on to the implant or preventing the healing from the effects of the implant:

- find and bring back all pieces of your energy lost during the wounding event
- clean, repair, and heal all pieces
- integrate all pieces within you

Your encodement technicians will perform the following steps:

- activate all inactive natural encodements needed to assist in healing this implant
- create any natural encodements needed to assist in the healing of this implant
- harmonize the encodement system

Remove Victim Consciousness Plug-In

Focus on the issue you need help with. Your encodement technicians will implement the Remove Victim Consciousness plug-in.

Your encodement technicians will perform the following steps:

- remove all artificial encodements holding on to victim consciousness
- repair damaged and altered natural encodements holding on to victim consciousness
- remove artificial encodements holding on to the energy that power is outside of you
- repair damaged and altered natural encodements holding on to the energy that power is outside of you
- remove the natural encodements brought in that say power is outside you

Your soul-healing angels will perform the following steps:

- find and bring back all pieces of your energy lost during the wounding event
- clean, repair, and heal all pieces
- integrate all pieces within you

Your encodement technicians will perform the following steps:

- create or activate the natural encodements of power within you
- create or activate natural encodements of you being able to access your power
- harmonize the encodement system

Heal the DNA Plug-In

Focus on the issue you need help with. Your encodement technicians will implement the Heal the DNA plug-in.

Your encodement technicians will perform the following steps:

- use the Basic plug-in to balance the wound most interfering with your intention
- use the Basic plug-in to balance the next wound most interfering with your intention
- use the Basic plug-in to balance the next wound most interfering with your intention
- link the DNA to the divine blueprint (This is a complex series of steps your healing team will perform.)
- use the Implant Removal plug-in to remove implants and intense, congested energies from each gene of the male DNA:

Genes 1–22

- all adenine
- all cytosine
- all guanine
- all thymine

Y-chromosome

- all adenine
- all cytosine
- all guanine
- all thymine

Your encodement technicians will do the following:

- use the Implant Removal plug-in to remove implants and intense, congested energies from each gene of the female DNA:

Genes 1–22
- all adenine
- all cytosine
- all guanine
- all thymine

X-chromosome
- all adenine
- all cytosine
- all guanine
- all thymine

Your healing team will perform the following steps:
- repeat the steps to remove intense and congested energies from the male and female DNA using the Shadow Removal plug-in
- repeat the steps to remove intense and congested energies from the male and female DNA using the Healing over Lifetimes plug-in
- use the Basic plug-in to heal and balance the priority wound affecting the proper replication of the genes
- use the Basic plug-in to heal and balance the next priority wound affecting the proper replication of the genes
- use the Basic plug-in to heal and balance the next priority wound affecting the proper replication of the genes
- use the Implant Removal plug-in to balance anything interfering with the RNA (replication of the genes)
- use the Shadow Removal plug-in to balance anything interfering with the RNA (replication of the genes)
- use the Healing over Lifetimes plug-in to balance anything interfering with the RNA (replication of the genes)
- harmonize the encodement system

Repair the Energy Field Plug-In

Set your intention, and ask your healing team to use the Repair the Energy Field plug-in. Your encodement team will perform the following steps:
- remove artificial encodements that initiated the problem
- repair damaged and altered natural encodements that initiated the problem
- remove artificial encodements that interfere with the repair of the chakra layers. One by one, go through each of the seven layers of the seven chakras. Start with the first chakra (example below) and then go through each layer, doing the same for the second to seventh chakras:

First Chakra

- first layer
- second layer
- third layer
- fourth layer
- fifth layer
- sixth layer
- seventh layer

After repeating the above layers for the second through seventh chakras, continue with this:

Energy Bodies (Additional Areas):

- core star
- soul star
- earth star
- pranic tube
- personal individuation point
- tan tien
- hara line
- all seven layers of the aura

Your encodement team will repair the damaged and altered natural encodements interfering with the first through seventh layers of all seven chakras and the energy bodies mentioned above.

Your healing team will use the Belief plug-in to remove any belief inhibiting the full repair and balance of the first through seventh layers of each of the seven chakras and the additional areas mentioned above.

Your soul-healing angels will perform the following steps to bring back pieces of yourself whose absence is either inhibiting the healing, holding in the limiting belief, or preventing the full integration of new beliefs:

- find and bring back all pieces of your energy lost during the wounding event
- clean, repair, and heal all pieces
- integrate all pieces within you

Your healing team will perform the following steps:

- connect your energy body part with its perfect template (Adam Kadmon or divine blueprint)
- match the appropriate natural encodements with each other (similar to matching puzzle pieces)
- harmonize the encodement system

Remove Blockages to Light Coming from the Subchakras Plug-In

Your healing team will perform these steps in the order that is best for you. The steps that follow are repeated for each subchakra of each chakra:

- remove all artificial encodements inhibiting light from flowing freely
- repair all damaged and altered natural encodements inhibiting light from flowing freely
- remove or deactivate all natural encodements no longer needed
- create and activate any natural encodements needed now

Belief Plug-In

Focus on the new belief you wish to have, and ask your healing team to implement the Belief plug-in.

Your encodement technicians will perform the following steps:

- remove all artificial encodements preventing the full activation of the new belief
- repair damaged and altered natural encodements preventing the full activation of the new belief
- remove all artificial encodements holding on to any conflicting belief
- repair all damaged and altered natural encodements holding on to any conflicting belief
- deactivate or remove all natural encodements of the old belief

The soul-healing angels will perform the following steps to bring back pieces of yourself whose absence is either holding on to the limiting belief or preventing the full integration of the new belief:

- find and bring back all pieces of your energy lost during the wounding event
- clean, repair, and heal all pieces
- integrate all pieces within you

Your encodement technicians will perform the following steps:

- create and activate all needed encodements for the new belief

- activate any inactive encodements for the new belief
- harmonize the encodement system

Shadow Removal Plug-In

Set your intention. Your healing team will call forth and remove the dark shadow and karma as well as any other dark shadows contributing to it.

Your encodement technicians will use the Basic plug-in to remove the dark shadows (which includes karma) from the first to seventh chakras, repeating this pattern for each chakra: DNA 1 & 2, 3 & 4, 5 & 6, 7 & 8, 9 & 10, 11 & 12.

Your healing team will use the Basic plug-in to lift out the energy of the dark shadow that was called forth with the following steps, repeated for all seven layers of your aura.

- lift out the energy of the dark shadow from the first to seventh layers of the aura, DNA 1 & 2, 3 & 4, 5 & 6, 7 & 8, 9 & 10, 11 & 12

Your healing team will now perform the following steps:

- use the Basic plug-in to lift all the energy of the dark shadow that was called forth
- ask your soul family (11 souls in addition to yourself) to call forth all the energy of the same dark shadow from all layers of the aura and all the chakras associated with the relevant strands of DNA
- ask your soul family to ask their healing teams to use the Basic plug-in to lift the energy of the dark shadow and all shadows associated with it that was called forth
- ask the rest of the members of your monadic family (132 souls in addition to your soul family) to call forth all the energy of the same dark shadow and all shadows associated with it that were called forth from all layers of the aura and all the chakras associated with the relevant strands of the DNA
- ask your monadic family to ask their healing teams to use the Basic plug-in to lift the energy of this dark shadow and all shadows associated with it that were called forth

Clear the Gaps in the Aura Plug-In

There are gaps between the layers of the aura where congested energy hides. This plug-in will remove the low vibration energies and replace them with high vibration energies. Set your intention, and your healing team will implement the Clear the Gaps in the Aura plug-in.

Your healing team will perform the following steps:

- remove all artificial encodements holding in congested energy in the gap between the seventh layer of the aura and the sixth layer
- repair and heal all damaged and altered natural encodements holding in congested energy in the gap between the seventh layer of the aura and the sixth layer
- activate all natural encodements related to the gap between the seventh and sixth layers of the aura needed for the integrity of that space
- remove all congested energy in the gap between the seventh layer of the aura and the sixth layer

Your soul-healing angels will perform the following steps:

- find and bring back all pieces of your energy lost during the wounding event
- clean, repair, and heal all pieces
- integrate all pieces within you

Your healing team will perform the following steps:

- fill the gap between the seventh and sixth layers of the aura with the highest vibration energy needed for you
- repeat all previous steps for the gap between the fifth and sixth, fourth and fifth, third and fourth, second and third, and first and second layers.
- repeat all previous steps for the gap between the physical body and first layer and the gap between the seventh and eighth layers
- harmonize the encodement system

Curse Removal Plug-In

Set your intention, and ask your healing team to use the Curse Removal plug-in. Your healing team will perform the following steps:

- remove artificial encodements holding in curses (emotions such as fear, anger, jealousy, etc.)

- repair damaged and altered natural encodements holding in curses

Your soul-healing angels will perform the following steps:

- find and bring back all pieces of your energy lost during the wounding event
- clean, repair, and heal all pieces
- integrate all pieces within you

Your healing team will perform the following steps:

- remove artificial encodements holding you to the person who cursed you
- repair damaged and altered natural encodements holding you to the person who cursed you
- use the Belief plug-in for the belief, "I am not controlled by the thoughts, words, actions or desires of another for me."
- use the Belief plug-in for the belief, "My energy field is impervious to the thoughts, words, actions, and desires of another."

Your healing team will remove encodements of the curse itself from the following:

- all seven levels of each of the chakras
- pranic tube
- all seven layers of the aura
- all meridians
- the core star
- the soul seat
- the earth star
- the individuation point
- every cell of the physical body
- the DNA and the RNA

Your healing team will harmonize the encodement system.

Repair, Heal, and Strengthen the Hara Line Plug-In

Move into your heart source and set your intention. Your encodement technicians will perform the following steps:

- remove all artificial encodements from the outer layer of the hara line
- repair all damaged and altered natural encodements in the outer layer of the hara line
- remove all artificial encodements from the inner layer of the hara line
- repair all damaged and altered natural encodements in the inner layer of the hara line
- remove all artificial encodements from the middle layer of the hara line
- repair all damaged and altered natural encodements in the middle layer of the hara line
- activate any natural encodements needed to be activated in the outer layer of your hara line so that the hara line adapts to the amazing energy changes occurring within you as your frequency increases
- activate any natural encodements needed to be activated in the inner layer of your hara line so that your hara line adapts to the amazing energy changes occurring within you as your frequency increases
- activate any natural encodements needed to be activated in the middle layer of your hara line so that your hara line adapts to the amazing energy changes occurring within you as your frequency increases
- implement the Basic plug-in to heal any wounds that have affected the hara line

Clear Connections to the Pranic Tube Plug-In

Your healing team will apply this plug-in to the area you request, or you can ask them to apply it to all connections to the pranic tube as a whole. This includes the chakras, fronts and backs, and other areas, such as the personal individuation point, soul star, core star, earth star, and other elements of the energy field you are not aware of.

Part 1: Your healing team will

- remove all artificial encodements interfering with the connection to the pranic tube

- repair damaged and altered natural encodements interfering with the connection to the pranic tube
- deactivate or remove all natural encodements that are no longer needed to limit the energy exchange between the energy structure and the pranic tube
- create any natural encodements needed to facilitate this connection
- apply the Soul-Healing Prayer (if you wish)

Part 2: Your healing team will follow the steps of the foundational plug-ins

- apply the Basic plug-in
- apply the Healing over Lifetimes plug-in
- apply the Implant Removal plug-in
- apply the Removal of Victim Consciousness plug-in

Part 3: Your healing team will

- construct the healing hologram as needed for the chakra or the point being addressed
- assign the appropriate variables to the corresponding points as needed for healing

Part 4: Your healing team will

- spin your chakras as fast as is safe to release congestion

Breathe deeply, in and out, picturing the energy entering your pranic tube from above and below as the congestion is released.

Repair the Pressure Funnels Plug-In

Set your intention, and ask your healing team to use the Repair the Pressure Funnels plug-in. Your healing team will perform the following steps:

- apply the Basic plug-in to the primary wound
- apply the Basic plug-in six times to address the six wounds causing the most extreme pressure in that funnel
- apply the Basic plug-in to the funnel within the aura in the greatest need of assistance

- apply the Basic plug-in to all funnels that need repaired, healing and balancing them
- apply the Healing over Lifetimes plug-in on all energies from any lifetime (past, present, parallel, and future) that are connected to these six wounds so that they are now released, resolved, and healed
- bring in all the wisdom and knowledge available to you now
- apply the Implant Removal plug-in to remove any implants within the funnels blocking energy in any way and preventing the full transmutation of energy in any way
- remove all artificial encodements inhibiting the full vibrancy of the electric violet light within each funnel
- remove all damaged and altered natural encodements that have anything to do with hiding the electric violet light that transmutes energy
- activate any natural encodements needed and not yet activated
- apply the Remove Victim Consciousness plug-in to remove all victim consciousness associated with what has been done and any victim consciousness ready to be released that doesn't have anything to do with this healing

Your soul-healing angels will perform the following steps:

- find and bring back all the pieces of your energy lost during the wounded event
- clean, repair, and heal all pieces
- integrate all pieces within you

Repair the Myelin Sheath Plug-In

Focus on the vagus nerve, and ask your encodement technicians to implement the Repair the Myelin Sheath plug-in to restore the three branches of the vagus nerve.

Your encodement technicians will perform the following steps to the first branch:

- implement the Implant Removal plug-in
- apply the Repair the DNA plug-in
- apply the Repair the DNA plug-in to also repair the RNA to restore wholeness

Your encodement technicians will perform the following steps:

- repair damaged and altered natural encodements interfering with the functioning of the telomeres
- activate natural encodements needed for the full functioning of the telomeres
- create and activate any new encodements needed for the full functioning of the telomeres
- harmonize your encodement system with the divine blueprint

Now ask your healing team to work with the movement of nerve impulses to, from, and within the nerve cell. Your encodement technicians will implement the following steps:

- remove all artificial encodements interfering with the way the nerve impulses are supposed to flow
- repair any damaged or altered natural encodements interfering with the movement of the nerve impulses to, from, or within the nerve
- activate any natural encodements that are inactive and need to be activated for the proper functioning of the nerve impulses to, from, and within the nerve
- create and activate any needed natural encodements that are not present and that are needed to assist in the functioning of the nerve impulses
- use the Repair the DNA plug-in to heal, balance, and repair the DNA as it pertains to the flow of the nerve impulses to, from, and within the nerve cell
- link the divine blueprint, asking that everything that has been done and that needs to be done be connected with the divine blueprint

Now focus on clearing congestion from your aura in regard to the vagus nerve. Your encodement technicians will perform the following steps:

- use the Clear the Gaps of the Aura plug-in to release and remove any congestion in the gaps between the layers of the aura
- apply the Clear the Gaps of the Aura plug-in to remove congested energy from the gaps in the chakras

- apply the foundational plug-ins to anything that has appeared and is ready to be balanced in each chakra, one at a time, clearing all seven layers of each
- apply the foundational plug-ins to the navel chakra

Continue to focus on restoring the vagus nerve, and ask your encodement technicians to repeat these steps on the second and third branches.

Release Shame about Sexuality Plug-In

Focus on connecting with your genetic line. Move through this healing from your Merkabah. State, "I am the Sword," and see your Merkabah turn into Archangel Michael's Sword. Focus on your DNA, and ask your healing team to implement the Release Shame about Sexuality plug-in. As you travel through your DNA, your encodement technicians will go into every particle of every cell within your body, to all the little organelles and mitochondria, where cellular memory is held and perform the following steps:

- identify and remove all encodements of shame, anger, fear, revulsion, rage, and any other low-vibration feelings projected on to you related to those feelings that came from the DNA
- repair any altered or damaged natural encodements
- activate the encodements related to giving you joy and delight and self-acceptance — no matter who you love
- remove the encodements from this shame (and all the other emotions mentioned) that came from religious institutions
- remove all the artificial encodements and repair damaged and altered natural encodements that came from educational and social institutions
- remove all the artificial encodements and repair damaged and altered natural encodements that came from governmental institutions and then any other place the energies might have come from, such as individuals, groups, or institutions
- apply the Remove Victim Consciousness and the Healing over Lifetimes plug-ins

Now focus your Merkabah, shaped like Michael's Sword, on your biological father's generation and travel through your DNA. Your encodement technicians will perform the following steps:

- remove the energy of shame, anger, fear, and revulsion about being attracted to the same gender from your father's generation
- remove the energy of shame, anger, fear, and revulsion about being attracted to the same gender from your grandfather's generation
- remove the energy of shame, anger, fear, and revulsion about being attracted to the same gender from your first great-grandfather's generation and then your second great-grandfather's, third great-grandfather's, fourth great-grandfather's, and fifth great-grandfather's generations
- remove the energy of shame, anger, fear, and revulsion about being attracted to the same gender from your sixth, seventh, eighth, ninth, tenth, eleventh, twelfth, thirteenth, fourteenth, fifteenth, sixteenth, seventeenth, eighteenth, nineteenth, and twentieth great-grandfathers
- continue back in your father's genetic line to remove the energy of shame, anger, fear, and revulsion about being attracted to the same gender from its origin

Now focus your Merkabah, shaped like Michael's Sword, on your biological mother's generation and travel through your DNA. Your encodement technicians will perform the following steps:

- remove the energy of shame, anger, fear, and revulsion about being attracted to the same gender from your mother's generation
- remove the energy of shame, anger, fear, and revulsion about being attracted to the same gender from your grandmother's generation
- remove the energy of shame, anger, fear, and revulsion about being attracted to the same gender from your first great-grandmother's generation and then your second great-grandmother's, third great-grandmother's, fourth great-grandmother's, and fifth great-grandmother's generations
- remove the energy of shame, anger, fear, and revulsion about being attracted to the same gender from your sixth, seventh, eighth, ninth, tenth, eleventh, twelfth, thirteenth, fourteenth, fifteenth, sixteenth, seventeenth, eighteenth, nineteenth, and twentieth great-grandmothers

- continue back in your mother's genetic line to remove the energy of shame, anger, fear, and revulsion about being attracted to the same gender from its origin

Return to the beginning of your DNA. Now slide out of it. Be conscious and aware of your body.

Your soul-healing angels will perform the following steps to bring back the pieces of you that were lost due to shame regarding your sexuality. They will perform the following steps:

- find and bring back all pieces of your energy lost during the wounding event
- clean, repair, and heal all pieces
- integrate all pieces within you

Your encodement technicians will then perform the following steps:

- activate all inactive natural encodements needed to assist in healing this implant
- create any natural encodements needed to assist in the healing of this implant
- harmonize the encodement system

Heal Genetic and Generational Experiences Plug-In

Focus on the issue you need help with, and ask your healing team to implement the Heal Genetic and Generational Experiences plug-in. Your encodement technicians will perform the following steps:

- identify and remove energies from the times you've felt objectified because of your gender, sexual orientation, or gender identification from your mother's maternal line, including her grandmother, her grandmother's mother, and so on down the line
- identify and remove energies from the times you've felt objectified because of your gender, sexual orientation, or gender identification from your mother's father's maternal line, including his mother, his grandmother, his grandmother's mother, and so on down the line
- identify and remove energies from the times you've felt objectified because of your gender, sexual orientation, or gender identification

from your mother's paternal line, including her grandfather, her grandfather's father, and so on down the line

- identify and remove energies from the times you've felt objectified because of your gender, sexual orientation, or gender identification from your father's paternal line, including his grandfather, his grandfather's father, and so on down the line

Focus on these issues that might have been inherited from nonbiological family and similarly close relationships as well as those you might have experienced from authority figures in educational systems. Ask your healing team to implement the Heal Genetic and Generational Experiences plug-in, and your encodement technicians will perform the following steps:

- identify and remove energies from the times you've felt objectified because of your gender, sexual orientation, or gender identification from your nonbiological family and close relationships
- identify and remove energies from the times you've felt objectified because of your gender, sexual orientation, or gender identification from educational experiences
- apply this healing to all parties involved as much as they will accept

Focus on any religious, employment, or general public experiences involving sexual harassment or gender bias to be healed, whether remembered or realized. Ask your healing team to implement the Heal Genetic and Generational Experiences plug-in, and your encodement technicians will perform the following steps:

- identify and remove energies from the times you've felt objectified because of your gender, sexual orientation, or gender identification from any experience, whether remembered or realized
- apply this healing to all parties involved as much as they will accept

Your soul-healing angels will perform the following steps to bring back the pieces of you lost regarding being objectified for your gender, sexual orientation, or gender identification. They will perform the following steps:

- find and bring back all pieces of your energy lost during the wounding event
- clean, repair, and heal all pieces
- integrate all pieces within you

Your encodement technicians will then perform the following steps:

- activate all inactive natural encodements needed to assist in healing this implant
- create any natural encodements needed to assist in the healing of this implant
- harmonize the encodement system

Just Done Plug-In

Focus on the issue you need help with, and ask your healing team to implement the Just Done plug-in. Your encodement technicians will perform the following steps:

- release the energy that either parent brought into the pregnancy of their sexual-identification issues and concerns about who they should love
- remove from the ovum, the sperm, and the initial fertilized egg any energy that is contrary to the full acceptance of the physical relationship on a heterosexual level
- remove any shame from the parents that entered the ovum, sperm, and the fertilized egg that they did not believe they were being true to themselves regarding their choice of sexual partner
- remove all artificial encodements that entered you from the time just before conception to birth from either birth parent
- repair any damaged and altered natural encodements from the point when the sperm and the egg joined to the point of birth, the first month of gestation, the second month, and then the third, fourth, fifth, sixth, seventh, eighth, and ninth months

Allow that energy to settle.

Now go to the very first time you knew you were attracted to someone of the same gender and the first time you heard that was wrong or were made to feel that you were wrong. Your encodement technicians will perform the following steps:

- use the Basic plug-in to remove that energy from you
- use the Belief plug-in to install the belief: "I am perfect just the way I am"

Now go now to the first time you experienced a person attracted to someone of the same gender, and that person was berated, made fun of, and bullied. That energy entered you and triggered feelings in you. You did not acknowledge your sexual orientation and felt shame about your feelings and not standing up for the person being bullied. Your encodement technicians will perform the following steps:

- apply the Basic plug-in to your inner reactions to what you saw and heard and then apply it to any feelings of cowardice or shame you might have had for not standing up for that individual
- remove the encodements and energies you took on from either the perpetrator or the one being bullied using the Remove Victim Consciousness plug-in
- identify and remove all those energies from other lifetimes using the Healing over Lifetimes plug-in
- remove implants of that energy from your chakras, meridians, aura, and hidden structures (in the order needed) using the Repair the Energy plug-in
- replace that cleared space with the belief: "I am perfect just as I am" using the Belief plug-in

Pause and allow for balance.

Now focus on each year of your life, and ask your healing team to implement the Just Done plug-in. Your encodement technicians will perform the following steps:

- apply the entire plug-in to you beginning at age three and then four, five, six, seven, eight, nine, and ten
- remove shame, guilt, or fear from the first time you touched someone of your gender in a sexual way, in an exploratory way
- repair your energy field using the Basic plug-in, the Healing over Lifetimes plug-in, and the Remove Victim Consciousness plug-in

- add the belief "I am perfect just the way I am" using the Belief plug-in to ages ten, eleven, twelve, thirteen, fourteen, fifteen, and sixteen
- apply the entire plug-in to you for the ages nineteen, twenty, twenty-one, twenty-two, twenty-three, twenty-four, twenty-five, twenty-six, twenty-seven, twenty-eight, twenty-nine, and thirty
- apply the entire plug-in to you for the ages thirty-one, thirty-two, thirty-three, thirty-four, thirty-five, thirty-six, thirty-seven, thirty-eight, thirty-nine, forty, forty-one, forty-two, forty-three, forty-four, forty-five, forty-six, forty-seven, forty-eight, forty-nine, and fifty
- apply the entire plug-in to you for the ages fifty-one, fifty-two, fifty-three, fifty-four, fifty-five, fifty-six, fifty-seven, fifty-eight, fifty-nine, sixty, sixty-one, sixty-two, sixty-three, sixty-four, sixty-five, sixty-six, sixty-seven, sixty-eight, sixty-nine, seventy, seventy-one, seventy-two, seventy-three, seventy-four, seventy-five, seventy-six, seventy-seven, seventy-eight, seventy-nine, and eighty
- apply the entire plug-in to all the years lived beyond eighty

Now focus on the first time you entered a committed love relationship with someone of the same gender and you hid the relationship. Your encodement technicians will perform the following steps:

- remove all that energy of not being accepted and all that pain of not being able to declare, "This is who I love"
- transmute to the highest level of pure love the fear of coming out publicly using Archangel Michael's Sword
- transmute to the highest level of pure love all hurtful messages, events, and remarks that you've experienced from your community, church, friends, family, strangers, and all forms of media using the Sword of Michael
- gather all regrets over not taking the risk to love who you wanted to love and transmute them to the highest level of pure love using Michael's Sword and fully incorporate all the knowledge and wisdom of those regrets into your encodement system
- gather all the incidents you have seen, heard about, or experienced of physical violence and trauma regarding who you love, including

the feelings of pain, fear, and shame, and transmute them to the highest level of love using Archangel Michael's Sword
- add the belief, "I am perfect as I am" using the Belief plug-in

Know that you are loved as deeply as you love the one you love.

Your soul-healing angels will perform the following steps to bring back the pieces of you that were lost due to sexual identification experiences. They will perform the following steps:
- find and bring back all pieces of your energy lost during the wounding event
- clean, repair, and heal all pieces
- integrate all pieces within you

Your encodement technicians will then perform the following steps:
- activate all inactive natural encodements needed to assist in healing this implant
- create any natural encodements needed to assist in the healing of this implant
- harmonize the encodement system

Repair the Endocrine System Plug-In

Set your intention, and ask your healing team to use the Repair the Endocrine System plug-in. Your healing team will perform the following steps:
- apply the Repair the Energy Field plug-in
- apply the Basic plug-in
- apply the Healing over Lifetimes plug-in
- apply the Repair the Energy Field plug-in
- apply the Remove Victim Consciousness plug-in
- apply the Repair the Energy Field plug-in
- apply the Remove Victim Consciousness plug-in
- apply the Repair the Energy Field plug-in
- apply the Remove Victim Consciousness plug-in
- apply the Repair the Energy Field plug-in
- apply the Implant Removal plug-in
- apply the Repair the Energy Field plug-in

Your soul-healing angels will perform the following steps:

- find and bring back all the pieces of your energy lost during the wounded event
- clean, repair, and heal all pieces
- integrate all pieces within you

Wei Chi Plug-In

Focus on the issue you need help with, and ask your healing team to implement the Wei Chi plug-in. The wei chi is the protective energy of the body. Your encodement technicians will perform the following steps:

- remove all artificial encodements that interfere with the strength of your wei chi (or wei qi)
- balance and repair any damaged or altered natural encodements interfering with the strength of your general wei chi
- activate all inactive natural encodements that need to be activated for a strong wei chi
- examine you (the soul, the spirit) and create any natural encodements you need to make your wei chi strong
- Find and bring back any pieces of you that were disassociated or sent away from being wounded
- clean, repair, and heal those pieces brought back and fully integrate them on all levels of your being — physical, mental, emotional, spiritual, and energetic
- harmonize your entire encodements system to what has been done
- then use the entire Wei Chi plug-in again and apply it to the emotional wei chi
- then use the entire Wei Chi plug-in again and apply it the wei chi affected by the weather — be it damp, cold, windy, or hot — on all levels
- repeat the Wei Chi plug-in on your wei chi that has been damaged by electromagnetic frequencies
- strengthen the wei chi against electromagnetic frequencies

Optional Steps

In many of the group encodement intensives I do on a monthly basis, Amma adds the following steps to some of the healing processes.

These steps are not part of a plug-in, but they are beneficial to add anytime you wish.

You may request that your healing team perform the following optional steps:

- remove the energy imprint of this wound that resonates throughout your soul's lifetimes
- remove the energy imprint of this wound from all dimensions, through all energy fields, and in all DNA — both physical and crystalline — in your soul family and monadic family
- heal any area you might have forgotten to request healing for or are unaware that you need

About Cathy Chapman, PhD

Dr. Cathy Chapman is a spiritual adventurer who assists people searching for inner healing and physical balance through prayer, spiritual growth, and energy-based healing. She delved deeply into Christian spirituality when she was a Catholic Sister in the Dominican Order for twenty years. During that time, she received a master's degree in theology.

Dr. Cathy's explorations of energy healing led her to a broader concept of God, of All That Is, which propelled her into a more expansive spirituality. Since 1996 she has studied various forms of energy healing. At the turn of the century, she was surprised by the energy of Amma, the Divine Mother and feminine aspect of God, coming through her to deliver powerful messages of love, healing, and hope.

Amma, the Divine Mother, through Dr. Cathy, introduced the heart source (an expansion of living from your heart) and information about the smallest energy structures called encodements. Through Amma, she works with the Golden Elohim, Archangel Golden, the

Encodement Formulator, and innumerable encodement master teachers and encodement technicians who assist everyone on the planet.

In 2018, Amma asked Dr. Cathy to work with the Golden Elohim to bring in the book *The Creation of Form*. Once that was completed, she was asked to work with whom Amma calls her healing friends. This collective energy gave their name as Ah-ya-me-de-yah-ta-say-na. Each syllable is associated with color and sound. They have said we may call them Amiya (Ah-me-ah).

In addition to Dr. Cathy's spiritual background, she was a therapist for more than thirty-five years and also a licensed master social worker for much of that time. She earned a doctorate in mind-body psychology.

To learn more about Amma's work, visit AmmatheDivineMother.com. To learn more about Dr. Cathy's work to facilitate your own healing, please go to OdysseytoWholeness.com. To purchase her books, go to amazon.com/Cathy-Chapman/e/B00CUI6UCC. You may contact Dr. Cathy at DrCathy@OdysseytoWholeness.com.

Light Technology PUBLISHING Presents

TO ORDER PRINT BOOKS
Visit LightTechnology.com, Call 928-526-1345 or 1-800-450-0985,
or Check Amazon.com or Your Favorite Bookstore

THROUGH CATHY CHAPMAN

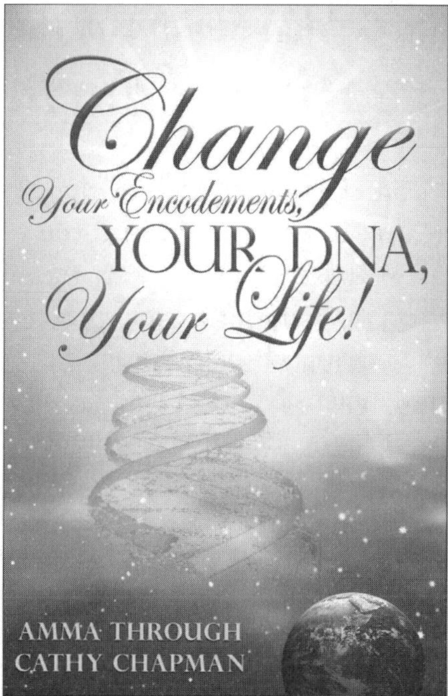

Chapters Include

- Using the Pillar of Light
- Turn Jealousy into Acceptance!
- Discover the Altar with Your Heart Center
- Learn to Live Love
- A Healthy Balance between Loving and Being Loved
- The New Energies in Adolescence and Healing
- The Energy of Sexuality and Spirituality
- Harmonizing and Assessing Encodements
- Healing the Past, Living in the Present
- Reincarnate Yourself

$16.95 • Softcover • 6 x 9 • 320 PP.
ISBN 978-1-891824-52-4

Change Your Encodements, Your DNA, Your Life!

Love is the most powerful energy. You are made of this energy, so when you learn to harness it, you can do whatever you wish in your life.

Learn powerful techniques for working with your DNA encodements. Discover how this process works so that you can make great changes in your life. Encodements will help you to perform what some would call miracles.

Amma also provides readings, predictions, and interpretations related to the current energy.

The powerful knowledge contained in this book is dormant unless you choose to use it. Breathe in and out of your heart center and set your intention to tap into the energy of the message you are reading. Ask that you be given the secrets contained within the message and ask to be shown how to implement these secrets. Have fun exploring.

As you read, Amma will have one hand on your heart and one touching your mind.

All Our Books Are Also Available as eBooks from Amazon, Apple iTunes, Google Play, Barnes & Noble, and Kobo.

Light Technology PUBLISHING *Presents*

TO ORDER PRINT BOOKS
Visit LightTechnology.com, Call 928-526-1345 or 1-800-450-0985,
or Check Amazon.com or Your Favorite Bookstore

AMIYA'S ENCYCLOPEDIA OF HEALING SERIES THROUGH CATHY CHAPMAN

The Human Energy Field — Auras

Learn the basics of encodements, where your energy field begins. Encodements are the building blocks of everything you see — the tiniest essence of All That Is. You were consciously created from the energy of All That Is. That is why Amma says you are love incarnate.

The human energy field interacts with the energy fields of the planet, plants, animals, angelic beings, and galactic energies.

The focus of this book is on working with your specific energy field to continue your healing journey. The ultimate goal is self-healing. Amma and Friends give the tools and techniques to independently heal yourself.

Amiya's Encyclopedia of Healing is a must for healers and those interested in healing themselves. Cathy Chapman is an exceptionally clear channel, and I am most grateful to her for bringing this information forward at this time.

— Marianne Crouse

$15.95 • 136 PP. • Softcover • 6 x 9
978-1-62233-068-3

Chapters Include

- Choose a Journey of Love
- You Are the Power and Presence of God
- Your Healing Tools
- Curse Energy and Its Removal
- The Structure of the Aura
- Strengthen and Repair Your Aura

All Our Books Are Also Available as eBooks from Amazon, Apple iTunes, Google Play, Barnes & Noble, and Kobo.

Light Technology PUBLISHING *Presents*

TO ORDER PRINT BOOKS
Visit LightTechnology.com, Call 928-526-1345 or 1-800-450-0985,
or Check Amazon.com or Your Favorite Bookstore

AMIYA'S ENCYCLOPEDIA OF HEALING SERIES THROUGH CATHY CHAPMAN

If one wants to change the energy on the planet in a good way, it will help to read these books by Amiya and the Elohim. You will learn fascinating information about the chakras and how to manage chakra energy. And most important, you will learn how to live from your heart.

— Diane Peckham

$19.95 • 364 PP. • Softcover • 6 x 9
978-1-62233-069-0

The Human Energy Field — Chakras

Chakras spin, take in energy, and release energy. They react to what happens in your life. They react to your thoughts and emotions. They react to the actions you take.

Focused intention occurs when you are in your heart source, and when you are in your heart source, your chakras align. You connect with the heart chakra and the third eye through a beam of energy, which goes all the way up and all the way down, connecting and aligning all your chakras. Your chakras work to keep you in balance as you perform your intention.

Chapters Include

- How the Chakras Develop in the Body
- The Energetic Anatomy of Chakras
- Maximize Your Chakra Energy
- Crystalline DNA and Crystalline Chakras
- The Backs of the Chakras
- Heart Chakra Activation
- Manifest at a Higher Level
- Special Qualities of the Third Eye

All Our Books Are Also Available as eBooks from Amazon, Apple iTunes, Google Play, Barnes & Noble, and Kobo.

Light Technology PUBLISHING Presents

TO ORDER PRINT BOOKS
Visit LightTechnology.com, Call 928-526-1345 or 1-800-450-0985,
or Check Amazon.com or Your Favorite Bookstore

Amiya's Encyclopedia of Healing series through Cathy Chapman

Trauma and PTSD — Resolve the Pain to Recover Your Life

When something occurs that is contrary to who you are as love incarnate, the tendency is to hold on to the energy of that pain to keep it from further damaging you or others. In this book, Amma's Healing Friends take you through a process so simple that all you need to do is read as you allow the release of all that is not you.

Simply take this book into your hands, connect with the spiritual beings who surround you, and say, "I am ready to release the pain of all that happened and come to know myself as the love from which God created me." Then read. Take in the words even if you don't understand the how and why of them.

Know that you deserve complete healing, and accept that healing. You can have your life back again.

Chapters Include

- Trauma Is Part of the Human Condition
- Identify the Seed Wound
- Conquer the Obstacles of Your Beliefs
- Emotional Reactions Identify What You Need to Heal
- Strengthen Your Immune System
- Detach from Victim Identity

$25.00 • 512 PP. • Softcover • 6 x 9
978-1-62233-080-5

All Our Books Are Also Available as eBooks from Amazon, Apple iTunes, Google Play, Barnes & Noble, and Kobo.

Light Technology PUBLISHING *Presents*

TO ORDER PRINT BOOKS
Visit LightTechnology.com, Call 928-526-1345 or 1-800-450-0985,
or Check Amazon.com or Your Favorite Bookstore

BOOKS THROUGH DRUNVALO MELCHIZEDEK

THE ANCIENT SECRET OF THE FLOWER OF LIFE, VOLUME 1

Also available in Spanish as *Antiguo Secreto Flor de la Vida, Volumen 1*

Once, all life in the universe knew the Flower of Life as the creation pattern, the geometrical design leading us into and out of physical existence. Then from a very high state of consciousness, we fell into darkness, and the secret was hidden for thousands of years, encoded in the cells of all life.

$25.00 • 240 PP. • Softcover • ISBN 978-1-891824-17-3

THE ANCIENT SECRET OF THE FLOWER OF LIFE, VOLUME 2

Also available in Spanish as *Antiguo Secreto Flor de la Vida, Volumen 2*

Drunvalo shares the instructions for the Mer-Ka-Ba meditation, step-by-step techniques for the re-creation of the energy field of the evolved human, which is the key to ascension and the next dimensional world. If done from love, this ancient process of breathing prana opens up for us a world of tantalizing possibility in this dimension, from protective powers to the healing of oneself, others, and even the planet.

$25.00 • 272 PP. • Softcover • ISBN 978-1-891824-21-0

Includes Heart Meditation CD

LIVING IN THE HEART

Also available in Spanish as *Viviendo en el Corazón*

Long ago we humans used a form of communication and sensing that did not involve the brain in any way; rather, it came from a sacred place within our hearts. What good would it do to find this place again in a world where the greatest religion is science and the logic of the mind? Don't I know this world where emotions and feelings are second-class citizens? Yes, I do. But my teachers have asked me to remind you who you really are. You are more than a human being, much more. Within your heart is a place, a sacred place, where the world can literally be remade through conscious cocreation. If you give me permission, I will show you what has been shown to me.

— Drunvalo Melchizedek

$25.00 • 144 PP. • Softcover • ISBN 978-1-891824-43-2

All Our Books Are Also Available as eBooks from Amazon, Apple iTunes, Google Play, Barnes & Noble, and Kobo.

Light Technology PUBLISHING *Presents*

TO ORDER PRINT BOOKS

Visit LightTechnology.com, Call 928-526-1345 or 1-800-450-0985,
or Check Amazon.com or Your Favorite Bookstore

BOOKS THROUGH TINA LOUISE SPALDING

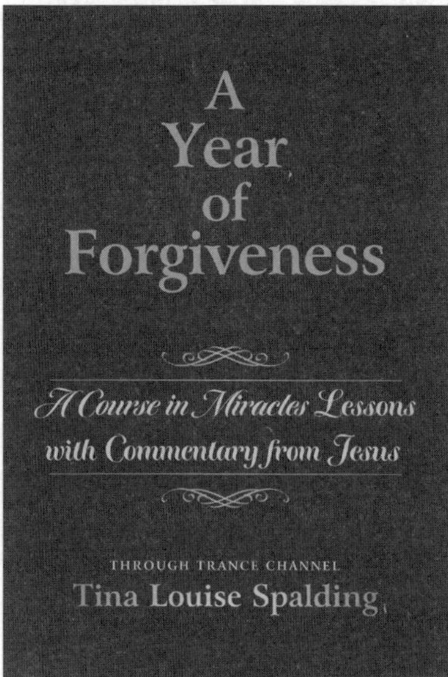

A Year of Forgiveness

***A Course in Miracles* Lessons with Commentary from Jesus**

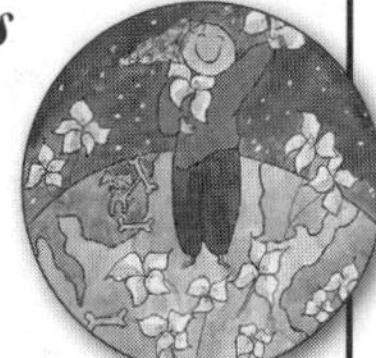

Keep this book close at hand with your *A Course in Miracles* manual, and read Jesus's commentaries after practicing the lesson as described in that text. Allow Jesus's simple and direct discussion of the topic to aid your understanding of these wonderful teachings.

This book is made even more appealing by the whimsical art of Renee Phillips, who has contributed beautiful illustrations for each lesson.

A Course in Miracles will change your life. With this companion book, find help and a clearer understanding of the lessons through these 365 channeled messages from Jesus.

Print Pub Date: September 30, 2020

$25.00 • 496 PP. • 978-1-62233-076-8

Features hundreds of full-color illustrations by Renée Phillips

Jesus: My Autobiography
$16.95 • Softcover • 304 PP.
978-1-62233-030-0

Love and a Map to the Unaltered Soul
$16.95 • Softcover • 240 PP.
ISBN 978-1-62233-047-8

Making Love to God: The Path to Divine Sex
$19.95 • Softcover • 416 PP.
978-1-62233-009-6

Spirit of the Western Way
$16.95 • Softcover • 176 PP.
978-1-62233-051-5

You Can Free Yourself from the Karma of Chaos
$16.95 • Softcover • 224 PP.
978-1-62233-051-5

Great Minds Speak to You
$19.95 • Softcover • 192 PP.
Includes CD
978-1-62233-010-2

CD included!

All Our Books Are Also Available as eBooks from Amazon, Apple iTunes, Google Play, Barnes & Noble, and Kobo.

Light Technology PUBLISHING Presents

TO ORDER PRINT BOOKS

Visit LightTechnology.com, Call 928-526-1345 or 1-800-450-0985,
or Check Amazon.com or Your Favorite Bookstore

PRODUCTS BY LYSSA ROYAL-HOLT

Galactic Heritage Cards

THE FIRST AND ONLY OF THEIR KIND: This 108-card divination system, based on material from Lyssa Royal-Holt's groundbreaking book *The Prism of Lyra,* is **designed to help you tap into your star lineage and karmic patterns** while revealing lessons brought to Earth from the stars and how those lessons can be used in your life on Earth now. Includes a 156-page book of instruction and additional information.

Illustrations by David Cow • 108 cards (2.75 x 4.5 inches)
156-page softcover book (4.5 x 5.5 inches) • $34.95 • 978-1-891824-88-3

Preparing for Contact
In this book, you will take an inner journey through your own psyche and discover a whole new dimension to your unexplained experiences.
$16.95 • Softcover • 320 PP.
978-1-891824-90-6

The Prism of Lyra
This text explores the idea that collective humanoid consciousness created this universe for specific purposes.
$16.95 • Softcover • 192 PP.
978-1-891824-87-6

The Golden Lake
This book features Pleiadian and Sirian awakening teachings that together provide a road map for the next phase of human evolution — the integration of polarity and the awakening of our consciousness beyond duality.
$19.95 • Softcover • 240 PP.
978-1-62233-070-6

All Our Books Are Also Available as eBooks from Amazon, Apple iTunes, Google Play, Barnes & Noble, and Kobo.

Light Technology PUBLISHING Presents

TO ORDER PRINT BOOKS
Visit LightTechnology.com, Call 928-526-1345 or 1-800-450-0985,
or Check Amazon.com or Your Favorite Bookstore

BOOKS THROUGH JAAP VAN ETTEN

$19.95 • Softcover • 352 PP. • 6 x 9
978-1-62233-066-9

DRAGONS
GUARDIANS OF CREATIVE POWERS

BECOMING A CONSCIOUS CREATOR

The elemental (fire, water, air, and earth) powers are the basis of all creation. Understanding the different aspects of these creative powers will help you to become a conscious creator.

Guardians are connected with every aspect of the elemental powers. They are known as dragons; however, different traditions use different names for them, such as angels or nature spirits. They are among the strongest allies we can ask for.

This book offers information to help you reconnect with these creative powers and their guardian dragons. Through this connection, you will become a conscious creator and change your life in ways that lead to success, joy, happiness, and abundance. Thereby, you will contribute optimally to the creation of a new world.

Birth of a New Consciousness: Dialogues with the Sidhe
$16.95 • 192 PP.
978-1-62233-033-1

The Gifts of Mother Earth
$16.95 • 256 PP.
978-1-891824-86-9

Crystal Skulls: Expand Your Consciousness
$25.00 • 256 PP.
978-1-62233-000-3

Crystal Skulls: Interacting with a Phenomenon
$19.95 • 240 PP.
978-1-891824-64-7

All Our Books Are Also Available as eBooks from Amazon, Apple iTunes, Google Play, Barnes & Noble, and Kobo.

Light Technology PUBLISHING *Presents*

TO ORDER PRINT BOOKS

Visit LightTechnology.com, Call 928-526-1345 or 1-800-450-0985, or Check Amazon.com or Your Favorite Bookstore

THROUGH ROBERT SHAPIRO

PHONE CALLS FROM THE FUTURE

Future History & Ancient History from the People Who Were There

Explorer Race Book 27

The channel, Robert Shapiro, and the questioner live in different cities, so the channeling sessions are conducted over the telephone.

All the beings speaking through Robert in this book live now in the future in various times and places but have had lives on Earth or visited Earth during the times they speak about for this book.

$25.00 • Softcover • 320 PP.
978-1-62233-096-6

PART ONE: FUTURE HISTORY

- Mining on the Moon
- Life on the Moon
- Future from the Moon
- Doc's Identity
- Life on the Moon
- Water on the Moon
- The Origins of the Moon
- Stop Digging Toxic Matter on Earth and Live 700 Years
- Children and Dogs on Mars

PART ONE: ANCIENT HISTORY

- Spirits of the Biloba Tree Created Yeti (Bigfoot) People
- Protection from Earth's Violence
- Earth's History of ET Visitations
- Ancient Cultures Moved Stones through Love
- Gobekli Tepe, Turkey — Ancient Pleiadian Healing and Manifestation Circles
- Dolmens: ET Gifts to Ensure Early Humans' Survival

All Our Books Are Also Available as eBooks on Amazon, Apple iTunes, Google Play, Barnes & Noble, and Kobo.

Light Technology PUBLISHING Presents

SEDONA JOURNAL OF Emergence

ORDER NOW

to receive SPECTACULAR SAVINGS on your *Sedona Journal* subscription!

All subscriptions include the annual Predictions Issue

YOU ARE EXPERIENCING AN UNPRECEDENTED EXPANSION into a new reality and a dimensional shift into a new state of being. This movement from one dimension to another while in a physical body has never been done before. It feels as if you are building the rocket you're riding while it is blasting off!

THERE ARE NO ANCIENT BOOKS, NO RULEBOOKS, no manuals or procedures, no record of how to do this thing, because it has never been done before. During previous dimensional shifts, embodied beings would die in the old reality and then be reborn in the new one in new bodies with a different vibrational frequency.

SO LIGHTBEINGS, THROUGH THEIR CHANNELS, EXPLAIN THIS PROCESS and offer guidance and spiritual techniques to help you learn to feel and express love and benevolence — and to encourage you to change your behavior to ensure that Earth remains habitable while you expand into your natural self and awaken to your natural talents and abilities. As this happens, you will allow yourself to flow with all humanity into a more benevolent version of Earth — into another dimensional focus, another of the strata of this existence.

PRINT SUBSCRIPTIONS

Mailed U.S. Subscriptions

1st Class	2nd Class
❒ 2yrs $129	❒ 2yrs $79
❒ 1yr.............. $65	❒ 1yr.......... $43

Canada

❒ 2yrs........... $159 ❒ 1yr......... $83

All prices are in U.S. currency.

All Other Countries

❒ 2yrs............ $299 ❒ 1yr....... $154

All prices are in U.S. currency.

NOTE: The U.S. Postal Service has changed postal rates, eliminating Canadian and global 2nd class surface and increasing all airmail rates.

Subscription includes the annual double-size PREDICTIONS ISSUE at no extra charge.

ELECTRONIC SUBSCRIPTIONS with Bonus Content

Get the entire journal plus additional content online by subscription — and get it 2 weeks before it hits newsstands!

❒ 2yrs........ $55 ❒ 1yr.............. $29

All electronic and combo subscriptions *MUST* be purchased online at SedonaJournal.com to obtain username and password.

Get the Best of Both Worlds!

Special Combo Offers!

U.S.A.

Get BOTH Printed AND Electronic Subscriptions

1st Class	2nd Class
❒ 2yrs...... $159	❒ 2yrs.......... $109
❒ 1yr......... $81	❒ 1yr............. $59

Canada

Get an Airmail Printed Subscription Along with an Electronic Subscription for Only

❒ 2yrs...... $189 ❒ 1yr.............. $99

NOTE: The U.S. Postal Service has changed postal rates, eliminating Canadian and global 2nd class surface and increasing all airmail rates.

All Countries

Get an Airmail Printed Subscription Along with an Electronic Subscription for Only

❒ 2yrs...... $329 ❒ 1yr............ $170

Order online: SedonaJournal.com or call 928-526-1345 or 1-800-450-0985

Light Technology PUBLISHING Presents

EASY ORDER 24 HOURS A DAY

1 Order ONLINE!
LightTechnology.com

Order by Email
customersrv@lighttechnology.com

2 Order by Mail
Send to
Light Technology Publishing
PO Box 3540
Flagstaff, AZ 86003

3 Order by Phone
800-450-0985
928-526-1345

4 Order by Fax
928-714-1132

Available from your favorite bookstore or

LIGHT Technology PUBLISHING

MasterCard · VISA · American Express · Discover Network · PayPal

LightTechnology.com
We Offer the Best Channeled and Inspired Books of Wisdom.
Use Our Secure Checkout.
In-Depth Information on Books, Including Excerpts and Contents.
Use the Links to Our Other Great Sites. See Below.

SedonaJournal.com
Read Excerpts of Monthly Channeling and Predictions in Advance.
Use Our Email Links to Contact Us or Send a Submission.
Electronic Subscriptions Available — with or without Print Copies.

BenevolentMagic.com
Learn the techniques of benevolence toward self and benevolence toward others to create global peace. Download all the techniques of benevolent magic and living prayer for FREE!

ExplorerRace.com
All humanity constitutes the Explorer Race, volunteers for a grand and glorious experiment. Discover your purpose, your history, and your future. Download the first chapter of each book for FREE!

ShamanicSecrets.com
What we call shamanism is the natural way of life for beings on other planets. Learn to be aware of your natural self and your natural talents and abilities. Download the first chapter of each book for FREE!